DECIDING THE PUBLIC GOOD

The Japan Center for International Exchange wishes to thank

The Nippon Foundation

DECIDING THE PUBLIC GOOD

Governance and Civil Society in Japan

edited by
Yamamoto Tadashi

JCIE

Tokyo · Japan Center for International Exchange · *New York*

Copyediting by Pamela J. Noda.
Cover and typographic design by Becky Davis, EDS Inc.,
Editorial & Design Services. Typesetting and production by EDS Inc.
Cover photograph of the people/crowd copyright © 1994 Yoav Levy/Phototake/PNI
Cover photograph of the Diet building copyright © Digital Archive Japan

Printed in Japan.
ISBN 4-88907-019-2

Distributed worldwide outside Japan by Brookings Institution Press,
1775 Massachusetts Avenue, N.W., Washington, D.C. 20036-2188 U.S.A.

Japan Center for International Exchange
9-17 Minami Azabu 4-chome, Minato-ku, Tokyo 106-0047 Japan
URL: http://www.jcie.or.jp
Japan Center for International Exchange, Inc. (JCIE/USA)
1251 Avenue of the Americas, New York, N.Y. 10020 U.S.A.

Contents

Foreword

IN THE FALL OF 1996, the Japan Center for International Exchange (JCIE) launched a multipronged study and dialogue project on the theme of "Globalization, Governance, and Civil Society" as an integral part of JCIE's Global ThinkNet Project, which is designed to promote international collaboration among policy research institutions and to strengthen Japan's participation in such international intellectual interaction. As the first phase of this project, JCIE assembled a group of leading intellectuals with diverse academic and professional backgrounds to focus on Japan's case of domestic governance and Japan's interaction with the world community. After two workshops among themselves, the authors presented their preliminary papers to JCIE's Global ThinkNet Tokyo Conference in February 1998, which brought together representatives of independent policy research institutions, foundations, and other civil society organizations throughout the world. On the basis of intense discussion at the conference, the papers were amplified and substantially revised. This volume, *Deciding the Public Good*, represents the final product of this project. A Japanese-language version of this volume, titled *Kan kara min e no pawā shifuto*, was published by TBS-Britannica in September 1998.

The overall objective of the study and dialogue project on "Globalization, Governance, and Civil Society" is based on the premise that more substantial exploration of the role of civil society organizations in the governance of society is needed for the full-fledged development of civil society in Japan. There is a critical need to explore such questions as how civil society responds to the challenges of newly emerging complex sociopolitical and economic issues brought about by the forces of globalization, what its comparative advantages and limitations are, and

7

how it interacts with other sectors, such as the bureaucracy and the corporate community.

Another premise of the project is that similar exploration on the role of civil society in governance is taking place in most of the countries around the world, and a comparative study will enable in-depth analysis of diverse factors stimulating and constraining the growth of civil society. While Japan can draw on the experience of other countries through such comparative analysis and international dialogue based on it, Japan's pattern of civil society development in the context of Japan's sociopolitical and cultural environments may offer a useful reference to other countries for the ongoing debate and exploration on the role of civil society in the governance of their respective societies.

The debate on the role of civil society and governance has been particularly intense in Japan in the past several years as the country has witnessed a breakdown in the system of governance that served Japan well during its modernization process. The forces of globalization have required Japan to undergo fundamental domestic adjustments and created complex social issues that have shaken the basic premise of the public-equals-official schema under which the bureaucracy was seen as the exclusive arbiter of the public interest. At the same time, there has been a growing recognition that civil society can play an active role in responding to pluralistic social needs as an effective innovative force for social change.

The Great Hanshin-Awaji Earthquake of January 1995, which took the lives of more than 6,400 people, galvanized the forces already at work attempting to build a stronger civil society. The sudden attention given to civil society, thanks, in large part, to the outpouring of support by over 1.3 million volunteers and a large number of nongovernmental organizations, paved the way for legislative proposals to facilitate the incorporation process and provide incentives for tax-deductible contributions. Traditional forces associated with the bureaucracy-dominated system of governance with strong control over civil society and emerging forces of civil society demanding more autonomous activities clashed throughout the ensuing legislative process. Some fundamental questions related to the system of governance raised in this process were, What is the public interest? Who defines the public interest? Who should serve the public interest?

While the NPO Law was passed in March 1998 and enacted on December 1, 1998, this debate on governance and civil society is far from over. *Deciding the Public Good* provides a comprehensive perspective on the changing nature of governance and the evolution of the role of civil society in Japan. Individual chapters analyze diverse dimensions of the subject of governance and civil society, including new challenges to the traditional pattern of governance; a historical perspective on individualism and civil society; the current evolution of civil society and its future challenges; the roles of the public and corporate sectors and civil society in management of the economy; and the role of nonstate actors in the process of internationalization of the society. Statistical data and an annotated bibliography on governance and civil society are also provided. It is hoped that this volume will serve the purpose of improving the quality of debate within Japan on the subject of governance and civil society. It is also hoped that this will provide foreign readers with a useful comparative perspective on this subject as well as an insight into the changing sociocultural and political dynamics of contemporary Japan.

Many people have made this book possible. First and foremost, I thank the authors of the papers, who made time in their busy schedules to take part in joint research. I wish to express my deepest appreciation to the Nippon Foundation for providing the financial support for the project from which this book emerged. My sincere gratitude goes to Kano Tsutomu for his masterful translation of the chapters by Yoshida Shin'ichi and Iokibe Makoto. I also thank Wordcraft Inc. and Geraldine Harcourt for their excellent respective translations of the chapters by Ōta Hiroko and Wada Jun. Finally, I wish to express my deep gratitude to Pamela J. Noda and the editorial staff of JCIE for their dedicated work in finalizing the manuscripts.

Yamamoto Tadashi
PRESIDENT
JAPAN CENTER FOR INTERNATIONAL EXCHANGE

DECIDING THE PUBLIC GOOD

CHAPTER ONE

Rethinking the Public Interest in Japan: Civil Society in the Making

Yoshida Shin'ichi

WHAT is the "public interest," or, for our purposes, the interests of the public? Who decides the ideas, policies, and activities that are formulated "for the common good," and how? What rules or criteria are used to determine priorities among various, often conflicting, interests of the people? These basic questions one might expect to be grappled with in any democratic society are just beginning to be asked in Japan today. For the first time in its modern history, this country now faces the challenge of reconsidering its whole approach to the public interest, along with many other long-held assumptions.

The following are the minimum three conditions a society requires to remain intact and viable: First, there must be recognition of interests that are public, transcending private and individual interests, and the members of the society must have a common desire to maintain and promote such interests. Second, a set of rules—and procedures and values —that the members accept as credible is necessary to determine and/or modify what they believe to be the constituents of the public interest in the context of their society. Third, someone, or some group, has to carry on the activities of protecting and advancing the public interest.

In modern Japan, the government has assumed the initiative in fulfilling all three conditions almost single-handedly. The central government bureaucracy, in particular, has maintained a virtual monopoly on decision-making authority and jurisdiction over the public interest. The resulting structure I call the "public-equals-official" society. Today, 130 years since the emergence of the modern Japanese state, however, the governing apparatus then established is beginning to show signs of institutional fatigue and operational dysfunction. In fact, the public-equals-official society is badly shaken and visibly crumbling. At the same time, an awareness is rapidly growing that autonomous citizens as individuals and in groups must be actively involved, alongside the government, in order to maintain social stability and promote as truly "public" those aspects of social life carried out for the common good in this country.

For now, let us define civil society as a spontaneous, concerned group of citizens who interact independently of government, while collaborating with it at certain times and opposing it at others. Japan today is experiencing the emergence of civil society in this sense, supported by the advent of a new public consciousness. This development has given fresh urgency to the question of who should determine, and how, what is in the interests of the public. In addition, a completely new kind of problem has appeared. It concerns priorities, how to assess and rank multiple and diverse public interests, including those designated by the government under established prerogatives, as well as those that have recently been gaining broad recognition in society. In short, Japanese society is being pressed not only to come up with a new concept of the public interest but also to reappraise what is "public" in the first place.

Attempts to define and manage the public interest in traditional ways become increasingly ineffective, prolonging political turmoil and aggravating economic recession. The prospects for achieving a national consensus on an alternative concept of the public interest and on new procedures and methods of decision making are, at least in the near future, extremely dim. It is going to be a long, uphill struggle to get anywhere near a consensus. Are Japanese really capable of making the mental shift that would be required if the government, which has held a monopoly on the public interest for so long, were to be relegated to relative status? Are they equipped to transform a society ruled by a bureaucracy and replace it with a new model built on their own initiative, according to their own logic? These questions are crucial, because nothing short of a revolution in the popular consciousness will be needed to accomplish the formidable task of reforming Japanese society.

This chapter presents an overview of the changing attitudes among Japanese toward the role of the government and examines the emerging tendencies toward civil society, focusing on how the concept of the

public interest is shifting and what "public" really stands for.[1] The first
section discusses the old patterns of thinking and approaches still being practiced by members of officialdom, taking as an example a recent
public works project involving river administration. This case study is
useful in analyzing the reactions and attitudes of residents in the area
concerned, which may be considered underlying factors in the per-
petuation of the official monopoly on the public interest.

The second section is devoted to a historical discussion of how,
conceptually, "public" became equated with "official" in the process of
Japan's modernization. This equation has found its way into the popular vocabulary and has permeated the popular subconscious, which is
one of the basic reasons why it is so difficult in Japanese society to make
even a dent in the bulwark of entrenched bureaucratic authority.

The third section employs some examples of political and economic
misjudgment to illustrate how the conjunction of "public" and "official"
in Japan's social structure has created serious symptoms of dysfunction.
Through this discussion I hope to demonstrate the need for Japanese to
reexamine and refurbish the decision-making system that determines
the public interest.

The fourth and final section focuses on the background factors that
have made redefinition of public interest unavoidable. It also reviews
how the changing roles of officialdom and shifts in popular consciousness have contributed to the rise of civil society and the reconsideration
of the public. I will conclude with a few thoughts on how these trends
might develop in the future.

The Riverside Park Project: A Case Study
UNWELCOME PUBLIC FACILITIES

The following case demonstrates the method that was traditionally used
to determine what constituted the public interest and how it should be
realized.[2]

The Fukushima prefectural government offices are located on the
edge of the Abukuma River in the center of the city of Fukushima. In the
Watari district across the river is a riverside park one kilometer in length
and eight hectares in area. Originally a dry riverbed, the land once lay
idle, covered with swamp grass inside a ten-meter-high embankment.
Part of it was a "no public access" area. In 1996, the Ministry of Construction spent ¥130 million to convert the land into a "public" park,

ostensibly for the benefit of local children. The slope from the top of the embankment down to the river's edge was made more gradual. Trees and grassy areas were planted, pebbles were spread along the banks, and a small inlet was created.

Behind this project was a new policy on river administration adopted in 1996 by the Construction Ministry. Its stated purpose was "to improve and manage rivers and their surroundings as safe, environmentally sound areas suitable for play and recreation, as well as for experience with outdoor life and nature study."

Residents in the Watari district, however, were not happy about the riverside park. According to city office sources, an informal decision on the project was first made on the basis of an unconfirmed report from the Fukushima Construction Office of the ministry to the effect that there was a need felt among local citizens for easy access to the river. Once the decision was made, albeit informal, the Construction Ministry went ahead with planning and budgetary appropriations.

It was not until after the construction expenses were earmarked in the national supplementary budget that a formal briefing was given to the local community. Residents were literally caught off guard by the news. They were worried about the safety of the area. A child had drowned in the river several years before. The teachers and parents of the children at the Watari Elementary School located right outside the embankment were particularly concerned about the dangers an easily accessible dry riverbed might pose to young children. As one teacher put it, "For years, we've been telling the children not to go close to the river, but now the government says we should 'make friends' with it. We just don't know what to tell them. . . ."

Despite these voices of concern from among the local citizens, the Construction Ministry carried on with the project; once the old wheels of the public-equals-official society were set in motion, no ordinary force could stop them. The members of the Watari community lodged no formal protest to the project.

Since the park was completed, the Watari Elementary School has occasionally taken students there for nature study as part of its science curriculum, but the school authorities strictly prohibit children from entering the area before and after school without an adult accompanying them. It is sheer nonsense that children are virtually barred from the "public" space ostensibly created for them to play freely.

Meanwhile, a large signboard was put up on the embankment, with

"Wanpaku hiroba" (literally, "open space for active, adventuresome kids") written on it in big letters. Suggesting all the various kinds of play that could be enjoyed in the park, the signboard invited children to "Have fun and play to your heart's content!" The fact that the children were not allowed the chance is an object lesson in the strange nature of the society they live in.

This ironical public works project demonstrated that the bureaucracy has the authority to determine what is in the public interest, and that official discretion takes precedence over the needs and desires of local residents in maintaining and promoting such interests. It also casts the public-equals-official formula in Japanese society into clear relief.

WHO DECIDES THE PUBLIC GOOD?

The Fukushima park is not an isolated case, but one of many similar projects being undertaken throughout the country. The Ministry of Construction plans to carry out such projects in altogether 1,000 locations. To be fair, I should add here that of the more than 100 projects already completed or under way, many did reflect the real needs of local residents. The Abukuma River fiasco may have been one of the relatively few cases where "both the government officials concerned and local people failed to make adequate efforts to communicate with each other" (an official in the river environment division of the Construction Ministry).

The greatest irony of the Abukuma and other similar cases is that these riverside park projects are the result of the ministry's change in policy objectives, a shift in what the bureaucrats consider to be *more* in the public interest. In other words, they were ostensibly devised to put an end to the one-sided official initiatives in river administration of the past.

Modern Japanese river administration had for years centered on flood control and other measures for river improvement. This policy was largely successful as far as flood prevention is concerned, but the scenery surrounding the nation's major watercourses, particularly in urban areas, was transformed completely, from natural to artificial, from organic to inorganic. In these areas, concrete river channels and fences now prevent people from getting anywhere close to the water. As consciousness of the environment heightened in the 1970s, popular sentiment objecting to such unfriendly rivers arose in several urban centers. In response to the outcry, some municipal governments did change their policy objectives, according attention to public access as well as flood control and to interaction between the river and citizens' lives, including safety from flooding.

As more and more local governments favored this new approach to river administration, the Construction Ministry belatedly decided to join the crowd. In 1995, the River Council, an advisory body to the construction minister, submitted a preliminary report recommending the reestablishment of a more congenial relationship between rivers and surrounding communities. The report admitted the lack of sufficient consideration in past riparian construction works for the many forms of natural life to be found in and along the river as well as for the beauty of the landscape. It also pointed out that river administration had, over the years, deprived local communities of a close relationship with their rivers. To rectify the situation, the council called for "communion between people and their rivers," and "improved communication with the local communities concerned" by the ministry (Council on Rivers 1995).

This preliminary report provided the basis for the final, more general report submitted in 1996, entitled "A Basic Orientation for Future River Improvement." It led to the revision of the River Act in the following year. Riverside park projects, in Fukushima and elsewhere, were most symbolic of the policy change.

Undoubtedly, this policy shift reflected the government's growing awareness that it could no longer respond adequately to social needs if public administration alone remained responsible for decision making on and the maintenance of the public interest. However, it is one thing for the central government to expound a new philosophy, but it is quite another for that philosophy to be translated into action on the local level. The way the Fukushima park project was planned and implemented, as we have seen, showed no departure from the old pattern. The established public-equals-official society effectively resisted the infusion of the new thinking into the project.

It was the bureaucracy, after all, that decided on the policy change. To analyze the motives behind the new bureaucratic thinking, let me quote a citizens'-movement activist who has long been involved in campaigns to restore the close relationship of people and rivers of the past and who continues to battle the Construction Ministry on the riverside park issue:

Nobody likes to see a river cemented with concrete on three sides. Such public works only repulse citizens. No amount of embankment works will prevent floods, after all, without the cooperation of local residents. We have been demanding, since the seventies, "software" improvements [that is, links between people and the river]. The bureaucrats have only begun advocating this policy now, having realized at long last that their exclusive control of rivers is deadlocked. For the Construction Ministry, the policy change was perhaps the only option left to keep public works projects alive. But if you look at the riverside park projects as they are being implemented in many parts of the country, they are basically hardware-oriented [that is, based on the mere construction of park facilities]. All the bureaucrats did was to tailor their public works projects to what they see as the needs of the times only for the purpose of continuing such projects.

On the surface, it looks as though the central government officials changed their policy, taking their cue from the attempts of some municipalities to respond to local citizens' needs. In reality, however, bureaucratic motivation lay elsewhere. Warnings about environmental destruction and calls for greater attention to the needs of local people are nothing new. They have been voiced since the 1970s. But officials in Tokyo had rarely bothered to listen to popular demands and complaints.

Around the time of the revision of policies in the mid-1990s, the drastic reduction of public works projects was a major issue on the agenda for fiscal retrenchment. Ultimately, the way the officials carry out their new policy is not new at all. As the Fukushima case demonstrates, the primary concern of the ministry is not so much local people's real needs as the execution of their construction plans and disposal of their budgets according to the predetermined schedule. The new "menu" for the public interest, therefore, was the brainchild of bureaucrats eager to preserve their vested interests and maintain their self-centered prestige.

PUBLIC ACCEPTANCE OF THE PUBLIC INTEREST

A review of what the Construction Ministry has tried to do with the "software" for the Fukushima project will reveal two distinct aspects of the public-equals-official formula at work in Japanese society. One is people's traditional obedience, submerged in the depths of the popular consciousness, to the public interest formulated for and imposed on them by officialdom. The other is the old-fashioned bureaucratic approach of indoctrinating the populace and mobilizing them to serve the public interest, as officials themselves define it.

As mentioned earlier, the people of the Watari district, including the teachers and the PTA members at the local primary school, were at first bewildered at the news about the riverside park project. The school itself, however, did not take action to press for any modification of the official plan, on the grounds that "we are in no position to say yes or no to the national government's river works projects, and besides, we had not been party to any discussion on the issue prior to the decision."

After the facilities were completed, the school decided to send a teacher, on a rotation basis, to the park once a morning and again in the afternoon on Sundays and national holidays to check whether any of its students were there without adult supervision or engaged in any dangerous activity. These patrols, though an extra burden on the staff, were deemed necessary to protect the interests of the school as a custodian of the children. Considered responsible for the lives of its students, the school has had to take this measure of self-defense, which boils down to discouraging the children from making use of the park facilities.

Members of the community, too, were initially unhappy about the plan decided upon over their heads, but ended up giving their ex post facto approval. An officer of the PTA interviewed said, "We all knew that the proposed park would entail a danger to our children, but who would dare to oppose the authorities? Almost no one said anything during the official briefing session. One senior member of our community played the role of the devil's advocate, so to speak, expressing our apprehensions." The older man's opinions had no real effect on the government plan, although they did help allay the residents' pent-up frustration. It is because of the people's deeply ingrained submissiveness and excessive deference to authority that officials can do as they please, imposing plans on the local community at their own discretion.

The stated objective of the park project, nevertheless, focused on the "software," that is, promoting human interaction with the river. Given the community's passive acceptance of the new facilities, one would expect its members to be reluctant to cooperate in their maintenance and management. Should that happen, the project would not accomplish the purposes it was implemented for. Strangely enough, however, people of the Watari district were converted soon after the completion of the riverside park from passive followers to active supporters, at least in form.

In the summer of 1996 when the project's "hardware" was finished, the Construction Ministry, working through the Fukushima city government and other channels, brought together representatives of the district's neighborhood associations and officials of the Fukushima Municipal Board of Education to urge their cooperation in administering the park facilities jointly with the ministry.

In November that year, the Watari Riverside Society was inaugurated for the management and programming of the park. Included in its membership were ministry officials from the Fukushima Construction Office, senior members of the municipal government staff, and the heads of neighborhood associations in the Watari district.

The Watari Riverside Society was quick to publish a PR bulletin aimed at local citizens in line with the objectives of the organization: "Our goal is to make the Riverside Park pleasant and accessible to citizens. To that end, we will see to it that close communication and connections be established between the government offices concerned, on the one hand, and members of the community, neighborhood associations, and local volunteer groups, on the other." Although with some time lag, the society began listing individuals who might serve as volunteer instructors for children in outdoor recreational activities. In 1997, periodic general cleaning of the park and mowing of weeds began to be organized by local residents.

In outward form, the Watari Riverside Society is a citizen-centered organization, or at least a "joint venture" of officials and private citizens. But all of its expenses are financed by subsidies from the Construction Ministry, a grant-giving foundation under the ministry's jurisdiction, and the Fukushima city government. The society's promotional materials, articles of incorporation and by-laws, and applications for financial assistance from the foundation were all prepared by ministry officials, and the society's secretariat is located in the River Section of the municipal office. An official in the section says, "Since the project was undertaken on such short notice, we [the city office] feel obliged to help out for a certain period of time."

Thus, what appears to be a local citizens' group is actually a government-sponsored nonprofit organization created on a model provided for in the ministry's project implementation plan. A neighborhood association leader says, "The ministry got everything ready, down to the last pencil, and then dropped the actual work in our laps. But the completed park itself looks all right, and we feel it would be a shame to leave it overrun with weeds."

Influential member of the community and head of the Watari Riverside Society Takano Izaemon says, "The local residents are now obliged to share some burden in the park's upkeep by cutting weeds, for example. So we should ask the city office for financial help, so that the people here will gradually feel closer to the park. I think that's best for the community. To restore the friendly river of the past is time-consuming, and we have to change our attitudes, too."

As observed already, for a project engineered by officials based on their own idea of the public interest, local residents find themselves mobilized before they know it, as if of their own volition, to represent and support the "public" cause. In this way, a government decision assumes the appearance of the public good that no one can dispute. The Fukushima project exemplifies what I have called the public-equals-official formula in Japanese society.

EXPOSURE OF INHERENT CONTRADICTIONS

In launching its "friendly river" program, the Construction Ministry was compelled to attach importance to the "software"—the cooperation of the local community—because of the problem of safety and liability for accidents.

As noted already, the Construction Ministry had previously pursued policies in its river administration that gave priority exclusively to flood control. This resulted in infrastructure and rules that severed the close ties that once existed between community life and local watercourses. Government responsibility for river management increased, and with it the state's financial liability for drownings and other fatal accidents. Under such circumstances, it was anticipated that the switch to the new policy of making rivers more accessible and "friendly" would entail even greater responsibility for the government to bear with regard to accidents.

The Construction Ministry held a series of study meetings, inviting outside specialists, to examine these eventualities. A number of preventative measures were suggested, but one of the main points stressed in the final report was the "need to cultivate a sense of self-responsibility" on the part of local people. Part of the study report reads as follows:

Rivers are essentially natural public domain available for free use by the general public. People should use such facilities at their own risk. In Western countries, citizens are accustomed to defending their own lives when they are of their own volition in a dangerous place. But in Japan . . . many accidents have taken place because of lack of imagination on the part of users about the possible risks they are taking. Hence it is crucial that we make an earnest effort to cultivate people's ability to understand potential dangers and perceptivity in responding to their own situation, thereby elevating awareness of responsibility for their own actions. (Research Committee on River Control 1996, 21)

The initial negative reactions of Fukushima citizens to the riverside park project focused on the issue of safety. They had been led to believe that the government is responsible for safety as the sole protector and executor of the public interest through its river conservation and flood-control measures. When suddenly told that the Abukuma River was once again to be part of their daily lives, it was only natural that they should be bewildered and apprehensive. A father of a primary school student expressed the honest feelings of many adults in the district: "I'm all for kids getting to know nature better, but the Abukuma is no gurgling brook. We don't need a park on the riverside there. It's as if we are being made the subjects of an experiment [that is, the government is using Watari residents to test whether citizens can develop enough responsibility for their own actions to prevent accidents]. That's kind of hard to accept."

The Construction Ministry's appeal for a greater sense of self-responsibility itself is ample evidence of how drastically the official monopoly on the public interest has destroyed the close symbiotic relationship between people and their rivers that once existed. The people's "lack of imagination" is at least in part the price the government has to pay for its own policy. Unintentional though it was, the Construction Ministry's revision of what it considers to be in the public interest has brought to the fore some of the contradictions inherent in the public-equals-official society of Japan. Those contradictions and flaws have manifested themselves at the lowest echelons of the bureaucratic hierarchy where most of the projects are implemented. Especially since the mid-1990s, they have spread nationwide, growing more

serious in degree and larger in scale. I will discuss these new developments and their backgrounds in section three of this chapter.

THE PUBLIC-OFFICIAL EQUATION
IN HISTORICAL PERSPECTIVE

KŌ AS GOVERNMENT

The standard Japanese translation of the word "public" is "*kō*," as in
kōeki (public interest). This Chinese character, as it has been used in
Japan during the modern period, has a dual meaning: It denotes "government" and "ruling authority" as well as "public." In fact, the former
connotation is stronger than the latter. Even today, most Japanese, when
they hear the word *kō*, will assume it means "government" before they
think of "public." The concept of public in its Western sense is still not
very familiar in Japan.

Behind the double meaning of the word *kō* and its weight toward the
meaning of "government" is a long historical process in which the pe-
culiarly Japanese social fabric has evolved, characterized by the public-
official equation. Originally, *kō* did not have the connotation of public
at all. Used in juxtaposition with *shi* (self or private), it meant, literally,
"righteousness devoid of selfish motives" or "impartiality." Some Si-
nologists say that the term had a connotation of public in ancient China,
but when the ideograph was imported to Japan in the sixth century, it
was used to represent the indigenous word *ōyake*, which means "man-
sion of the lord." Hence, the *kō-shi* pair came to take on the nuance of a
ruler-subject relationship. One of the articles of Prince Shōtoku's (574–
622) Seventeen-Article Constitution reads: "To turn away from that
which is private [*shi*], and to set our faces toward that which is public
[*kō*]—this is the path of a minister."

During the Edo period (1603–1867), the appellation *daikōgi* (Great
Authority) was used in reference to the Tokugawa shogun at the apex
of the hierarchy, while domanial daimyo (feudal lords) were called *kōgi*
(authorities). Throughout the modern period, at least until 1945, the
phrase *messhi hōkō* (literally, self-annihilation for the sake of one's country) was frequently and widely used in the context of hierarchical social
relations. These usages of the word *kō* clearly indicate that the meaning
of *kō* as "ruling authority" is deeply embedded in the Japanese psyche as well as vocabulary (see Mito 1976 and Katō 1992). Depending
on the historical era and social context, "the term generally meant the

monarch, government, or some other superior authority" (Maruyama 1986). In its Edo-period usage, *kōgi* was a common noun meaning government (Watanabe 1997).

The Meiji Restoration of 1868 put the emperor at the apex of both the spiritual hierarchy and the power structure. The term *kō* then came to mean the imperial government and/or the state itself. Under the system where the monarch represented the ultimate, absolute *kō*, the imperial subjects were required to "courageously sacrifice themselves for the state in a national crisis" (Imperial Rescript on Education). The phrase *messhi hōkō* was often used in slogans calling for "selfless loyalty to the state." In this way, a nationwide network was created mobilizing popular energy for service to the *kō* as the state, both spiritually and materially. This system of national mobilization was instrumental in propelling the country's modernization drive, but it also paved the way for the rise of ultranationalism in the 1930s, and subsequently for Japan's catastrophic plunge into World War II.

Even more important for our purposes here is that the concept *kō* became identified with a very specific entity—the government bureaucracy. This was because the "emperor's officials" took upon their shoulders the task of nation building and administering the affairs of the state. Government documents have come to be known as *kōbunsho*, and archives as *kōbunsho-kan*. Even the vehicles officials use are called *kōyōsha*. As these usages indicate, the word *kō* became synonymous with the government and its officials in the course of modern Japanese history.

Under Japan's centralized system of government, the ministry officials at the top of the bureaucratic hierarchy not only made decisions on matters of the national interest but dictated the public interest for prefectural and municipal administrations, in descending order. It was thus no wonder that the whole structure of decision making on matters of the public interest was one and the same with the bureaucratic hierarchy.

KŌ AS PUBLIC

Early Meiji intellectuals who introduced Western ideas and philosophies had a hard time trying to find a Japanese equivalent to the word "public." Public is a horizontal or lateral concept, as opposed to the vertical or hierarchical concept of *kō*, in that it is premised on the presence of values divorced from the state and common to all members of a society or people (Maruyama 1986). Such a concept or word denoting it had not existed in pre-Meiji Japan.

The same was true for the word "society," which implies a horizontal, spontaneous association of individuals. The whole notion was foreign to Japan at the time. A wide variety of words or phrases were tried before *"shakai"* took root as the standard rendering of "society" (see Katō 1992 and Maruyama 1986). The absence of Japanese equivalents for "public" and "society" is symbolic. The modern state may be one thought to be founded upon a civil society independent of the state itself and where the concept of "public" is indispensable, but Japan started out its modernization process without either of these.

The modernizing efforts by Meiji Japan involved not only the task of putting together the façade of a modern state, including the establishment of a centralized government. A national society had to be created at all cost, transplanting modern economic systems and reorganizing the decentralized domains and small local communities. The Meiji government tried to instill new social values in the population through the national education system, while organizing many civic groups under its auspices (government-sponsored nonprofit organizations) in an attempt to mold a "society," at least in outward form. In other words, the Meiji state artificially created what looked like a modern civil society with a semblance of a "public."

Whatever the reality, the word *kō* did take on the additional connotation of public at that point. But both *shakai* (society) or *kō* as public, set out as hastily patched together, half-baked concepts, continued to suffer thereafter from a heavy dependence on and influence from the state and government. *Kō* as public has never been free from the imprint of *kō* as government.

OFFICIALLY DESIGNATED PARKS

One evidence of that imprint is in the deep-rooted national mentality that the government should control everything in the public domain and, conversely, that that which the government controls is the public domain. To explain this mentality, let me briefly review the history of parks in this country and official and popular attitudes toward them.[3]

During the latter half of the 19th century, the Meiji government made a desperate effort to transplant or create those institutions and facilities that Japan did not have but that it considered indispensable for the country's Westernization. One such facility was the kind of public garden found in European cities. In a flurry to adopt things Western, the government decided on a system in 1873 whereby many open spaces and shrine or temple compounds were officially designated as parks. These were the places where ordinary folk had thronged for cherry-blossom viewing, picnics, or festivals. The designation system helped to increase the number of parks, at least on paper. The Meiji regime also built Western-style parks in big cities, such as Hibiya Park in the heart of Tokyo. All the while, use of recreation spots that the authorities deemed unsuitable or undesirable was abolished under government pressure.

These newly created or newly designated facilities were first called *yūen* (pleasure grounds or amusement parks), but eventually *kōen* (literally, public/official gardens) became the official term. The dissemination of this term greatly facilitated the popular acceptance of *kō* as being synonymous with "public." In reality, however, the *kō* in *kōen* did not signify "public" but "official." It is more fitting, therefore, to call these facilities *kan'en* (official gardens) than *kōen*.

Symbolic is the story of the opening day of Hibiya Park, the country's first European-style park, completed in June 1903. The police prohibited eating and drinking inside the park and refused to allow street performers to enter. So, outside the park, hundreds of open-air stalls were lined up where visitors who had come to see the new park enjoyed eating and drinking. Hibiya Park was not a public garden but literally an official garden.

The net result of the government initiative in building parks is the distorted belief that only those facilities designated as *kōen* by the government are real parks. This notion is very much alive today, and the number of *kōen* keeps increasing, not so much in response to the needs of citizens as the result of the execution of central or local government plans and the expansion of budgets. The underlying pattern of thinking behind these park projects is that government approval or authorization alone puts social overhead capital in line with the public interest. The riverside park project discussed in the preceding section typically demonstrates this logic.

The nature of Japanese parks as "official gardens" has given rise to the notion that the government is responsible for the management and care of the parks. This notion, firmly anchored in the people's mind-set, has undermined the popular understanding of *kō* as public. Shirahata

Yōzaburō, professor at the International Research Center for Japanese Studies, is one scholar who has consistently criticized the official park policy in this country, noting, for example, that the general cleanup of the parks is conducted by "volunteers" recruited and organized by the government! Based on his extensive analysis of the history of Japanese parks, Shirahata concludes that official initiative and control have produced the following twofold mentality: (1) that only those facilities created through bureaucratic channels and approved and authorized officially qualify as *kō*; and (2) that *kō* is free of cost, because citizen participation in or personal financial burdens for the maintenance of the facilities are not required. This mentality assumes the a priori existence of the government and total dependence on its support. The "heteronomous" society thus created was the price the Japanese public have had to pay for leaving the public-equals-official model in place for so long.

All this would be quite understandable if we were just talking about prewar Japan where the state controlled the whole society. The democratization of Japan since 1945, however, has made it possible for the popular will (what the public wants) to be reflected in governmental processes through various institutional and legal apparatuses. Why is it, then, that officialdom has been able to hold a virtual monopoly on the interpretation and implementation of the public interest even through the postwar period? The answer to this question lies, as we have seen in the riverside park issue and the history of parks in Japan, in the decline of the people's sense of independence and the insufficient autonomy of society itself.

For about 15 years after the end of World War II, until the nationwide uproar over the revised U.S.-Japan Security Treaty issue in 1960, "what the public interest should be" was often the focal point of political debate and confrontation, especially as it related to the economic system and foreign policy. Even then, the Japanese people's psychology of dependency on the government authorities had not really changed since before the war. Another element of continuity from the prewar to the postwar period was the Japanese preoccupation with the national goal of catching up with the West, that is, modernizing Japan after the model of the advanced West. The bureaucracy survived Japan's defeat at the hands of the Allied Powers, and as a team of specialists in the pursuit of the national goal, it tackled the task of economic reconstruction. The political parties, on the other hand, barred from sound growth before the war under the emperor system, remained incapable of defining the public interest and mustering popular support for their policies without the help and guidance of the bureaucracy. They simply lacked the necessary intellectual resources and organizational strength.

Under these circumstances, the central government bureaucrats were able to consolidate their position as the guardians of the public interest in postwar Japan. Whereas "a wealthy nation, a strong military" had been the prewar slogan of the public interest, "economic growth" became the key phrase after 1945. By virtue of their technical acumen, ministry officials have virtually run the government, using politicians for their own purposes, and continued to mobilize the necessary social resources to implement their policies under the centralized system of public administration. In this way, the subordination of society to the state, a prominent feature of modern Japan, has not only remained intact, but has been taken for granted by the government and bureaucracy, as well as the politicians and people.

The Established Order on Trial

System Crumbling, Credibility Eroding

The whole system aimed at serving the public interest—the decision-making process, order of priorities, and credibility of the decisions made—began to collapse in the middle of the 1990s. Recent political and economic confusion in Japan is closely related to the collapse of this system.

Japanese politics has been in turmoil since the one-party rule of the Liberal Democratic Party (LDP) ended in 1993 and its replacement by a succession of coalition cabinets. The coalition between the Liberal Democrats and the Social Democrats is now a thing of the past. Meanwhile, out-of-power groups continue to realign themselves in a constant meeting and parting of the ways. Politics is an arena of open competition for various public interests, but the system of public interests the parties competed to pursue has disintegrated, and they are unable to find any alternative.

As the chaotic situation continues in the political arena, voter support for parties has drastically diminished, with about one-half of the entire electorate having no party of preference. The nonpartisan group has doubled over the past ten years. The turnout of voters in national elections has steadily declined since 1992, each time marking a new

record low. In the House of Councillors election of 1995, the turnout
was below 45 percent, and even in the House of Representatives election of the following year it did not reach 60 percent. Both explicitly and
implicitly, popular support for the old systems for defining and maintaining the public interest is fast eroding.

The current turmoil, however, has gradually made clear exactly what
the issue is. The viability of the established order of the public interest
is now being subjected to fundamental scrutiny.

WHAT IS THE PUBLIC INTEREST?

A number of controversial issues came into the limelight in 1996 that
shook the systems serving the public interest at their very foundations.
Their dysfunctions were obvious for all to see. A leading case that particularly aroused public indignation was the proposed use of taxpayers'
money to help settle the irrecoverable debts of seven housing loan
companies.

The seven companies, which had heavily invested in real estate
during the period of the overheated economy in the late 1980s, were
burdened with massive credit accounts that became uncollectable after
the bubble burst and land prices plunged. Because these loan companies were partly financed by agricultural cooperatives, the government attempted to infuse them with ¥680 billion from national coffers
under pressure from the ruling parties, which wanted by all means to
maintain their bastions of support among the rural voters who custom-
arily deposit their savings in the agricultural cooperatives. This move
aroused vehement protest from the media and general public. The widespread reaction was, Why should taxpayers' money be used to help out
private businesses which have gotten into trouble through their own
misjudgment and inept management?

The government's rationale for the infusion was its behest to maintain a stable financial system, which it claimed was in the public interest.
But the administration could not even offer a coherent explanation for
what it had based the proposed figure on; ¥680 billion was the amount
decided upon through a political compromise between the financial institutions concerned (banks, agricultural cooperatives, and others) and
the finance and agriculture ministries. Nor did the government disclose
the total figure of irrecoverable credits the housing loan companies
held, lest such information trigger financial panic.

The critics, meanwhile, argued that the proposed measure was simply intended to salvage certain banking institutions such as the agricultural cooperatives, and that the real "public interest" in this case lay in making clear exactly who was responsible and making them account for their own failures and wrongdoings. In the end, the bill for a special appropriation of ¥680 billion was forced through the Diet by the majority.

What this case demonstrated beyond doubt is the changing attitude of the Japanese people toward the public interest. An official policy in pursuit of the so-called public interest met with stiff opposition, the government could not present any convincing argument for the proposed measure, and its accountability was squarely and repeatedly questioned. The official monopoly on the public interest was indeed being challenged on an unprecedented scale.

This nightmarish experience with the housing loan company issue made the Japanese government exceedingly hesitant to deal squarely and effectively with the massive uncollectable credits weighing down banks and other financial institutions. The financial instability that arose as a major issue in 1997 onward was the result. Toward the end of that year, the government decided on the infusion of ¥30 trillion from public funds into the financial sector. The amount was incomparably larger than the ¥680 billion appropriated for the housing loan companies. But more important was whether this new measure was really in the public interest. Even within the ruling party criticism mounted over the accountability of the Ministry of Finance and inadequate public disclosure of corporate data and information.

The Great Hanshin-Awaji Earthquake that hit the Kobe-Osaka area in January 1995, with a final death toll of more than 6,400 people, prompted many to question what the government is for, whose interests it supposedly serves, and what, ultimately, the public interest is. These questions came to the fore in 1996 after more than a year of reconstruction and relief work.

Two-hundred-fifty thousand houses were completely destroyed or partially damaged and at least 320,000 people were obliged to evacuate their homes in the wake of the disaster. Many lost both their residence and their place of work. Apart from the emergency relief following the quake, financial aid provided to the victims came from exclusively private sources. A maximum of ¥500,000 was sent to each household.

Official assistance was limited to low-interest-rate loans and the provision of public housing units. No direct relief funds were made available from the Treasury. Victims have had a hard time trying to restore their lives to normal. Nearly three years after the disaster, as of October 1998, 9,563 families still lived in temporary shelters hastily built in the aftermath of the quake. The shortage of public funding and the delay in the availability of housing units in the Kobe-Osaka area are the main reasons for this unfortunate situation.

The Japanese government has firmly held to the principle that "victims of natural disasters should deal with the damage on their own resources" (Prime Minister Hashimoto Ryūtarō), and consistently refuses to provide any financial aid from public coffers. "No compensation by the government for private assets lost" is in line with the classical concept of the public interest maintained by officialdom.

A citizens' group launched a campaign in 1996 for new legislation on behalf of the earthquake victims. The group argues, Why does a government that rescues financial institutions with taxpayers' money refuse to help citizens whose lives have been completely devastated? It calls for public assistance of up to ¥5 million per household, and has collected about 25 million signatures from around the country in support of the proposed legislation.

The group's campaign bore fruit when several sympathetic members of the Diet submitted a bill for the use of public funds to aid victims of natural disasters. It was the first nationwide movement to present an alternative to the government's version of the public interest from the citizens' viewpoint.

In a separate move, the National Prefectural Governors' Association called on the central government to create a special relief fund to compensate for damage caused by natural disasters. Their reasoning is that a large-scale calamity like the Great Hanshin-Awaji Earthquake requires public aid for reconstruction and rehabilitation. Here, too, we find the public interest of the local governments diverging from that of the central administration.

The bill was enacted in May 1998 as the Law for Livelihood Rehabilitation of Natural Disaster Victims, which stipulated the provision of up to ¥1 million for those families whose houses have been completely destroyed in a natural disaster. The relief provisions of the law were made applicable to the victims of the earthquake retroactively. This legislation meant that a new type of public interest was written into law on the basis of actual needs, and it also brought to light the fictitious nature of the official concept of the public interest.

ORDER OF PRIORITIES

Insofar as there are many kinds of public interest, the question arises as to how to determine the order of priorities. A series of epoch-making phenomena occurred in the 1990s that amounted to an open revolt by local communities against the central government's idea of what constituted the national and public interest. Their means of resistance was referendums at the prefectural and municipal levels. This turn of events unambiguously shows that the established hierarchy with the state at the top and towns and villages at the bottom is crumbling, and with it the system of officially determined public interest.

The rape of a 12-year-old Okinawan schoolgirl by three Marines in September 1995 triggered a new anti-U.S. base campaign, demanding reduction and scaling down of the U.S. military presence on the islands. Ōta Masahide, governor of Okinawa Prefecture, subsequently refused to sign a new lease on some of the private land appropriated for U.S. bases. The case was brought all the way to the Supreme Court. Through the lawsuit against the state, the governor was asking the government in Tokyo to ease the excessive burden on Okinawa, where 75 percent of U.S. military installations on Japanese soil are concentrated under the bilateral security treaty.

In April 1996, the two countries agreed at a bilateral summit on a package for consolidating and reducing American military facilities in Okinawa, including the return of Futenma Air Station. Ōta did not change his basic position even then, but the government had no recourse but to impose the national interest on Okinawa and make the expired lease on land legal through the Supreme Court ruling in favor of the state.

Soon thereafter, in September, Okinawa Prefecture held a referendum on the issue. Approximately 90 percent of those who voted were in favor of the consolidation and reduction of the U.S. bases there. The governor conducted a series of negotiations with Tokyo on behalf of the "public interest" of the Okinawan people made explicit through the referendum. "What is Japan's national interest," asks Ōta, "if so much of the burden must be forced on Okinawa? Shouldn't real national interest reflect a wide spectrum of public opinion?" Clearly, his view of the public interest is remote from that of the bureaucrats in Tokyo.

One month before the voting in Okinawa, the Maki township in Nii-gata Prefecture held a referendum on the issue of locating a nuclear power plant there. It was the first referendum in Japan. The town had already been chosen as one of the sites in the government's Basic Plan for the Development of Power Resources. Nearly 90 percent of the eligible voters in the town cast their ballots, and the great majority was against the construction of a power plant. Mayor Sasaguchi Takaaki immediately declared that he would not sell the town-owned land for building facilities for nuclear-power generation. Here again, the public interest of the local townspeople challenged the national policy drawn up in Tokyo.

Japan-U.S. mutual security arrangements are "public goods" based on national consensus, to cite Prime Minister Hashimoto Ryūtarō. It is probably safe to say that development of power resources, too, is a major component in the national interest, particularly for a resource-poor country like Japan. Up until 1996, the government had somehow managed to get local areas to accept, albeit reluctantly at times, its "national policy" programs, taking full advantage of bureaucratic prerogatives and the submissiveness of the people to authority. When there was organized opposition to the government plan, various economic benefits such as subsidies were offered to compensate for the losses that might be incurred and to mollify the concerns and dissatisfaction of local residents.

In Okinawa Prefecture and Maki township, neither of these approaches worked. Both of the traditional, experientially proven systems of public interests and economic benefits had vanished from people's purview. Instead, they pitted their own "public interest" against the national interest.

Noteworthy here is the fact that the government resorted to all kinds of means prior to the voting, including door-to-door visits of its representatives, to persuade the townspeople of Maki to support its policy. The results of the referendum proved that when the local public interest was openly pitted against the national interest, the government did not know how to sway public opinion for the sake of the latter. Kajiyama Seiroku, then chief cabinet secretary, deplored the refusal of the people of Maki, saying, "Sometimes I wonder if we could not build a nuclear power plant in Tokyo."

These facts amply show a major gap in the traditional Japanese style of governance. As was revealed in the handling of the housing loan issue described earlier, the government was not equipped to offer a plausible rationale for its policy decision. Under the official monopoly on the public interest, it has seldom occurred to the bureaucrats that they have to explain their decisions, much less persuade the local people concerned. Nor have they ever acquired an effective technique of persuasion. Moreover, they lack the wisdom and know-how necessary to compare different sets of public interests in an open setting and decide on an order of priorities through the presentation of convincing background and arguments.

Confusion in the system of public interests gave rise to a new style of political bargaining. In March 1998, Governor of Aomori Prefecture Kimura Morio suddenly announced his intention to refuse the entry into the Mutsu Ogawara port of a vessel carrying high-level radioactive waste. He reasoned that he could not give a convincing explanation to the people of his prefecture. It was a show of a prefectural governor's resistance to the central government's policy. The governor backed down rather quickly in this case, so it was generally taken as a case of political grandstanding. The incident nevertheless proved that the local public interest can legally assert itself against the central government authorities.

Modern Japan's structure of governance is premised on the public-equals-official mentality, in that local obedience to national policy is taken for granted. But the cases of Okinawa, Niigata, and Aomori cited here show that local governments have various "weapons" at their disposal with which to resist or act in defiance of the central authorities. We can perhaps say that the local public interest is the gunpowder for these weapons.

CAN OFFICIALS REPRESENT THE PUBLIC INTEREST?

A series of scandals broke out in 1995 involving high-ranking Ministry of Finance officials. The former chief of the Tokyo Custom-House and the former deputy chief of the Budget Bureau were found to have colluded with dubious money brokers. They resigned under the pressure of public outcry.

Then in 1996, startling facts began coming to public attention at the Ministry of Health and Welfare. It was found that officials of the government had deliberately neglected that highest priority in the realm of the public interest—the safety of people's lives. Through misjudgment and neglect on the part of the ministry, about 2,000 people were infected by HIV-contaminated blood plasma products that ministry officials had continued to insist were safe.

The crucial data and documents, the existence of which the ministry had consistently denied for seven years in the course of civil trials (AIDS patients and HIV carriers vs. the pharmaceutical companies that imported and sold blood plasma products and the state that approved those products and their sale), turned up under the direction of a non-LDP minister of health and welfare. These records provided undeniable evidence that the ministry officials in charge had been aware of possible infection at a fairly early stage and had chosen not to take any action to remove the imported blood plasma products from the market, thereby allowing the spread of fatal infection for a number of years.

This revelation was quickly followed by a formal apology from the minister of health and welfare to the HIV carriers and AIDS patients concerned, and settlement of the civil suits that had been brought. The medical scientists and pharmaceutical company executives who had been sued for murder were arrested on charges of involuntary manslaughter. A top-ranking bureaucrat, who was a section chief in the mid-1980s, was also arrested on the same charge. This was the first arrest in modern Japanese history of a bureaucrat personally accused of administrative negligence.

In December that year (1996), the Health Ministry's top official—administrative vice-minister—was arrested on charges of graft in a separate case of corruption. He had received a substantial amount in bribes from the owner of several welfare facilities for the elderly.

Successive revelations of cases of corruption, negligence, and incompetence among elite bureaucrats since the mid-1990s raised the basic question of their competence to act in the public interest, and whether citizens should continue to entrust decisions on the public interest and their execution to officialdom, as had always been done in the past. The "public" consciousness, if any, that bureaucrats possess also came under scrutiny.

Debate was quickly to emerge over the pros and cons of legislation for a code of ethics for public servants. The government was at first reluctant to enact a new law, saying that an internal code was sufficient. Hashimoto expressed his view that "rather than regulating their conduct by law, I would prefer to trust the sense of shame, conscientiousness, and spirit of service to the people of the overwhelming majority of officials." The National Public Service Law already stipulates, "[Government officials] may not act in any way as to harm the reputation of their offices or to be a dishonor to officialdom as a whole." The government argued that this provision was sufficient to punish disgraceful conduct by officials.

Police investigation beginning in 1997 into bribery scandals in financial institutions, however, led to the arrest of Finance Ministry officials in January 1998. The repeated corruption of the most powerful and prestigious of all government agencies rendered meaningless the claim that officials should be the sole arbiter of the public interest. Hashimoto was forced to change his stance in favor of the legislation of an ethical code of conduct. He was quoted as saying, "I cannot but feel betrayed." One of the major issues during the ordinary Diet session in 1998 was a bill forbidding officials to be entertained by any business concern falling within their jurisdiction and requiring them to report any case of entertainment exceeding ¥5,000.

Why did the prime minister vacillate in his stance on the code of ethics? Obviously he himself had fallen prey to the peculiar sense of responsibility characteristic of the public-equals-official society. The above-mentioned provisions of the National Public Service Law are intended not to protect the interests of the people but to safeguard the reputation and honor of officialdom itself. Officials are subject to punishment when they commit acts damaging to the credibility and prestige of the bureaucracy. But according to the logic of this code, it is officialdom itself that is seen as the victim of malfeasance, where in fact, it is the people, the taxpayers, who are betrayed. There is no mechanism for punishing officials either for their failure to respond to the needs of the people or for undermining the popular trust. In other words, bureaucrats are considered responsible primarily to their own organization, not to the people or the public.

Through the post–World War II reforms, Japan's officials became "public servants," a change in status from the prewar "officials of the emperor." But there was no mechanism built in to check and guarantee their spirit of service to the people. Even under the democratic system of the civil service, the public-equals-official society survived to preserve the bureaucratic sanctuary.

DISCOVERY OF NEW HORIZONS OF THE PUBLIC
RELATIVIZATION OF GOVERNMENT

The fissures in the public-equals-official edifice that were brought to light one by one in 1996 did not appear all of a sudden, of course. Among the factors behind them were the quantitative increase in wealth during the extended period of economic growth, and the accompanying diversification of social values and expansion of social activities of all kinds. Since the early 1980s, moreover, with the fiscal deadlock and rising calls for deregulation, the role of the government began to be limited and reduced. People gradually came to recognize that there is a certain realm of the public that the government does not control, or cannot directly control. In broad perspective, we can say that the structure of modern Japan, in which the government builds the society and manages it, had started to collapse—both in actuality and on the level of the popular consciousness—as the result of the maturation of society and the "relativization" of government authority (see Sakamoto 1997).

The epochal event in the relativization of government was the establishment in the 1980s of the Ad-hoc Commission on Administrative Reform, an advisory organ to the prime minister, which embarked upon administrative reform under the slogan of "government-private burden sharing." The commission was led by members of the business community seriously concerned about the threat of fiscal bankruptcy with the advent of the low-growth period and the rapidly aging population. One major purpose of the reform was to streamline the administration. A consensus had been forming among business leaders that the government, although it had contributed to sustaining rapid economic growth, was becoming increasingly inefficient and wasteful and therefore had to be streamlined for the sake of the expanding and globalizing national economy.

The focus in the Ad-hoc Commission was on the reorganization and reduction of the many government regulations that placed restraint on private activities. Deregulation became firmly established as a political task by the end of the 1980s, and even after that, deregulation continued to be among the basic demands of the business world vis-à-vis the government. Until the early 1980s, regulations had been a fundamental part of the government's "public benefit" activities, or in collaboration between government and business. The deregulation approach demonstrated that the government, the old patron of the nation's business and industry, was now seen as a major impediment to the growth of the economy.

Officialdom, centering on the Ministry of Finance, did ostensibly follow the Ad-hoc Commission line of "fiscal reconstruction without tax increase." But the government was incapable of casting off its

long-indulged habit of lavishing money on public works projects and
welfare programs. It finally introduced a consumption tax in 1989.Thus,
although the times were calling on the government to revise its policies
vis-à-vis the public interest, the bureaucracy still sought to avoid the
issue by making minimal adjustments. By combining the gradual reduction of vested interests with the gradual increase of financial burden, the government adopted a policy line that it considered would
assure a soft landing for the rapidly aging society.

However, the people's instinctive opposition to the increased burden, and their indignation at the continuing revelations of political corruption, as well as the government's failure to effectively manage the
economy as reflected in the economic bubble, triggered political turmoil, as outlined earlier, and the onset of a series of unstable coalition
governments. Then, as the people grew distrustful of officialdom because of its handling of the housing loan company problem and the
spread of HIV infection through contaminated blood products, the political parties and politicians that had depended on the bureaucracy for
so long began the unprecedented move of distancing themselves from it.

The fact that the Hashimoto administration made reorganization
of government agencies a major campaign pledge in the 1996 general
election and that heated debate has continued within the ruling parties
on the subdivision of the Ministry of Finance, the very kingpin of the
bureaucracy (a debate which shook the coalition government in 1997
and 1998), reflects an irreversible trend in which politicians are gradually weaning themselves from dependency on the bureaucracy, although
in some cases the reorganization and consolidation of government agencies is tainted by vote-seeking tactics. Hashimoto forcibly replaced the
vice-minister of finance at the apex of the government bureaucracy in
connection with the financial scandals of 1998. It was an "epoch-making
incident," commented Katō Kōichi, then secretary-general of the LDP,
"testifying to the shifting balance of power between politicians and bureaucrats."

For politicians and political parties, the new "public interest" and
new public symbols are necessary not only to win in elections under the
party-centered single-seat constituency system recently adopted for
the House of Representatives, but also to survive the fierce realignment
struggle among the parties. In a society with such a strong tradition
equating the public with the official, distance from officialdom will be
seen as new and fresh. Exemplary of that trend, leading politicians of

conservative background have begun advocating "civil rights" and "civil interests," which are new symbols of the public interest vis-à-vis the "official." The public-equals-official governing system, or what is called the union of politics and the bureaucracy, is being reappraised from the political side as well.

SELF-DISCOVERY OF "PUBLIC"

The onset of an age of increasing burdens came all too soon after Japanese had begun to enjoy the fruits of hard-won affluence. Dramatic changes in popular attitudes as a result have been another unmistakable factor in the relativization of government.

The attitudes of taxpayers who in the 1980s strongly resisted the introduction of the consumption tax on principle changed in quality during the 1990s to concern for and resistance to the way the tax collected from them was being used. That shift can be seen in the ramifications of the public information disclosure movement and its growing importance in society.

Institutionalization of information disclosure in Japan began in the early 1980s on the local government level. Systems for information disclosure were instituted in one local government after another on the momentum of the then-fashionable "age of regionalism" and "citizens-first priorities." As of 1998, such systems had been instituted in all 47 of Japan's prefectural governments as well as in nearly 18 percent of local governments lower down on the municipal level.

The information disclosure system is the embodiment of popular sovereignty, and as such holds special meaning in the rhetoric of the public-equals-official society. As formally stated in the information disclosure ordinances of some local governments, the system is a framework for disclosure (literally, opening to the public) of public documents (*kōbunsho*), and, as noted earlier, traditionally "public documents" meant "government documents," that is, the records kept and information compiled by government officials. Here the concepts of *kō* as government and as public curiously overlap. Whether or not the government will really disclose the information it holds and the system will properly function depends, in the final analysis, on whether the concept of *kō* as public can replace that of *kō* as government.

This system can be said to be in the process of changing people's attitudes. The establishment of information disclosure systems on the local level set in motion in the mid-1990s movements by taxpayers to expose cases of account-book juggling in local governments. The revelations that emerged at this time dealt a heavy blow to the public-equals-official society. It was found that local government officials had made a common practice of siphoning off public funds through manipulation of accounts billed under such categories as official trips and extra hires, using the funds to entertain visiting officials from the ministries in Tokyo as a means of soliciting generous subsidies from the central government. Revelations of such government corruption and scandals made through applications for disclosure of public documents by citizens' groups and local residents' ombudsmen had been found in 25 different prefectures by 1996, and ¥7.8 billion in public funds discovered to have been siphoned off by local officials in 14 prefectures was to be refunded from individual salaries (Asahi Shimbun 1997, 388).

In Akita Prefecture, where it was found that false public documents had been handed over for fear of the discovery of illegal disbursements, the subsequent public outcry was so intense that the governor was forced to resign. In Miyagi Prefecture, under strong pressure from citizens' groups, prefectural authorities were forced to reveal the names of central government officials who had been "entertained" by local officials, information until then not subject to public disclosure. It was in Miyagi that the incumbent governor, who had switched to a stance of strong support for public disclosure in the gubernatorial elections in the fall of 1997, defeated by a large margin the challenger for his post backed by the two largest conservative parties (the LDP and the New Frontier Party) as well as big business organizations. It was while they witnessed this series of revelations of the true quality of government under the public-equals-official society that local citizens began to realize that "public" meant they themselves and awareness of *kō* as public began to take root.

The waves of change that had shaken local governments began to be felt in the offices of the central government ministries as well. Although the central ministries flatly rejected public information disclosure systems a few years ago on the grounds that they would further complicate administration, they have finally come under the terms of the Freedom of Information Law proposed to the Diet during 1998. The institution of systems by which the government will be accountable to the people for all its actions and the adoption of legal systems for monitoring of public administration by citizens and enhancing popular participation in government has been possible because the government recognizes that they are indispensable if it is to maintain even a minimum of credibility with the people. We have entered the stage in the crack-up of the public-equals-official society in which people will not be convinced of the public interest until they can see what officials are really doing.

PRIVATE PUBLIC VS. PUBLIC PUBLIC

The rise of "public" consciousness goes hand in hand with the growth of citizens' activism, as shown in the case of the disclosure issue. Detailed data on nonprofit organizations (NPOs) and nongovernmental organizations (NGOs) in Japan are not yet available, but according to a September 1996 survey by the Economic Planning Agency, there exist about 85,000 groups involved in a wide range of activities from welfare and education to human rights, peace, and international cooperation.

The number of NGOs established for the purpose of engaging in international cooperation, for example, has increased rapidly since the 1980s, according to data from the Japanese NGO Center for International Cooperation: 7 at the end of the 1960s; 33 at the close of the 1970s; 132 at the end of the 1980s; and 190 so far in the 1990s. Whether organized or not, a large number of volunteers participated in relief activities after the Great Hanshin-Awaji Earthquake of 1995 (1.3 million people) and when thousands of tons of crude oil leaked from a wrecked Russian tanker drifted ashore on the Sea of Japan coast in 1997 (270,000 volunteer workers).

Japan now finds itself, along with many other countries, in the midst of the global trend toward rapid expansion of the nongovernmental sector that Lester M. Salamon calls the "associational revolution" (1994). Japan, too, has an increasing number of "ordinary people who decide to take matters into their own hands and organize to improve their conditions or seek basic rights" (112). It is the activities of these people that are beginning to bring to the surface the problematic nature of the system of serving the public interest that has been distorted by the public-equals-official schema. At long last, these activists are breaking the spell of government that has bound people throughout Japan's modern period.

One important thing we have to consider here is what the growth of the nongovernmental sector really means for the relativization of government in Japan. It means that relativization must go far beyond the call for a "small government" aimed at ensuring freer, less-regulated economic activities or the demand for only qualitative improvements in public administration, such as disclosure of information. In other words, it is no longer sufficient for the government to make itself more efficient and more democratic.

The growth of the nongovernmental sector is itself proof that the kind of public realm that the government is either unwilling or unable to handle is rapidly expanding. In both consciousness and reality, the public realm is growing ever wider, but the government can no longer be responsible for everything. This is another crucial factor accelerating the relativization of government. The simple truth is that our world has reached a point where the public-equals-official schema is no longer viable.

International cooperation for development assistance and global environmental issues are well-known examples of the areas in the public realm that government alone cannot take care of. But there are an increasing number of domestic problems that defy official control of public concerns. The problems of waste disposal and recycling are good examples.

In Japan's urban areas, trash collection and disposal have been handled by local governments, free of charge to citizens in most cases. More recently, however, as resource conservation has become a major issue and garbage disposal capacity has nearly reached its limits in urban centers, a new awareness and new approaches have emerged. A number of cities have begun to separate the collection of glassware, plastics, metals, and so on for purposes of recycling. They also urge citizens to keep their trash to a minimum, and in some areas the municipal authorities charge for waste collection in hopes of reducing the amounts of trash people produce.

In urban life, at least, waste disposal is one public realm that affects everyone. Providing such a service free of charge was in a way typical of a society like Japan's, where public has been equated with official. But now, partly because the necessity for resource conservation has gained societal acceptance as a new kind of common good, people are obliged to take part in such "public" activities as separating their garbage by type of material and working to reduce the amount of trash they produce. Corporations, too, are now actively involved in recycling efforts and trying to lessen their waste output. In many cities, citizens have launched campaigns to promote recycling.

In any case, we find today many private citizens and private enterprises taking on some "public" endeavors. The equation is shifting from the old public-official pattern to "public equals citizens plus companies," which in turn means "private."

As I pointed out in the second section of this chapter, *kō* (official-cum-public) has traditionally been paired with *shi* (private) in Japan. Another dichotomy that has prevailed in this country is *kan* (government officials) and *min* (people). Where *kō* was equated with *kan, min* and *shi* were identified as one and the same. The dominant notion in modern Japan has been that people are essentially private, divorced from either the public or the official.

But the problem of urban waste disposal defies this kind of dichotomous thinking. Yorimoto Katsumi, who teaches at Waseda University and is himself an activist in a citizens' movement for solution of the waste disposal issue, says that there are two kinds of public: "private public" and "public public." What is at stake for Japan, he writes, is how to establish the realm of private public, and how the two realms (that is, government and the realm of private public) can work together. In other words, the primary question is "what the role sharing should be between *min* (people) and *kan* (officials)" (Yorimoto 1994, 8–10). That a scholar had to coin the term "private public," which is self-contradictory, is eloquent testimony to the deep-rooted grip of the public-equals-official tradition on people's consciousnesses and the urgent necessity for the country to shed that premodern mentality.

Another problem the public-equals-official mentality no longer copes with effectively is that of a rapidly aging society, coupled with the decreasing birthrate. The most pressing issue involves the kind of public services to provide the elderly, and here, too, we see the emergence of "private public."

In its interim report of March 1996, the government Committee for the Promotion of Decentralization stresses the necessity of a new system incorporating private-sector and citizen participation in meeting the increasing demand for public services for the aged. The report states in part: "Local government officials alone can no longer provide effective services. It is necessary to establish a joint network of public-private cooperation in which various public service corporations, nonprofit organizations, volunteer groups, and even private enterprises take part" (Committee for the Promotion of Decentralization 1996, 6–7). In this new scheme, "private" is recognized as an independent entity capable of pursuing the public interest, as a partner equal to "official" rather than just the latter's auxiliary force. As the committee's report indicates, the government is now groping for a new pattern of citizen participation in order to respond to the needs of the times. Such a pattern must clearly "go beyond the old pattern of local resident participation" (Kawashima 1998, 62). The "official" monopoly on "public" is now becoming a thing of the past.

CONCLUSION: CHALLENGE OF CIVIL SOCIETY

As we have seen in the above discussion, fundamental questions about the meaning of "public" now haunt the old public-equals-official society, challenging Japanese to redefine the very meaning of the word. Behind those questions is the awakening of popular consciousness of bonds among citizens in a spontaneous, self-conscious group: civil society. The discovery of a new concept of public—a new meaning for the common good—is in the process of opening up the prospects for a repositioning of the government as just part of the public sector. The realization of such a prospect would be historic because it would mean a dramatic change in the traditional concept of governance.

The more historic such a revolution in perceptions, however, the greater the obstacles to its realization. Conscious and unconscious resistance will be very strong from the very officialdom that will be required to change its role as the central actor in government. Another problem will be the deep-rooted distrust of the "private" fostered under the aegis of the public-equals-official society.

As suggested by its accommodation to the establishment of systems for disclosure of public information, the bureaucracy is fully aware of the challenges the changing times present it. To quote from a draft position paper on administrative reform prepared unofficially by young officials at the direction of senior officials in the Ministry of International Trade and Industry (1997) in March 1997:

> Revelations regarding the policy decision-making process vis-à-vis use of public funds for dealing with the defunct housing loan companies and on the official misjudgments on potentially HIV-contaminated blood plasma products shocked and angered citizens, laying before their eyes the extremely murky, secretive nature of administration. . . . There has never been such a tremendous outcry about the absence of checks and participation

from the citizen side on the policy formulation process assumed by the government and about the failure of the government to make available public information that would make such involvement possible.

Failures or inadequacies on the part of government caused by lack of professionalism or specialized know-how have become more frequent and noticeable, arousing concerns among the people about whether they can really trust it to handle the administration of their country. In some fields, moreover, the private sector has come to possess superior technology, and this has given rise to doubts about the justification for public administration.

The outbreak of recent scandals has heightened distrust of government and strengthened doubts about government capacity for self-reform and self-purification, planting the seeds of doubt in people's minds about the very legitimacy of government. (1–4)

This report reflects the clear and candid awareness regarding a crisis in the legitimacy of government. This awareness, however, has not been linked to constructive action, nor has it led to a new set of behavioral norms for the bureaucrats. As Hashimoto sought to make headway in administrative reform, the central government agencies bustled around mobilizing related organizations and Diet members with close ties to the ministries (*zoku giin*) to defend and maintain the organizational structures and powers they had garnered over the years. They fought to protect the public interest in the old sense, keeping a death grip on the deeply entrenched systems of old-style government control. The new reform plan ended up mainly a reshuffling of the administration, with little changed.

The fact that officials took such actions in the face of a crisis in their very raison d'être demonstrates two well-established principles: that, particularly in times of transition, officialdom lacks the capacity to devise new forms of the public interest conforming to the needs of the times, and that the megastructures that are the vessels of the order of established public interests are not invested with the necessary vision and vitality to change that order. What they demonstrated in readily comprehensible form is that the bureaucracy does not have the capacity to engineer change in the public-equals-official society.

If that be so, can the private sector engineer such a change? Herein lies the great challenge for Japanese society today.

In the public-equals-official society, horizontal channels linking people without the mediation of officialdom are few and frail. This is because of the mentality fostered in this society that anything that has not passed through official hands or obtained its stamp of approval cannot be confidently trusted by society. In other words, while the government/public sector has enjoyed unconditional trust, the private sector is always suspect of not being completely trustworthy.

But we need not be too pessimistic. There are definite signs of departure from dependence on officialdom and of the development of a new modus vivendi for society. A typical example is the NPO Law, which won Diet approval in March 1998. The concept for the NPO Law, designed to provide incorporated status and tax exemptions to citizens' groups engaged in nonprofit activities, was sparked by the vigorous volunteer activities that sprang up following the Great Hanshin-Awaji Earthquake.

The concept of "public-interest corporation" exists in Japan in the texts of the Civil Code and other laws, but confirmation of an organization's public-interest orientation by the central government authorities is the condition for authorization of its legal status. Even after incorporation, such organizations are under the guidance and supervision of the ministries. There are 26,000 such public-interest corporations today, and many of them, providing postretirement employment for career civil servants, help to buttress the public-equals-official structure. The idea behind the NPO Law was to create public-interest organizations not subject to official control, paving the way for citizen-led activities in a freer context.

However, support for the law was hobbled by concerns of the old public-equals-official school about who (or what agency) will approve organizations as engaging in activities for the public interest, fears that they may be used for tax evasion, and whether any such organizations should be permitted that are not supervised by the government. People's thinking has still not moved away from the suspicion that anything "private" and left to its own devices will sooner or later violate the public interest.

In 1996, the ruling parties finally reached agreement on a revised NPO bill, omitting tax-benefits measures and renaming it the Law for Promotion of Citizens' Activities. However, further opposition arose from within the LDP declaring that the term "citizen's activities" was too closely associated with activities critical of the government, so another revision was done, entitling the bill Law to Promote Specified Nonprofit Activities. The whole legislative process represented competition between the public-equals-official society and the forces for freedom from the fetters of that society.

The bill was finally passed into law through the patient and wide-ranging support and pressure exerted by numerous citizens' groups for prompt legislation. These activities, coupled with the slow but steady changes in the popular consciousness, have had an impact on the thinking of some LDP leaders about the advent of a new era in which citizens' groups are to play a variety of political roles and functions.[4] It is symbolic that the NPO Law was passed unanimously.

Who is to decide what is in the public interest? Whose job is it to maintain and promote the public interest? Does it have to be the government? Can it be some other person or organization? Fundamental questions such as these, which were not discussed in the process of legislation, are now on the table for open political debate. These are questions Japanese society can no longer avoid. Today, indeed, the public-equals-official society is at a crucial crossroads.

NOTES

1. Unless otherwise stated, quoted material is from interviews by the author.

2. The material for this case study comes from research done by the Reform and the Citizens Research Team at the Asahi Shimbun in 1997 (of which the author was chief). I am particularly indebted to the findings of Takano Yuzuru, one of the reporters on the team.

3. Iinuma and Shirahata (1993), Shirahata (1991), and interviews by the author with Shirahata.

4. Cf. interpellation by Katō Kōichi, secretary-general of the LDP, during the 1998 ordinary Diet session, February 18.

BIBLIOGRAPHY

Asahi Shimbun, ed. 1997. *Asahi nenkan 1997* (Asahi yearbook 1997). Tokyo: Asahi Shimbun Sha.

Committee for the Promotion of Decentralization. 1996. "Chūkan hōkoku—bunkengata shakai no sōzō" (Creation of a decentralized society: An interim report). Unpublished.

Council on Rivers. 1995. "Concerning River Environments from Now to the Future." Unpublished report.

Iinuma Jirō and Shirahata Yōzaburō. 1993. *Nihon bunka toshite no kōen* (Parks in Japanese culture). Tokyo: Yasaka Shobō.

Kawashima Masahide. 1998. "Kankoku no seiji-teki ichi wo saguru" (An inquiry into the political significance of the recommendations). *Jurist*, no. 1127 (February): 57–62.

Katō Tetsuro. 1992. *Shakai to kokka* (Society and the state). Tokyo: Iwanami Shoten.

Maruyama Masao. 1986. *"Bunmeiron no gairyaku" wo yomu, jo* (Reading Fukuzawa Yukichi's "An Outline of Civilization," vol. 1). Tokyo: Iwanami Shoten.

Ministry of International Trade and Industry. 1997. "Gyōsei kaikaku no ichi kōsatsu" (A study of administrative reform). Tentative draft of unpublished document.

Mito Tadashi. 1976. *Kō to shi* (Public and private). Tokyo: Miraisha.

Research Committee on River Control, Ministry of Construction. 1996. "Shinsui shisetsu ni okeru anzen taisaku no kihonteki kangaekata ni tsuite" (Fundamental considerations for safety measures in 'friendly river' facilities). Unpublished report.

Sakamoto Yoshikazu. 1997. "Sōtaika no jidai" (The Age of Relativization). *Sekai*, no. 630 (January): 35–67.

Salamon, Lester M. 1994. "The Rise of the Nonprofit Sector." *Foreign Affairs* 70(4): 109–122.

Shirahata Yōzaburō. 1991. *"Nihonjin ni totte no 'kurashiyosa' to wa* (What Japanese consider "good living"). *Asteion*, no. 22 (Autumn): 62–70.

Watanabe Hiroshi. 1997. *Higashi Ajia no ōken to shisō* (Royal authority and political ideas in East Asia). Tokyo: Tokyo Daigaku Shuppankai.

Yorimoto Katsumi. 1994. "Genba kara mita bunkenron" (The meaning of decentralization from the field). Tokyo: Japan Research Institute for Local Government.

CHAPTER TWO

Japan's Civil Society: An Historical Overview

Iokibe Makoto

THE TRADITION of respect for authority and disdain for the masses (*kanson minpi*) is deep-rooted in Japan. Officialdom monopolizes the public realm while the people, the masses, are permitted the pursuit of private gain, personal welfare, and individual happiness insofar as these things lie within the legal and political frameworks dictated by the government. This tradition has largely demarcated the realms of public and private in Japanese society.

Considering such a tradition, any attempt to examine Japan's history in terms of the notion of "civil society" might seem a futile exercise. After all, the applications of this term, which have recently been the focus of considerable attention, are quite broad. A civil society can denote a private organization on the one hand and a civic community on the other, but the concept goes beyond those meanings as well. It refers to organizations that act for the public and the public benefit even though they are part of the private rather than the government sector. Although not formally invested with any official prerogatives, such organizations support the welfare of people in general and carry out activities for the community as a whole with a strong sense of commitment.

Any independent organization or private individual so impertinent as to attempt such activities in the Tokugawa period (also called the Edo period; 1603–1867) would have been instantly suspected of posing a threat to the ruling authorities. In those times, it was believed that all aspects of government had to be monopolized by *kōgi* (government

51

authority), which was, at that time, the *bakufu,* or shogunal government headed by the Tokugawa clan. From the viewpoint of the feudal system of domains under shogunal control (*bakuhan taisei*) and the then-prevailing Confucianist view of social order, for private individuals to trespass the boundaries of their status in society and intervene in the realm of activity deemed to belong to the government was considered a form of revolt. After the founding of the modern state of Meiji in 1868, anyone who wanted to establish an organization to contribute to the good of others was subject to laws and ordinances established by one government agency or another, as well as to often-numerous constraints clamped onto them through bureaucratic guidance. Under these conditions, there was very little that might have encouraged the development of civil society in Japan, either in terms of the social environment or human and intellectual resources.

Even today, few public-interest corporations (*kōeki hōjin*) are completely independent of the government. On the contrary, in many cases they are either auxiliary organs of the government or virtually under its control, accepting official regulations to obtain the privileged status of public-interest corporation. There are numerous occasions, of course, when the government calls upon the support and cooperation of people or groups in the private sector in order to fulfill public goals or needs. In these endeavors, while the private individuals or organizations are given a chance to contribute to the public welfare, the scope and purpose of their activities can unfold only within areas prescribed and determined by the powers that be. It goes without saying that there are self-motivated and self-respecting people in Japan who have contributed to society in the spirit of service for the public good. Particularly in recent years, the dramatic increase in the number of nongovernmental organizations (NGOs), nonprofit organizations (NPOs), independent foundations, and research or educational institutions can be considered nothing less than revolutionary.

In this chapter, I will examine the conditions that held the development of civil society in Japan in abeyance and look at what it is that is now in the process of changing.

Preconditions of Civil Society

The following three conditions can be considered requisite for civil society to develop: the presence of a pluralistic society, recognition of the intrinsic value of the "private," and popular awareness of the public interest.

A PLURALISTIC SOCIETY

Under a dictatorship or authoritarian regime—whether it be the Nazi dictatorship or pre–1945 Japanese militarism or developmental authoritarianism—civil society is soon suffocated. The presence of a pluralistic society is the preeminent condition for the free activity of private groups and associations.

Generally speaking, social pluralism is the product of economic development and is considered fundamental for the functioning of democracy. During the post–World War II period, rapid economic growth produced a new middle class in Japan and provided the conditions under which the vast majority of citizens acquired a middle-class consciousness. The same development has occurred in Taiwan and in the Republic of Korea, providing the social foundations for the transition to a democratic system. It is likely that the member countries of the Association of Southeast Asian Nations will undergo a similar process of change, or so it is expected. Should that be the case, the development-oriented authoritarian regimes, which carry out "development" coercively, by undemocratic means, are sure to bring about their own demise through development's success, which makes the democratization of their societies inevitable.

In this sense, the optimistic view that social diversification is currently in progress in East Asia and that it will provide the foundations for democratization and nurture civil society in the region is probably not wrong in the long run. History, however, rejects simplistic determinism. It was immediately after the heydays of Weimar democracy in Germany and Taishō democracy in Japan (1912–1926) were brought to an end by the Great Depression that the forces of Nazism and militarism took control. There is no promise that economic development in East Asia will lead to peace and democracy in some predestined fashion. Should responses to economic crisis err, either domestically or internationally, terrible consequences could result. Nonetheless, in the long-range view, I believe it is correct to assume that mature advanced societies enjoy pluralism, democracy, and the growth of civil society.

Decentralization in Tokugawa Society
Social pluralism of a sort did exist in premodern times as well. Modern

centralized states were born by destroying the decentralized feudal regimes of medieval and premodern times. In the case of Japan's Tokugawa
society, the shogunate controlled the center of government authority.
The domains, which were granted the right to control local areas by
swearing fealty to the *bakufu*, could participate in this government
authority and its dominions. They formed small-scale shogunate-like
regimes throughout the country.

During the Tokugawa period, the emperor, who was the source of
ruling legitimacy, was reduced to the position of a figurehead, while the
shogunate became the custodian of government authority. The latter
controlled the semi-independent domains and retained the power to
reduce or take away the holdings of domanial lords who did not follow
its rules. The farmers governed under this system frequently revolted
against heavy taxation and corrupt government (approximately 2,800
incidents occurred during the Tokugawa period). Invariably, these up-
risings were suppressed by the local lord and their leaders executed,
but if the shogunate found that the unrest had been caused by bad government, it could also lead to penalties for the domain. The leaders of
these rebellions literally put their lives on the line to appeal to the higher
authority of the shogunate for redress of their grievances (Inoguchi
1988).

In any society, the ruler and ruled are aware, at least latently, of the
public interest and the issue of governance. If the ruler ignores the public good, it may not be able to avoid the outbreak of protests that violate
the law. In 1837, a rebellion broke out in Osaka led by Ōshio Heihachirō,
a middle-ranking local official and Wang Yang-ming Confucian scholar
inspired by a strong sense of justice and devotion to the people. This rebellion was a case where a man literally staked his life to make a statement about the responsibilities of government. The Wang Yang-ming
school of Confucianism, established in the 16th century in Ming China
to advocate the translation of truth into reality through subjective acts,
inspired the action-oriented revolutionary spirit of Ōshio Heihachirō,
and later Yoshida Shōin (1830–1859).

The Tokugawa shogunate, by contrast, had adopted and promoted
so-called Neo-Confucian orthodoxy soon after it seized control of the
whole country in the early 17th century, putting an end to a prolonged
period of civil war. Neo-Confucianism, based on the teachings of 12th-
century scholar Chu Hsi (1130–1200), stressed the static order of the
universe, hence the shogunate considered it helpful in securing a

lasting and stable domestic order. The models of human relations taught in Neo-Confucianism are predominantly vertical, such as those between parent and child, elder and younger brothers, teacher and disciple, and lord and vassal. (The only exception is the horizontal relationship of "friends.") Special emphasis was placed on obedience and fidelity shown by those in inferior positions (child, younger brother, disciple, vassal) vis-à-vis their superiors (parent, elder brother, teacher, lord). The Confucian ideology prized by the Tokugawa shogunate and the succeeding Meiji government attached more importance to the individual moral training of the ruled than the high moral leadership of the ruler.

From one point of view, the feudal system created a society of many divisions. It was divided vertically into the samurai, farmer, artisan, and merchant classes and horizontally into more than 270 semi-independent domains. Each domain had its own ethos and culture and competed in the realms of scholarship, martial arts, and local products. The ethos of the Satsuma domain in Kyushu, for example, stressed martial spirit and action and looked down on assiduous study and logical argument. By contrast, the Saga domain, located not far away, inculcated its youth with a thoroughgoing devotion to learning.

Another domain, the size of a pea in comparison with the nearby mammoth Satsuma, was Obi (now just one part of the city of Nichinan in Miyazaki Prefecture). This tiny domain toughly resisted the hegemony of its giant neighbor over the centuries. By skillful use of an alliance with Toyotomi Hideyoshi (1537–1598), who was in the process of unifying Japan's warring provincialities, and other diplomatic means, Obi managed to maintain its independence. One young man who studied in the domain school for the sons of local samurai was Komura Jutarō (1855–1911), who later played a leading role in Japan's diplomacy at the time of the Russo-Japanese War of 1904–1905. No doubt putting to use the survival tactics developed by a small domain in dealing with a powerful one, Komura's diplomacy was responsible for Japan's survival in the life-or-death struggle with the great continental military power, Russia, by skillful reliance on diplomatic relations with faraway powers like Britain and the United States.

In any case, the 270-odd domains were the source of tremendous cultural and industrial diversity. Premodern Japan's social hierarchy was another source of diversity. Over time, the merchant and artisan classes attained a degree of autonomy—based on economic strength—from the political authority monopolized by the samurai class. A freewheeling urban culture flourished in the cities and castletowns sustained by the merchant and artisan classes. In addition to the domain-run schools (*hankō*) for the sons of samurai, approximately 10,000 popular schools (*terakoya*) attended by members of the other classes operated throughout the country, and in the cities there were also a variety of private academies, or *shijuku*. The *shijuku* of the late Tokugawa period included the Tekijuku of Osaka, led by Rangaku (Dutch learning) scholar Ogata Kōan (1810–1863), and the Shōka Sonjuku school where Yoshida Shōin taught his ideas of revolution. These schools generated the shock waves that helped to open the way for the Meiji Restoration of 1868. Any search for civil society in Tokugawa Japan would be in vain, but it did provide the space in which people could enjoy cultural diversity; such pluralism proved to be a precious resource from the beginning of the Meiji era (1868–1912) onward.

All the same, in the face of the social crisis that resulted following the arrival of Commodore Matthew C. Perry's "black ships" in the early 1850s, it was almost exclusively members of the samurai class who were able to suggest strategies and policy proposals and actively participated in political campaigns for or against the government. Only they, after all, had had any training in dealing with issues of governance and the public interest. And in the face of an age of drastic change, it was not so much the senior officials as the young men and not so much the high-ranking samurai as those of lower ranks who provided the new ideas and the energy to engineer the transition.

DIGNITY OF THE PEOPLE

Under the authoritarian state, the government represents the *whole*, the authority embodying the public, and the people are considered simply parts that are individually pursuing their private interests under that authority. Until this definition of public and private is overcome and replaced by an awareness that the people themselves are worthy of respect and have value on their own terms, civil society will not emerge.

Novelist Shiba Ryōtarō (1923–1996) once noted that until 1871, when popular-rights advocate Nakae Chōmin (1847–1901) brought back from France the ideas of Jean Jacques Rousseau (*The Social Contract*), Japan had virtually no concept of "the people." In that sense, Shiba said, the intellectual soil in Japan at the end of the Tokugawa period and in the early Meiji period was quite barren (Shiba 1989). Why did the idea of "the people" exist in the West yet remain so underdeveloped in Japan? Furthermore, does that mean that respect for the people and the emergence of civil society in Japan and other non-Western societies is unlikely? Discussion of this issue is continuing even today.

Honma Masaaki, a professor of economics at Osaka University who has been studying NPO activities since 1978, says that his findings are often rebutted with the argument that the volunteer spirit is a Western tradition based on Christian teachings and could not possibly take root in Japan. Honma's view, however, is that volunteerism is part of a humanistic global trend characterized by an economic and social rationalism that by no means excludes Japan. Today, with the outburst of volunteer activity since the Great Hanshin-Awaji Earthquake of January 1995, when 1.3 million volunteers turned out to help deal with its aftermath, and the enactment of the Law to Promote Specified Nonprofit Activities, or the NPO Law, that facilitates incorporation of NPOs, Honma's assertion has been supported by reality.

Here I believe we should make a clear distinction between two things. It is one thing that the idea of "the people" has been fostered most aggressively in the West, but it is quite another that an attractive idea spreads beyond its place of origin and, propelled by its universality, takes root in other places in specific guises influenced by the local context.

The Idea of "the People" in the Christian World

In the West, the concept of "the people" is premised on the concept of the "person" or individual, and the impact of Christianity in the shaping of this concept in Western civilization is undeniable. Christian thinkers defined the human being as being in the image of God and taught that each person must be respected to the utmost because he or she was endowed with the divine nature.

In *Summa Theologica,* St. Thomas Aquinas cites Boethius's definition of the *persona:* "an individual substance of a rational nature." Here "rational" meant possessing a nature resembling that of God and "individual substance" meant a unique and irreplaceable entity not dependent upon or accessory to others. The impact on real politics and society of this theological concept proved considerable through the ideas and actions of the Protestant denominations following the Reformation. The well-known ultrarepublican movements of the Levellers and the Diggers at the time of the Puritan Revolution based their claims to political legitimacy on new interpretations of Christian theology.

George Fox, leader of a new religious sect that arose during the mid-17th century in England, taught that "there is that of God in every man" and that since all people equally possess the Inner Light of the divine spirit the dignity and equality of all human beings should be respected. In line with that view, his sect did not distinguish between clergy and layman and in congregations or meetings, leadership of which was taken by turns among the participants, each person recounted his or her experiences of encounter with the Inner Light. The group stressed the sharing of these experiences among its members. They called for social reforms that would guarantee the dignity and equality of people.

The idea of the dignity of each individual person under God paved the way for the belief in the dignity of all people, and in the course of time, the source of legitimacy ceased to be traced to the Christian principle of the individual "under God." Respect for humanity, popular thought, and fundamental human rights came to be expounded in the realms of natural law, humanism, and political theory. Be that as it may, it is clear that the concepts of "the person" and "the people" were sustained by Christianity, which the people of Western civilization believe to be the common source of their values.

In the mechanistic view of social relations, the relation of government to individuals is that of whole to parts, and in this scheme it was logical that the whole should have precedence over the parts. However, the introduction of the idea of human dignity in this context brings into being a realm of basic human rights of the individual that even the government representing the whole may not violate. Moreover, if that which is most valued in a society is humanity (which is in God's image), then it follows that it is the people who make up the whole and whose primacy must be respected. Here the government does not take the leading role, exercising the powers of life and death, or of giving or taking away; it becomes a functional body intended to serve "the people." Historically, there were attempts to legitimize absolute rule according to the concept of the divine right of kings, but the mainstream development, from Christianity to humanism, and thence to democratic government, ultimately made the society where officialdom is exalted and the people despised untenable, and laid the foundation for the dignity of the people.

Other religions besides Christianity included doctrines of respect

for humanity. It is believed in Buddhism that Shakyamuni, the historical Buddha, sang at his birth, "I alone am honored / In heaven and on
earth." This verse does not advocate selfishness but calls for respect for
each individual as a precious and irreplaceable existence. The Lotus
Sutra tells of the Bodhisattva Never Disparaging (in Sanskrit, Sadapari-
bhūta), who bows low before each and every person he meets, saying,
"Please accept my deepest respects, because within you is the Buddha."
People found his behavior so odd and suspicious that they stoned him
to death and the bodhisattva became a martyr to the doctrine of the
"Buddha within all persons."

The inner Buddha and the inner Christ are similar, although, unlike
in the West, this former idea did not crystallize into a doctrine of "the
people" in society and politics in Asia and did not evolve into a theory of
democratic principles. Indeed, it was an idea that has been transmitted
through the generations, settling in the deepest layers of the Japanese
spirit. Buddhist thought, which teaches love and compassion for all living things, had a tremendous impact on the ethos of Japan's traditional
animism, the indigenous belief in a broad pantheon of deities, including
those of the mountains, the sea, the forest, the well, and the fields. The
spiritual tradition in Japan that prizes gentleness toward others (people)
must have been even further strengthened by the Buddhist teaching of
universal compassion. This was the spiritual layer that later absorbed
the Confucian teaching of "every person has a sympathetic heart," that
in modern and contemporary times responded to Christian ideas and
democracy, and that more recently fueled the impulses that turn Japanese to engage in voluntary activity with unprecedented energy.

The ideas of treasuring the splendor of life and of compassion for
all individuals without discrimination were therefore deeply imbedded
in the Japanese spirit, and people who were capable of treating others
in that spirit were highly respected. But the principle of universal compassion did not come into play in the realities of politics and government. There were religious leaders like Priest Nichiren (1222–1282) who
fiercely demanded that secular rule be subject to Buddhist laws, and
there were religious cults such as the Ikkō (Jōdo Shin) sect of Buddhism
that engaged in fanatic armed campaigns. Rulers saw the danger of political turmoil in such extremist ideas. Especially in the Tokugawa period,
the shogunate was successful in containing them within the framework
of the Confucian view of social order.

The Tokugawa government, which brought to a close a century and a half of war and civil strife by placing top priority on peace and order, banned Christianity and allowed the Buddhist sects to survive insofar as they submitted to incorporation within the structure of its rule. Thus, under the feudal regime, through which the shogunate controlled the semi-independent domains throughout the country, the spirit of compassion to all living things universalized by the transmission of Buddhist teachings was respected only in that private realm insofar as it did not conflict with the official structures of the Confucian view of social order. The ideas of the dignity of the individual and respect for the people, therefore, could not be legitimized either socially or politically; even if they were, they could only be subordinate concepts.

POPULAR AWARENESS OF THE PUBLIC INTEREST

The public interest is served by that which is to the common good of the communal group as a whole. The legitimacy of authority is heightened by the degree to which it conforms to that public interest and diminished by the degree to which it is arbitrary. No dictatorial regime will prevail for long after it ceases to conform to the public interest. And no matter how well established the custom of reverence for officialdom and contempt for the masses in a society, when the regime ceases to promote the safety and well-being of the people or when it engages in government tainted by the pursuit of personal gain, it will not be long before the regime is brought to an end, either by the chorus of popular censure or by a national catastrophe of some sort.

Here we may identify a number of phases with regard to the government versus the public interest relationship. The first is the phase in which officialdom (the government) monopolizes all matters in the public interest. On this level, even should officialdom violate the public interest, any criticism or opposition is considered a crime against the state. This is the government-decides-all type of society that does not recognize the people (and the nongovernmental sector) as capable of independent undertakings in the public interest. In the second phase, while officialdom is the exclusive actor in the realm of the public interest, individual rights are guaranteed in a constitution so that it is possible to refuse intervention of the government in the private realm. At the third phase, the people hold the power to challenge the government if it is not conducting government in conformity with the public interest; in other words, at this level the power of the people to change those in authority, when they believe government is not being conducted properly, is institutionalized. At the fourth phase, the people not only hold the power of approval regarding the government's actions in the public interest, they themselves are conscious of their responsibility to act in the public interest as private citizens, and this awareness is recognized by the government.

As shown above, pluralism is an important element of the social infrastructure for civil society to be able to emerge, and respect for humanity and the individual is also absolutely necessary as the spiritual and philosophical condition for it to flourish. In addition, it is only if there is willingness on the part of the people, no less than the government, to contribute to the public interest and the common good that civil society gains both vitality and validity.

RELATIONSHIP OF PUBLIC AND PRIVATE IN MODERN JAPAN

In the mid-19th century, the Tokugawa government that had ruled Japan since 1603 felt the full impact of the arrival of Western civilization on its doorstep, as symbolized by the appearance of the "black ships" in 1853. Commodore Matthew C. Perry (1794–1858) and his fleet arrived in Tokyo Bay and forced Japan to end more than two centuries of national seclusion. In what direction did that encounter turn Tokugawa society, which had been shaped by a decentralized, feudal system? Was the advent of Western civilization fortuitous for the people? The answers to these questions are two-faceted. The modern, centralized state that the Meiji-era leaders sought to build had to be two different things: It had to be both a "strong state" and a "more democratic state" based on the rule of law.

On the one hand, therefore, the Meiji state faced the task of abolishing the decentralized feudal system and of building a strong centralized state. As the modern navies of the Western colonial powers began to appear in the waters around the Japanese archipelago, self-defense and survival became Japan's most urgent business. Insofar as India had been placed under colonial rule and even parts of China were controlled by the Western powers in semicolonial fashion, it was clear that maintaining independence would not be easy. When samurai struck out in xenophobic pride and blind patriotism, killing an Englishman at Namamugi in 1862, the city of Kagoshima was bombarded by British naval forces, and the forces of the Chōshū domain started an attack on all Western

ships in 1863, only to be defeated by a fleet of four Western nations
that occupied the Shimonoseki Strait region in 1864. Driving out the
foreigners was obviously impossible. To challenge the Western powers
without sufficient strength could, on the contrary, hand them the opportunity to take over Japan completely.

Ultimately, Japan had but one logical recourse: It could only adopt
what Arnold J. Toynbee later dubbed "Herodism." It had to open its
doors and, by conducting trade and studying the secrets of the strength
of foreign civilizations and acquiring those strengths for itself, hope
eventually to overcome the challenge of those outside powers. Thus,
the task of Meiji Japan was to master enough of Western civilization to
build up its strength to the level of its challengers.

Not only as far as military might was concerned but in other areas,
Japan would have to be a centralized state that could control and mobilize the people as a united force if it was to maintain independence from
the colonialist powers. To fend off exploitation by advanced states that
had already undergone "bourgeois" revolutions and the industrial revolution, Japan had to rapidly forge a society to the same effect, and that
had to be implemented efficiently from above. Meiji Japan tackled this
effort under the slogan of "enrich the country and strengthen its arms,"
or *fukoku kyōhei*. The slogan reflected leaders' appreciation of the fact
that without vigorous industrial strength Japan could not sustain strong
military forces. Becoming a strong nation was paramount; national survival was at stake.

On the other hand, the modern states of the West were not simply
strong, centralized states; they were founded on different social principles. During the mid-19th century, the nation-states of the West had
reached the point where the creed of universal human rights, parliamentary institutions based on the rational contractual principle of no
taxation without representation, and assertion of the right of self-rule
had become well-established. It had become widely accepted that state
authority had to be limited in this fashion. In the advanced societies of
the time, constitutional governments were being established based on
the premise that state power should not be unlimited and that it should
go hand in hand with the basic rights of the individual and the people.
Under constitutional government, both the individual and the state were
subject to law.

There was also recognition that all power corrupts, and absolute
power corrupts absolutely. State power, therefore, should not be unitary,

but separated and balanced out through the checking of power between different branches of government. The exercise of power by the executive branch would be checked by the high authority of the legislative branch reflecting the will of the people, and the judiciary established to administer justice under the law would be separate from both the executive and legislative branches. The process of building strong centralized states, but created on the basis of democratic principles (namely, respect for the individual and respect for the will of the majority of the people), of constitutionalism and representation, and the institutionalization of the separation and limitation of power, had taken place first in Great Britain, France, and the United States.

Then, by the mid-19th century, Germany and Italy had finally managed to unite the diverse principalities within their borders and had begun to emerge as modern nation-states. It was at this time that Japan's interlude of peaceful isolation was broken and it determined to leave its Asian neighbors behind and somehow catch up with the advanced powers of the West. Officially, the new Meiji government declared noble aims: that it would seek knowledge widely throughout the world, that the "four classes"—samurai, farmers, artisans, and merchants—were equal, and that all things would be decided through public debate. But, given the international circumstances, would it be able to stick to the high ideal of building an egalitarian society with a constitutional government and a parliamentary system?

OVERWHELMING SUPERIORITY OF OFFICIALDOM

While the advanced Western states that were the models for the building of the Meiji state had built themselves into strong sovereign states and nurtured institutions limiting state power through law and popular participation in government, did Japan adopt both those aspects of nation building? If it did learn both aspects, which one received the greater attention?

The Meiji period is often portrayed as a time when reverence for government and contempt for the masses prevailed, and indeed the greatest energy was invested in the building of a strong centralized state dominated by the overwhelming power of the bureaucracy. Why was this the case? Part of the reason was more or less the result of the general conditions in the world at the time. But part of the reason had to do with Japan's own specific circumstances.

At the end of the 19th and the beginning of the 20th century, the functions of states in the West were expanding and growing stronger. At one time, the theory was advanced that government should be limited to keeping the domestic peace—the so-called nightwatch state. That represented the extreme, of course, but it was widely considered that the minimum responsibilities of government included national security, foreign relations, domestic peace, and management of the currency.

In 18th-century Europe, the plight of the masses was extreme. The poverty of English workers during the industrial revolution convinced Karl Marx that exploitation of labor was a universal and immutable feature of capitalism. Starting in the early 18th century, unseasonable weather and famine assailed all of Europe and starvation repeatedly swept the continent thereafter, leaving death and misery in its wake. No one except the members of the nobility and the wealthy enjoyed the luxury of eating meat or dairy products; others subsisted on meager diets mainly of grain. The French Revolution erupted against the backdrop of this dire suffering of the 18th-century masses.

After the devastating famine in the mid-19th century that struck not only Ireland but also areas of northern Europe with a high rate of dependency on potatoes, however, the problem of famine was overcome in Europe, and people came to enjoy the nutritious and abundant food supply that Asians tend to think of as typical of the West. Famine was conquered partly because industrialization resulted in improved diets, but it was also because, prompted by popular protests and riots that continued until the February Revolution of 1848, governments began to realize that society would not stabilize until the state guaranteed not only human freedom under the law but also a minimum standard of living for the people. Thereafter, from the 19th and into the 20th century, social security and welfare gradually became the responsibility of the state, and citizens were considered entitled to the right to life and social rights.

The expansion of the functions of the state from the end of the 19th century to the beginning of the 20th, therefore, was explosive. States now undertook not only the redistribution of wealth but created government agencies for every aspect of national life. Advances in science and technology, industrialization, and the emergence of the mass society revolutionized not only civilian life but the scale and intensity of wars. It was also the age of imperialism, and states that could not meet these challenges did not survive. By the time of the two world wars of the 20th century, states had burgeoned to grotesque proportions that evoked the great beasts of myth and folklore, Behemoth and Leviathan.

Such was the international environment into which Japan plunged as it abandoned national isolation and embarked upon its nation-building effort. Japan was more or less obsessed by the idea that it could not survive internationally without building a powerful state and that it could not be accepted among the world powers unless it revised the unequal treaties signed in the 1850s and 1860s.

In the case of Japan, there were other, particular reasons in addition to the international conditions in which states in general were growing large and powerful. Those reasons derived from the fact that Japan had been a late starter in the modernization process. Strong governmental authority was required to overcome the resistance to modernization of a traditional society to which Western civilization was inherently alien. While Tokugawa society was already quite an advanced society culturally, it would have taken quite a long time if industrialization, modernization of laws, establishment of a public school system, and building of modern military power had been left to the spontaneous action of the private sector. But Meiji Japan could not wait. Ultimately, modern institutions modeled after those of the West had to be transplanted under the leadership of the state. The government orchestrated a national drive through which modern institutions were grafted onto Japanese society from above.

Except for the advanced nations that achieved modernization in a gradual, endogenous process, all others could only do their best to catch up through such state-led modernization implemented by government decree. In contrast to the first group of advanced nations (Britain, France, and the United States), the second group of states to modernize—Germany, Italy, and Japan—achieved their success by authoritarian (Prussian-style) means. The emergence of the communist system in the 20th century, too, was in response to the urgent need for nations to catch up by committing themselves to planned economic development under one-party dictatorship. The developmental authoritarianism of post–World War II East Asia is also a product of the need for countries lagging behind to catch up as rapidly as possible.

The above-described circumstances, compounded by the tradition in Japan in which the samurai class had monopolized government authority since the 12th century, contributed to the creation of an overwhelmingly state-led body politic in modern Japan. The job of rebuilding traditional society in conformity with the models of the modern West presented a real crisis for Japanese identity. There was much talk of *wakon-yōsai*, or preserving the "Japanese spirit" while acquiring "Western arts (technology)," but in practice people were irresistibly attracted to the philosophy of Rousseau, John Locke, and others, and not a few were converted to Christianity. Many people became uncertain about the validity of the notion of Japanese spirit. The greater people's misgivings about Japan's distinctiveness, the greater the effectiveness of the emperor system as the traditional symbol of unity. Inasmuch as modern Japan had no choice but to follow the Herodian path of studying the secrets of Western power to preserve itself, it was inevitable that Westernization should leave its mark in every corner of society. Considering the traumas of that experience, holding aloft the banner of the emperor system proved to be a valuable spiritual counterbalance.

The Imperial Rescript on Education issued in 1890 clearly demonstrated the emperor system's counterbalancing role. It declared the creation of a structure sustained by the Confucian worldview under the banner of the traditional symbol of the emperor system, which had for centuries been remote from the actual exercise of government. It was the embodiment of modern Japan, rooted in tradition, struggling to establish national unity and order so that it could cope with the double-edged challenge of both learning from and defending itself against the West.

FUKUZAWA YUKICHI AND THE IDEA OF "THE PEOPLE"

In the early Meiji era, even before Nakae Chōmin brought back from France Rousseau's ideas about popular rights and "the people," Western political thought had begun to flow into Japan. The man who indisputably played the greatest role in introducing individualism and the self-respect of the people independent of the government was Fukuzawa Yukichi (1835–1901).

As recounted in Fukuzawa's famous autobiography *Fukuō jiden* (The Autobiography of Fukuzawa Yukichi), he grew up in the Nakatsu domain of Kyushu and received an education centered around the study of Chinese classics, but later entered Tekijuku, Ogata Kōan's school of Dutch studies in Osaka, where he advanced to the position of chief instructor. In 1859, a few years after the opening of the treaty ports, however, Fukuzawa happened to visit Yokohama where he was shocked to discover that the Dutch language he had worked so long to master was useless in communicating with the foreigners he encountered there. He immediately began to study English. He boarded the first ship to cross the Pacific under Japanese command, the *Kanrinmaru,* as part of a Japanese mission. He visited the United States and Europe a total of three times and purchased many English books. He described the experience of coming into close contact with both Western civilization and the traditional society of Japan as having lived "two lives in one."

Fukuzawa wrote bluntly about his disdain for the two types of arrogance devoid of substance he observed among Japanese. The first type of arrogance was that bandied about in the final days of the shogunate under the slogan of "expel the foreigners" (*jōi*), although its advocates usually knew nothing of the West. He wrote, "The more widely these uncivilized fellows carried on arrogantly about 'driving out the foreigners,' the more they sapped the strength of Japan. To think of what could happen to this country as a result filled me with despair."

The other type of arrogance was that displayed by government officials. The "way shogunate officials boasted and blustered," although they were without exception "ignorant and incompetent," Fukuzawa later wrote, "is completely unimaginable today." Ultimately the shogunate fell and the new government adopted a policy of opening Japan's doors to the West. That was all very well, but then the officials of the new government turned out to be just as arrogant as those of the old. "Everywhere throughout the land," Fukuzawa complained, "officials build unnecessary distinctions between the high and the low, the illustrious and the lowly, contriving in every possible way to make it seem as if officials and the people are of completely different races. Since the government is considered worthy of the highest esteem, those who enter its service are automatically considered to be highly esteemed and begin to take on airs of superiority. . . . Once you join the company of such officials you will find yourself adopting the same arrogant behavior before you know it."

Fukuzawa thus clearly saw how the "respect for authority/contempt for the masses" tradition was passed on from the old feudal regime to the new Meiji government. This was the reason he refused to take any government appointment. He argued that the common belief among Japanese that "the only road to success lies in the government" was a "misguided holdover" from the old society. Convinced that people ought to realize the error of this behavior, Fukuzawa was eager to "show them from his own example that they should learn the truth about advanced civilization and culture," and inspired by what he had learned, he chose to remain a private, individual citizen throughout his life. "I do not want to rely on the government nor do I want to be indebted to its officials." Japan would only have a future, he categorically declared, through the fulfillment of society brought into being by an independent-minded citizenry determined not to depend on the government and not to rely on government officials.

Even in the Meiji state, where authority and officialdom were unquestionably ascendant, there were independent thinkers like Fukuzawa. Now let us look at how the balance between these two sides fluctuated during the history of modern Japan.

OFFICIAL AND PRIVATE IN THE MEIJI ERA

The Meiji system continued until the end of World War II in 1945. Here let us evaluate the relationship between official and private during that period in terms of two indicators.

The first indicator is school textbooks, which clearly exhibit how the government sought to inculcate certain values among the people.[1] The second indicator of the official-private relationship is the number of private organizations formed during the modern period.[2]

Looking back over the history of school textbooks, we soon discover that during the period before World War II, textbooks were most liberal, enlightened, and dynamic in the early Meiji period. The Ministry of Education was established in 1871, and in the following year the Education Order of 1872 (Gakusei) was promulgated, which set up a system of eight years of elementary education divided into upper and lower levels of four years each. The ministry drew up guidelines for primary-level schooling, stipulated the content of instruction, and in time began to write and publish textbooks of its own.

This early period was remarkable for the free and wide-ranging publishing by individual scholars of many textbooks, and for the fact that the Education Ministry encouraged this activity as well as competitive publishing of good textbooks. Most of these publications introduced the society, thought, ethics, and famous personalities of Europe and the United States. There were also many cases when well-received books originally published for a general readership by respected authors of the day were reissued as school textbooks. Examples include the famous translation by Nakamura Masanao of Samuel Smiles's *Self Help* and Fukuzawa Yukichi's translation of Robert Chambers's *Moral Class Book*. Fresh and informative books like these, which introduced

Western ideas on humanity and society and portrayed the exemplary lives of important figures, were taken up as textbooks.

Smiles's treatise showed that England's strength lay in the spirit of self-help that characterized its people and explained how English society was sustained by the strong aspiration to nobility and heroism not only among its noble and heroic but equally among the nameless and unknown.

The Fukuzawa translation contained the story of Benjamin Franklin, the son of a Boston candlemaker who became a central figure in the American revolution. Franklin's success in the printing industry and his achievements in community and public service led him eventually, as in the case of Fukuzawa himself, to open an academy for advanced study. Fukuzawa's enthusiasm for this book, which portrayed Franklin's meritorious achievements in France as ambassador while the colonies went to war with Great Britain, is clearly evident. It was stimulating stories of world achievement and adventure such as this that became textbooks in the early Meiji period.

The Meiji government, realizing the urgency of launching a new approach to education and training a new brand of teacher, sought the advice of New York–born educator David Murray (1830–1905). It is said that the classroom scene so familiar to Japanese even today, with its blackboard at the front, modest teacher's podium, and small individual desks for pupils, was introduced directly from the Boston area by Murray (Kōsaka 1996). In 1872, a teacher's college was established in Tokyo, and the training of teachers in Japan was begun. At the recommendation of Murray, Marion Scott, who had been a school principal in San Francisco, became its head. In the early Meiji era, education reflected the enlightened, liberal models of the West under the strong influence of U.S., British, and French education. Teaching resources included many translations of civics texts used in the modern West.

According to a study by Muramatsu, Itō, and Tsujinaka (1986) of the formation of private organizations before and after World War II, the first type to be established were so-called sector organizations rooted in key industries in various fields. Next came the "policy-beneficiary" organizations related to the distribution of government subsidies and other resources. The "value-promotion" organizations devoted to furthering particular ideas or movements were the last to emerge.

Of course, sector organizations were not the only such groups created in the early Meiji period. In addition to federations in key

industries, such as the Dai-Nihon Nōkai (Greater Japan Agricultural
Association) and the Bōseki Rengōkai (Federation of Spinning Manu-
facturers), all manner of academic and cultural societies were founded,
including the Teikoku Gakushiin (Imperial Academy; today the Japan
Academy), Kōjunsha (an association of intellectuals established by
Fukuzawa Yukichi), and the Meirokusha (an intellectual society started
by statesman Mori Arinori [1847–1889] that published the liberal journal *Meiroku zasshi*). In the early Meiji era, many societies to promote
particular ideas or values were founded that drew on knowledge from
around the world and played an important role in the dissemination of
enlightened thinking in Japan.

The liberal and open era of "civilization and enlightenment," however, proved to be unexpectedly short-lived. In 1877, the Satsuma
Rebellion in southwestern Japan led by Saigō Takamori (1827–1877),
was crushed by the Meiji government under the leadership of Ōkubo
Toshimichi (1830–1878). This turned out to be the last attempt at
armed insurrection by the old guard against Ōkubo's modernization
reforms. In its place, the popular rights movement (*jiyū minken undō*)
gained momentum and demonstrations calling for adoption of a constitutional government and formation of a national legislature spread
throughout the country. There was another pattern of antigovernment
movement. As evidenced by the assassination of Ōkubo in 1878, isolated acts of terrorism occurred intermittently throughout the pre–
World War II period.

The Meiji government struck back hard at both challenges to its
authority, particularly against the popular rights movement. Measures
to maintain peace and order were tightened, and in 1880 the Public
Assembly Ordinance was issued in an attempt to control antigovernment activities by restricting freedom of speech and assembly. In addition to these measures of physical restraint, the authorities undertook
to guide popular attitudes relating to ideas and education in what they
considered favorable directions. The policy of active encouragement of
free publishing of textbooks of the early Meiji era was abandoned and
steps taken to strengthen state supervision. In regard to content as well,
the government moved to bring an end to the introduction of quality
books of Western ethics and philosophy and inculcate the people instead with a sense of order and obedience to the state by revival of Confucian thought.

The Imperial Will on Education of 1879 (Kyōiku-seishi) marked a

clear turning point in education policy. Convinced that liberal education on Western models was a factor contributing to antigovernment
movements, the Meiji government switched to a policy of suppression
of Western books on morals and ethics as textbooks, declaring that
they "threatened public security and corrupted popular morals." For
example, citing the passage in Abe Taizō's highly reputed translation
of American clergyman and educator Francis Wayland's *Elements of
Moral Science* that goes, "When officials in the government are corrupt,
and cruel and brutal in their actions, there is no way to stop their impe-
riousness except revolt and civil protest," it prohibited further use of
the work as a textbook. Discussion of ideas that recognized the initiative of the people or approved of the right of the people to resist bad
government or revolt against authority was prohibited; instead the government vigorously stressed Confucian ethics and traditional Japanese
customs. Education policy was clearly designed to inculcate a uniform
morality centering around "the loyal subject, righteous man, filial child,
and faithful woman" from an early age.

With issuance of the Revised Education Order of 1880, the local
autonomy that had been permitted in regional education was with-
drawn. The state strengthened fundamental educational standards and
the Ministry of Education established the Henshūkyoku (Editorial Bureau) and began to compile and publish ethics textbooks based on its
own new policies. The following year, all schools were required to report
to the ministry what textbooks they were using. In 1883, the ministry
issued an order stating that no textbooks could be used without obtain-
ing its prior permission. In 1886, the year after the inauguration of the
cabinet system, this official approval system was further revised with the
institution of the textbook authorization system. At that time, the national public education system was completed on the basis of the Elementary School Law, the Middle School Law, the Teachers' College
Law, and the Imperial University Law, and the new system for over-
seeing textbooks meant that the entire system was now totally under
the control of the government.

With the political crisis of 1881, the government came under new
leadership. Fulfilling public pledges, the government of Itō Hirobumi
(1841–1909) adopted the Meiji Constitution in 1889 and the following
year convened the Diet for the first time. These developments were in
part responses to the liberalism of the early Meiji period and the pressures brought by the popular rights movement. At the same time,

however, they represented the success of the Meiji government in containing such popular and liberal forces within the framework of government-led institutions. The new emperor-granted Constitution stated that "Japanese subjects shall, within the limits of law, enjoy the liberty of speech, writing, publication, public meetings, and associations" (Article 29), but "within the limits of law" was prescribed by the Newspapers Ordinance, the above-mentioned Public Assembly Ordinance, and the Public Peace and Order Ordinance. The Imperial Rescript on Education issued the same year as the Diet was first convened as an edict based on the spiritual principles of the Confucian social order that made the duty of children to obey their parents the starting point for loyalty of citizens to the state. Two years later, elementary school morals textbooks written in accordance with these principles began to be used in the schools throughout the country.

In the field of education, any remaining freedom for private or individual spontaneity was being rapidly eclipsed as government controls were clamped down one by one. The textbook authorization system led to widespread cases of bribery and corruption, however, and in 1902 a scandal erupted over textbook publishing that forced the government to "rethink" its practices. The upshot was the decision to allow only state-designated textbook publishing. Only three publishers were permitted to produce textbooks: Nihon Shoseki, Tokyo Shoseki, and Osaka Shoseki. Adoption of this system made it possible for the educational policy and ideology of the state to be directly reflected in the content of school textbooks.

The government-led modernization drive of the Meiji period was supported by the strong loyalty and diligent endeavors of the people. Under the Tokugawa regime, government had been monopolized by the samurai class. While forced to pay heavy annual taxes, participation in politics by the farming class was out of the question, and the people had had no way of expressing their political will save by staking their lives through revolt or insurrection. By comparison, the vast majority of the people were better off even under the bureaucrat-led Meiji regime. Under the system for elections, there was room for expression of political will and it was possible for the people to join the power elite, either by seeking candidacy for election to the Diet or by gaining a position in the bureaucracy through academic achievement.

As long as it was moving toward the apparently attractive goals of modernization, economic development, and raising the image of the country on the international stage, the government was able to count on the cooperation and contribution of the people in its endeavors. The Japanese were an easy people to govern and they did not make excessive demands on the government. One aspect of traditional values was the spirit of self-sacrifice for a larger public objective (*hoshigarimasen katsu made wa*, "we will relinquish everything until victory"), and the Confucian-inspired educational policies instituted from the second decade of the Meiji era (the 1870s) were carefully worked out to mobilize even further the unconditional loyalty of the people to the emperor-system state.

Throughout the period of the Sino-Japanese War (1894–1895) and the Russo-Japanese War, the Japanese people worked themselves to the bone, as has been depicted in the stories of Oshin and of the young women who toiled in the textile factories. Not only members of the former samurai class but the people in general practiced high moral standards and their sense of civic duty was of a standard equal to that of any other society in the world. The people as a whole supported and were united in the consciousness of their duty to prevent their new nation from falling prey to the imperialist powers and their determination to modernize and build up their country to rival the world powers of the time. Sustained by this endogenous nationalism, the Meiji government was successful in its aims. The success of the centralized Meiji state would not have been possible without the diverse and abundant human resources nurtured in the heterogeneous society of the Tokugawa period and by the extraordinarily high sense of public mission and responsibility of the people.

TAISHŌ DEMOCRACY AND THE "ASSOCIATIONAL REVOLUTION"

With its victory in the Russo-Japanese War, Japan was finally able to put behind it the sense of crisis in being a newly developing state whose very survival was at stake. It attained recognized status as Asia's sole imperial power. It no longer had to unilaterally demand the limitless loyalty of its citizens, but had reached a stage at which several national objectives could be posited and Japanese society could enjoy a certain diversification of values. The ensuing period of peace provided an environment for the growth of private activity.

With the political crisis of 1913 in which the upsurge of popular sentiment under the first movement to protect constitutional government brought down an unpopular cabinet, Japanese society put behind it for the time being the era of excessive concern with the external threat to Japan's security and of national mobilization to achieve state goals. The times were ripe for the fulfillment of the potential of civil society.

In a sense, this development in Japanese society presaged the international trends of the post–World War I period. The experience of the first war in history that involved not only armies but the entire populace of nations in an international conflict dealt a profound blow to the societies of Europe and North America, and they began to seek a new kind of society and a new kind of world. Pacificism, democracy, and socialism were the order of the day. In Japan as well, the era of party politics began with the skillful leadership of politician Hara Takashi (1856–1921), and for eight years from 1924 through 1932 the government alternated between two major political parties, the Seiyūkai (Political Friends Association) and the Kenseikai (Constitutional Politics Association). Shidehara Kijūrō (1872–1951), ambassador to the United States from 1919 to 1922 and Japan's representative at the Washington Conference, pursued a cooperative and conciliatory foreign policy under the post–World War I Washington system that offered the country some relief from the tensions of earlier years. It was the era of scholar Yoshino Sakuzō's (1878–1933) prolific writing on democracy and government by the people. In the field of literature, the Shirakaba coterie of writers presided over a new optimism and internationalism.

The impact of changing currents in thought was not lost on school textbooks. Around 1918, textbooks and teaching methods began reflecting the ideas of the so-called New Education Movement stressing the spontaneous activity of children and free approaches to learning. Then in 1925, with passage of the universal (manhood) suffrage act and the quadrupling of the number of voters to 12 million, people became keenly aware of the need to acquire objective knowledge of their own society, and efforts were stepped up to introduce not only morals appropriate to virtuous "subjects (*shinmin*) of the Empire" but to "citizens" (*kōmin*) holding certain rights under the constitutional system (Matsuno 1996).

The emergence of the new educational trends reflecting the conditions of liberal Taishō democracy, however, aroused considerable alarm among traditionalist educators and bureaucrats who believed that the spiritual supports of the state could only be assured by a doctrine of loyalty and patriotism. As efforts to open up a new "civic" education in response to the needs of democracy confronted conservatives' moves to restrengthen state-centered education pivoting on traditional values, the short heyday of post–World War I democracy of the 1920s came to an end. The year after the Manchurian Incident in 1931, when elements of the Japanese Imperial Army launched the conquest of Manchuria, textbooks reverted to their earlier support for nationalist values. Under the National People's School System (Kokumin Gakkō Seidō) instituted in 1941, control of education by the state became complete and the inculcation of the imperial subjects with the values of self-sacrifice in the service of the nation for the all-out war with the United States and Great Britain became pervasive.

Looking at the rise and fall of private-sector organizations, we can see that the prewar peak falls roughly in the period centering around the 1920s, between the Taishō Political Crisis (1913) and the Manchurian Incident. In terms of numbers, there was an eruption of private organizations formed before the war, an "associational revolution" in its time; and they were tremendously diverse in purpose and type. Not only were there business-related groups such as the Japan Chamber of Commerce and Industry, but numerous labor unions and welfare societies in every field of industry, the Japan Fabian Society and ideologically inspired organizations such as the National Federation of Levellers, and cultural and academic societies and international exchange groups such as the Pacific Society. The proliferation of nonprofit as well as "value-promotion" organizations was phenomenal.

However, like Taishō democracy itself, the privately initiated endeavors of this period were troubled by the inherent vulnerability of greenhouse-cultivated plants. They had not put down the sturdy roots that were needed to endure the cruel assault of ultranationalism and militarism that swept the country following the Manchurian Incident.

A case described by Hayashi Yūjirō (1997) vividly portrays the "noble" birth of these private organizations in the best of times before the outbreak of the war as well as the way they were treated by the state. In 1923, in Ibaraki Prefecture, the Saitō Foundation was founded. Its founder, Saitō Zen'emon, described its purpose as follows:

Human beings are caused, through the awesome power of the grace of the gods or buddhas, to work for the advancement of world civilization, and the fruits of these labors belong to heaven. They should not be private possessions but be offered for the happiness of all humankind. Based on this idea, I set aside a 3 million yen endowment for a foundation for public programs "for the repayment of divine favors" (*hōon*). The foundation's trustees were to administer the funds fairly in such a way as not to betray the will and spirit of heaven and without the least concern for the benefit of the Saitō family. Even if the Saitō family should perish, the family will never touch the original endowment, and insofar as family business prospered, the family will endeavor to increase the fund in perpetuity. Some people criticized me for being stingy, but I have always lived simply and frugally and I could not bear to see the fruits of what I have gained simply squandered.

What is evidenced here is the awakening of the public spirit in a private citizen and his very noble aspiration to do good for the world without discrimination in return for the divine favor he has enjoyed.

But when the Saitō Foundation was approved as a public-interest corporation under the jurisdiction of the Ministry of Education, its by-laws came out (in part) as follows:

Article 1. The purpose of the said Foundation is to conduct and/or assist programs that are deemed spiritually and physically necessary to contribute to furthering the fortunes of the state . . .

Article 3. . . . . facilities needed to increase the happiness of society by enlightening and guiding people's thought and propagating the concept of the state.

After undergoing the ritual of approval by the competent authorities, Saitō's ideas of the "happiness of all humankind" and the "spirit of heaven" in founding the foundation were so transformed as to seem to have been placed under an evil spell. The foundation's purposes were now defined as "furthering the fortunes of the state" and "propagating the concept of the state," narrowly defined notions that could hardly have been further from the intentions of the founder (Hayashi 1997).

From the point of view of the Meiji state, the public good could be none other than that which conformed with the objectives of the state. Only the state was capable of defining with authority and responsibility the nature of "public" and the "public interest." That which the government did not approve and which went against the will of the government would not be recognized as of value. Anything that sought to be good for the public had to show that it contributed to the interests of the state. This pattern of thought was so deeply entrenched that even the brief flourishing of Taishō democracy could not change it. Indeed, it may be said that after the end of World War II, liberation from the old state-centered ideas has still been quite limited.

CIVIL SOCIETY IN THE POSTWAR PERIOD
LIBERATION OF THE PRIVATE REALM
AND CONTINUITY OF OFFICIALDOM

The principle of the pendulum seemed to be at work in modern Japan. Periods of enchantment with things Western and obsession with the "catch-up" mentality alternated with eras of "return-to-Japan" introspection characterized by reappraisal of tradition and preoccupation with self-identity, often accompanied by antiforeign belligerence toward the outside world. At the risk of oversimplification, we might describe these swings as moving between modernization and domestic reform at one extreme and war with other countries at the other.

Prior to World War II, Japan was at war with one country or another once every ten years. Nationalistic sentiment would arise among the people with the outbreak of the conflict and all available resources—material, financial, and human—would be poured into the war effort. Once hostilities were over, however, the pendulum swung back, while the country "recharged" itself, so to speak, through a resurgence of civilian economic vigor. Popular energy thus released sought its outlet in individualism, democracy, liberalism, and internationalism. In short, mobilization for waging of war and improvement of the economic life of the nation stood in a kind of trade-off relationship vis-à-vis the country's limited resources.

The same pattern of shift occurred in the transition from wartime to the postwar period after 1945. Given that inherent tendency in modern Japanese history, it was practically inevitable that the pendulum would swing back to emphasis on civilian economic strength. Not only did the state's all-out mobilization for the war culminate in disastrous defeat and devastation but the international environment itself had changed dramatically. The age of imperialism had ended in the course of the two world wars and, with the advent of the nuclear age marked by the atomic bombings of Hiroshima and Nagasaki, the settling of international disputes by military means became increasingly unfeasible and ineffective.

In terms of the historical stresses between "mobilization for war" and "emphasis on civilian economic strength," the postwar environment was decidedly favorable to the latter—toward civil society and democracy. Even more basic, the fundamental principle governing the nation—the national polity—underwent a drastic transformation through the postwar reforms. The emperor system did survive, though only after having been divested of its absolute authority and relegated to an institution whose role was mainly symbolic and ceremonial. Sovereignty no longer rests with the throne but with the people under the new Constitution that went into effect in 1947.

Alongside popular sovereignty, the postwar Constitution firmly guarantees the autonomy and dignity of the individual in the name of basic human rights. It sets forth the principle of respect for private rights. Whereas the prewar Meiji Constitution restrained individual freedom "as provided by law," the postwar charter guarantees it insofar as it conforms to the "public welfare." Human rights are not subordinate to the state; both the state and individual are subject equally to the public welfare.

In post–World War II society worldwide, the role of the sovereign state entered into a phase of decline. Japan was no exception, especially with the demise of imperialism. Modernization carried out from above by the state had been more or less completed. That did not mean, however, that a powerful state apparatus was no longer necessary for Japan.

Even after the war's end, the Japanese state retained its authoritarian control over the people and the supremacy of officialdom persisted. One reason for this continuity was that the Allied Occupation's reform programs and purge of leaders in positions of official responsibility dealt a devastating blow to all the prewar/wartime establishment, except for the bureaucracy. Apart from the military and the Home Ministry, which were abolished, most government servants came away virtually unscathed.

General Douglas MacArthur, Supreme Commander for the Allied Powers (SCAP), opted for "indirect rule" in implementing his Occupation policy "through the emperor and the Japanese government." The government here meant those officials and politicians who escaped the purge. Except for a few high-ranking bureaucrats who had served the wartime government, the overwhelming majority of officials were allowed to continue their careers.

SCAP's approach enabled younger bureaucrats to work closely with the Occupation authorities and accumulate much expertise. It was these bureaucrats who filled the gap created by the absence of party politics that had been destroyed by the wartime militarist regime. They also served as a major source of high-caliber political leadership in the prewar period.

The bureaucracy was given an important role to play in reconstructing the war-devastated country. The modernization program carried out since the Meiji period was continued in a different guise for economic development and new nation-building. The leadership necessary for Japan's rise to economic power status from the ruins of the war was provided by such bureaucrat-turned-politician figures as Yoshida Shigeru (1878–1967), Kishi Nobusuke (1896–1987), Ikeda Hayato (1899–1965), and Satō Eisaku (1901–1975), and their policies were executed by the bureaucracy. In the crucial early postwar years, many political leaders with nonbureaucratic backgrounds were purged from office. For these reasons, the "modernization from above" continued during the postwar years, despite the fact that objective conditions were ripe for ending the traditional preponderance of official over private.

THE NEW GROUPISM

Despite all the democratic provisions of the postwar Constitution, individuation did not occur easily in Japanese society, nor was the private accorded due respect as smoothly as one might have thought. The preponderance of officialdom persisted tenaciously in Japan's body politic. Meanwhile, two new types of groupism emerged to take a firm grip on the Japanese public: "people's democracy" and "company first-ism."

The people's democracy brand of groupism was practiced primarily by members of the Japan Communist Party and its sympathizers. By virtue of its wartime resistance against the military regime, the party made a heroic comeback on the political scene after the war. The fact that most of its leaders and activists had been either in jail or in exile during the war greatly enhanced its prestige. Communists preached that capitalism was doomed and a communist revolution was inevitable, hence people should actively commit themselves to the class struggle according to this scientific law of history. Individual self-fulfillment can be achieved, they argued, only by carrying out the historic mission of the proletariat.

From today's vantage point, it may seem unbelievable, but many serious, courageous young people took the communist doctrine at face value and plunged themselves into subversive activism, armed with real weapons and often forced underground. From the late 1940s—the time of the "absolute impoverishment" of the people—to the early 1960s, radical students, unionists, and others were ready to sacrifice themselves for the revolutionary cause.

The free development of individual character and the principles of democracy were part of this radical ideology, but in actual practice individuals were commanded to submerge their personal well-being in the larger interest of the group. A person's existence was considered meaningful only insofar as he or she faithfully followed the a priori dogma that dictated participation in the revolutionary movement.

In those days, any young man or woman who showed serious interest in philanthropic and/or volunteer activities for the common good of the people would have been vehemently criticized and ridiculed by followers of the people's democracy as indulging in intellectual naiveté and petit-bourgeois complacency. Such activities, they argued, would serve only to gloss over the real sources of social injustice and widespread poverty.

Up until 1960, when massive demonstrations occurred protesting the ratification of the revised U.S.-Japan Security Treaty, Japan's political processes were dominated by ideological confrontation between the left-wing reformist forces and the traditional nationalists led by Kishi (who was prime minister from 1957 to 1960) and others who advocated constitutional revision and rearmament. Neither of these ideological positions was successful in fostering respect for human dignity or providing a firm rationale for the importance of private initiatives. Buffeted by these two ideologies, the maturation of a modern civil consciousness based on the concept of individual rights remained on hold in the nation's political life.

Behind the open ideological confrontation of the late 1950s, a new pattern of political process was quietly and steadily developing. In 1955 at the strong recommendation of business groupings like Keidanren (Japan Federation of Economic Organizations), two conservative parties merged to form the Liberal Democratic Party (LDP), while the left-wing and right-wing socialist groups were unified under the Japan Socialist Party (JSP). That same year, Japan's GNP reached the prewar all-time high and the period of rapid economic growth began. The ruling LDP took full advantage of the booming economy to devise a method of consolidating its base of political support by handing out benefits to various interest groups—business, farming, medical, veterans' groups, etc.—through skillful channeling of subsidies and budgetary allocations as well as legal protection. When Prime Minister Ikeda announced his income-doubling plan in 1960, after the downfall of the Kishi administration, interest politics clearly replaced the ideological politics of the previous decade as the dominant vehicle of the political process in Japan.

ECONOMISM OF THE 1960S

In the 1960s, economics became the primary concern in Japan. For Japanese, this meant the relativization and decline of the two dominant political ideologies of the fifties—the traditional view of the state and people's democracy. Moreover, the inauguration of John F. Kennedy as president of the United States in 1961 and his appointment of Edwin O. Reischauer as ambassador to Japan provided a new context for political perceptions to evolve among Japanese.

A well-known Japanologist, Reischauer presented a positive view of Japan and a new direction for Japan-U.S. relations. Postwar Japan, he argued, was on the road to a remarkable success in both economic development and in the building of a democratic society. In fact, Japan stands out as a model of industrialization and democratization in the modern and recent history of the world. Modernization is a universal phenomenon, as Japan proved by successfully building an advanced society in Asia. With regard to bilateral relations, Reischauer said that the United States and Japan were no longer victor and vanquished, developed and developing nations. Moving beyond a vertical relationship, as advanced industrial democracies the two countries had to become equal partners.

Reischauer's message to the Japanese public was in basic conformity with Ikeda's policy of pursuing rapid economic growth and building a national consensus on political issues. This policy line originated with Prime Minister Yoshida, who signed the San Francisco Peace Treaty with the countries of the Western bloc (i.e., without the Soviet-bloc countries) and the U.S.-Japan Security Treaty (which allowed the continued stationing of American forces on Japanese soil) in 1951. His choice put Japan on a clear course of reconstruction as a trading nation, placing top priority on economics and entrusting national security to the United States. This policy line bore fruit in the 1960s with Japan's emergence as an economic power.

Ikeda enunciated the concept of the "trilateralism" of Japan, the United States, and Europe. For him, the trilateral idea was a declaration of Japan's identity and integrity as an economic power, rather than merely a member of the Western bloc of nations under the cold war schema.

In 1964, political scientist Kōsaka Masataka published an article rationalizing Japan's choice of the option to grow as a maritime, economic nation and acknowledging Yoshida's leadership in making that decision. Novelist Shiba Ryōtarō is another who endorsed postwar Japan's adoption of economism. In his best-selling saga *Ryōma ga yuku* (There Goes Sakamoto Ryōma), published between 1962 and 1966, Shiba credited Sakamoto, one of the chief architects of the Meiji Restoration, with recognizing at that early stage that Japan's prosperity would be as a maritime, mercantile nation.

Economism, however, gave rise to the other type of groupism mentioned earlier. It produced many men who became corporate "soldiers." For Japanese who grew up hungry and cold in the ruins of the nation's defeat, working for one of the country's top corporations was a matter of great pride and joy. Once thus enlisted, they became "zealous employees" (*mōretsu shain*), driven by their sense of responsibility to their families, strong aspiration for promotion up the corporate ladder, and total devotion to the traditional virtue of diligence. Management, taking full advantage of this mind-set, adopted policies to enhance their loyalty to the company and spur their competitive spirit.

The strong sense of belonging and loyalty to "our company" exhibited by the postwar Japanese corporate warrior was vividly reminiscent of that of the vassals of the feudal lords (daimyo) of early modern times. For these modern-day samurai, the company meant everything. Given the widespread custom of exchanging business cards upon a first encounter in any context, the company one works for and the position one holds became more important than what kind of person one was as an individual. It was this mentality that fostered another brand of groupism, what may be called "company first-ism." These workaholic corporate soldiers, who were literally ready to die for their companies, sustained Japan's "economic miracle" in the 1960s.

Where this kind of groupism prevailed there was, needless to say, little room for autonomy of the individual and growth of the civil society. True, with a decade of political confrontation behind them, people had much greater freedom to pursue personal benefits and were beginning to enjoy some affluence, fitting out their homes with the full array of household appliances and even purchasing their own automobiles. The object of their self-identification shifted from political entities to the private enterprise. Selfless devotion to country was replaced by workaholism, as each person became one of innumerable cogs in the corporate machine.

In the long-range perspective of social diversification, however, groupism centered on the corporation, too, was a passing phenomenon. If the economy continued to grow at a rapid pace, it was anticipated that the society would become truly affluent and more permissive toward the self-assertions of the well-educated, highly diverse new middle class.

Indeed, by the end of the 1960s the term "my home-ism" had gained currency in Japan. It reflected the changing attitudes of a relatively small but increasing number of company employees who, rather than being workaholics, sought to give priority to the happiness of their nuclear families. A popular song written and composed by a young female singer of those days begins with "If I had a house built . . ." and goes on to describe the house of her dreams and her image of a happy home. The song ends with: "I want you to be there with me." It perfectly captured the spirit of my home-ism, which was a product of the rapid growth period.

It must be added here that ideologically inspired movements did not disappear completely. During the latter half of the sixties, left-wing groups staged campaigns for reversion of Okinawa to Japan along the lines of their anti-American, antigovernment stance, while the conservative Satō administration sought reversion of the southern islands through diplomatic negotiations with Washington. This was around the time the United States was being drawn into the quagmire of the Vietnam War and the Cultural Revolution was raging in China under the slogan "There is reason in revolution." The international environment seemed to be moving toward intensification of the cold war. If the Satō government had failed to secure the return of Okinawa through bilateral cooperation, the LDP might have fallen from power by the early 1970s, bringing an earlier end to the 1955 system under which the conservatives held the majority and the socialists remained a perpetual minority in the Diet.

Nevertheless, the elements of old-style anti-establishment resistance had lost their vigor and appeal in the course of rapid economic growth. The anti–Vietnam War movement had much broader popular support because it was able to capture the hearts and minds—the civic consciousness—of people who desired peace and gentleness toward others. The antiwar folk song of 1969, "The Case of Francine," was symbolic of such a mood. The May Revolution in France in 1968 and the campus disputes of the late 1960s occurred with similar broad bases of support. All were political struggles at the core but won a broader popular sympathy because of their roots in the counter-culture ethos that sought to challenge the established authority and order as well as in the civic culture of advanced industrial societies seeking self-government, participation in governance, and protection of the environment.

Toward the end of the 1960s, movements of local residents erupted in many parts of Japan involving welfare, the environment, and other issues that had been neglected during the period of rapid growth. Antipollution activism became intense, forcing the government to create the Environment Agency in the early 1970s to confront pollution problems. Another notable development of the decade was the election of reformist governors and mayors in various urban centers through the combined support of reformist parties and citizens' groups. This itself reflected the diversification of values accompanying phenomenal economic growth.

Similar trends were observed in other industrialized nations. In fact, the 1970s witnessed frequent power changes in many countries. In Japan, too, voter support for the ruling LDP had been steadily declining along with the rise of pluralistic tendencies in society as a result of successful economic development. From the conservative-reformist parity of the early seventies, it seemed all but inevitable that the reformist forces would soon gain a majority in the national legislature. That expectation was shattered by two crises that threatened the very foundation of Japan's prosperity. One was President Richard M. Nixon's new economic policy that took the U.S. dollar off the gold standard and put an end to the fixed exchange-rate system. The other was the oil crisis of 1973, whereby the price of crude oil quadrupled overnight. Both these crises jeopardized the systems of free trade and U.S.-Japan cooperation upon which Japan's economic survival rested.

For a resource-poor country like Japan, access to imported oil is a matter of vital concern. Indeed, the fear that Japan could no longer import foreign oil, cut off through the ABCD encirclement[3] in 1941, was what triggered the attack on Pearl Harbor and war against the United States. The impact of the 1973 oil crisis was so strong that the whole country had to return to the original point of departure where "national unity" and "diligence" were the norm. The concerted effort to assure the nation's survival affected labor as well. Trade unions, departing from their confrontational policies to cooperation with management, accepted only half the wage increases they had been accustomed to demanding. When the survival of the whole economy was at stake, they reasoned, there was no point in demanding a greater share of the profit at the risk of destroying their companies altogether.

The economic crises of the seventies dampened a tendency that had been accelerating toward formation of a coalition of citizens' movements and reformist forces. Under the conservative government's policy of economic revival, the Japanese people reverted once again to their workaholic mode and devotion to the corporation.

The sense of crisis and concerted effort for survival led to a high level of energy conservation, better quality control, and higher productivity in Japanese industry. Most symbolic of this was the production of energy-efficient, environment-friendly cars by Japanese auto makers. Japan's competitiveness in foreign markets increased tremendously as a result, which enabled the country to rise to economic superpower status in the 1980s. That the country successfully coped with the economic crises of the seventies restored confidence and composure among the people in the new decade, in turn paving the way for the rise of civil society in Japan.

RIPENING CONDITIONS FOR CIVIL SOCIETY: THE 1980S

The decade of the 1980s was the era of the new conservatism as represented by the politics of Ronald Reagan, Margaret Thatcher, and Nakasone Yasuhiro. Neo-conservatism was anti-Soviet, anticommunist, and hawkish military expansionist in external policy. In domestic policy, it advocated private-sector participation in public projects and privatization of public enterprises, stressing the market economy and small government. In contrast to the 1960s, when efforts to achieve social equality had concentrated on expansion of citizens' rights movements and welfare services in line with the public objectives of the "great society," the 1980s was a decade of devotion to the self-activating mechanisms of the market and effort within the private sector to solve problems and encourage private, individual initiatives.

No less than the commitment to further the public interest of the 1960s, the determination in the 1980s to invigorate the private sector without relying on the government provided important conditions for the development of civil society. If the transition from reliance on the "policy-beneficiary" organizations that received government subsidies to "value-promotion" organizations whose objective is to advance the public interest without relying on government is a prerequisite for civil society, Japan had to develop the spirit of "self-help" in the private sector.

What factors in the 1980s worked to awaken awareness in the private sector of service to the public interest? There were a number of significant developments resulting from Japan's growth into a mammoth economy. The unprecedented expansion of the trade surplus forced Japan to seek some measures for recycling the surplus. A dramatic increase in direct overseas investment not only contributed to expanding profits but eventually gave Japanese businesspeople on-site experience in European and American societies where contributing to local society and nonprofit organization activities in the public interest are emphasized. Although engagement with such activities was initially motivated by the desire to assure acceptance of their factories and enterprises in foreign locales, many of these companies were converted to support for the principles of corporate citizenship and philanthropy that underlie civil society, and they began to introduce these activities and ideas into Japanese society.

Also, partly in response to the need to recycle the trade surplus, from the latter part of the 1970s Japanese official development assistance (ODA) expanded spectacularly. By extending ODA to developing countries, Japan was obviously motivated by the expectation that its generosity would strengthen friendly relations with their governments and that it would contribute to building economic resource infrastructures advantageous to Japan. However, as the complexity of international interdependence deepened, a view of "enlightened self-interest" of nations gained sway based on the recognition that the stability and development of the economies and societies of partner countries would also build the foundations for regional and global peace and prosperity, thereby contributing to the national interest of Japan in the long run. In other words, contributing to the welfare of one country came to be seen as an investment in the international public interest, which, in the natural course of events, would circulate and eventually be recompensed. The noblesse-oblige idea that the economically strong had a responsibility to serve the international public interest became widespread among Japanese in the course of this expansion of Japan's foreign aid programs.

Part of Japan's ODA included the Japan Overseas Cooperation Volunteers, through which young people were sent abroad to work closely with local people, contributing to development programs through person-to-person exchange. These programs, which paralleled the purposes of many NGOs devoted to international cooperation, helped to spread understanding of the concept of citizen-level activity in line with the public interest.

Also during this period, damage caused by acid rain and global warming resulting from destruction of the ozone layer began to receive widespread attention, and issues relating to the global environment awakened awareness of the shared destiny of humanity and the earth itself. The two chief conditions that fostered environmentalism are the increasing gravity of pollution and the overall tranquillity and affluence in society. In the 1980s, those two conditions were fulfilled in Japan. It was also a time when experts studying issues of global public concern formed an intellectual community. The dissemination of the results of their research worldwide was instrumental in building a world community of shared perceptions. Research institutions, which serve as the intellectual searchlights of society, came to acquire particular importance in matters of governance in the global age.

Another important factor that promoted the advance of civil society in the 1980s was the rising level of educational achievement, including among women. With increased affluence, it became economically possible for women as well as men to continue their studies on the university and postgraduate level. Men with university educations continued to seek careers in secure jobs in the large, well-established corporations, whereas women tended to feel more at home with work in NGOs, NPOs, and other fields in civil society.

GOVERNANCE AND CIVIL SOCIETY:
THE POST–COLD WAR ERA

More than any other factor, however, it was the ending of the cold war that finally released the forces capable of propagating civil society in Japan. Humankind was liberated from the strategic obsessions of the cold war era. In its place, there was now much talk of "economic confrontation" and of the "clash of civilizations." Both were based on slightly old-fashioned premises, however. Once the walls came down among groups of nation-states, it was found that the barriers between nations were open everywhere. Not only the borderless economy, but borderless security and borderless culture had already become an everyday affair in the advanced societies of North America, Europe, and Japan. The importance of the state was by no means eclipsed, but as society developed greater depth and complexity through the process of internationalization, the proportion of issues the state could readily deal with markedly decreased. As Daniel Bell pointed out, the state was too small a body to adequately deal with global problems but too big a presence to take care of the concerns of individuals and local communities.

Dealing with the problems that cannot be adequately handled by the state comes under the rubric of "governance." In the absence of a well-developed civil society, all kinds of problems, from global environmental destruction and regional development to matters related to the individual psyche, would be left unsolved. The times are such that the public good cannot be realized unless both the private sector and the government both deal with issues of a public nature. A country where the ethos of civil society is poorly developed cannot become a first-rate nation or earn the respect of the international community. The fundamental challenge of the 21st century is to build societies where the private sector flourishes and that possess a wealth of individuals and private groups with the knowledge and expertise to solve problems and the capacity to express themselves on an international level.

The event that impressed the world with the role of NGOs in an era when governments are either too big or too small was the Earth Summit (United Nations Conference on Environment and Development) in Rio de Janeiro in 1992. This was the product of international trends, however, and in Japan at that stage, no one expected much of NGO, NPO, or volunteer activities of any sort.

All the more amazing, therefore, were the tremendous forces of volunteer energy in Japan that welled forth following the Great Hanshin-Awaji Earthquake. I myself was witness to this phenomenon from within, although what sparked such a change in Japanese society still strikes me as somewhat of a puzzle.

Kobe University alone lost 39 students to the quake. The students in my seminar at the time moved quickly to ascertain the safety of their fellows, and two days later a female student who played a leading role in liaison efforts came to my house with two others to report the news that with the exception of two students, all the others in my seminar had been accounted for. Right after that I received a telephone call informing me that one of the two had been found dead by his father in the rubble of his boardinghouse.

At a memorial service held in the nearby city of Sakai three days later where families and friends gathered to mourn the student of my seminar who had died, 15 other members who had survived the disaster also gathered. After the ceremony I talked with each of them, asking what they had experienced, and it was then that I learned that more than half were ready to volunteer to help deal with the aftermath of the quake. One young man was so overcome with grief at the loss of his classmate that he said doing volunteer work was the only thing that would save his sanity. The two American students in the group, I noticed, pitched in to help as if it was the obvious thing to do. In no time, the network that had been created to check classmates' safety had become a network for volunteer work.

Given the traditions of Japanese society, one might ask about the safety of friends, teachers, or acquaintances, but beyond that, it was the norm to withdraw and take care of one's own situation, not becoming involved in the affairs of others. For the first time, the students in Kobe turned their energies to volunteer efforts based on the kind of civic consciousness we associate with American society.

Not only students but the victims of the quake themselves went out of their way to help each other. Back in 1923, at the time of the Great Kantō Earthquake that struck Tokyo, antiforeign rumors had set off group hysteria that resulted in the murder and maltreatment of Korean residents. In Kobe as well, there were people who were concerned only with the protection of themselves and their families, and in some cases government-level responses had virtually criminal results because of reliance on routine rules even in the face of crisis and lack of an adequate crisis-management policy. On the whole, however, the level of private, individual initiative in dealing with the catastrophe was unprecedented. This came not only from the victims themselves and others in the area but from the 1.3 million volunteers who came forth to help, and the astronomical sum of emergency relief aid that poured in from private sources around the world.

Certainly the information revolution and internationalization contributed greatly to this unexpected manifestation of civic consciousness in Japan. Conditions in the devastated area immediately became known throughout the world, and reporting on the quake was heard throughout Japan and in the disaster zone itself. Distorted views and mistaken responses could be corrected through international communication. When the remark of the governor of a neighboring prefecture, in responding to requests for relief assistance, to the effect that Kobe should basically look out for itself, was taken up in the news, it unwittingly revealed both how poor his understanding of the circumstances and how meager his civic spirit were.

When it was reported from Ministry of Finance sources that the government would not provide relief assistance from public funds for individual quake victims for fear of conflicting with the letter of the law, we shuddered at the unchanged horror of officials who considered it their responsibility to the state to put the logic of the bureaucracy above the lives of citizens. It made us all the more grateful for the praise we read in the newspapers penned by novelist Shiba Ryōtarō, who observed from the sight of victims sharing what little food and supplies they had, that "[the people of] Kobe had lost a great deal, but at least they had not lost their 'hearts.'" I was also very encouraged when I read an article entitled "Thank you, People of Kobe," by then Washington-based *Asahi Shimbun* bureau chief Funabashi Yōichi, who reported that the U.S. media were quite impressed with the courageous handling of the disaster by the victims of the quake.

Of course, the above anecdote is just a personal experience, but I do believe that our internationalized media communications have made it possible for us to see ourselves as if in a mirror and to correct our own behavior as necessary. I am convinced that it played a significant role in guiding the responses not only of the victims and other local citizens but of the nation as a whole.

Behind the phenomena that came to the fore with the Kobe disaster were the maturation of conditions that I have examined in this chapter. Tracing its roots to the modernization period and nourished after World War II, particularly during the 1960s and 1980s, the ethos of civil society has developed to such an unexpectedly high standard since the ending of the cold war that it can easily rise to the surface in an emergency.

CONCLUSION

When Japanese political scientists use the term "civil society," it is usually as the abstract concept of the society of citizens in contrast to the apparatus of the state. The same term may remind Americans of more specific, nongovernmental private organizations. The society of citizens and private organizations are not conflicting concepts. Associated among Japanese with the society of citizens, civil society is still thought of as displaying the indispensable elements of independent individuals and their autonomous private organizations. When seen, as among Americans, as referring to private organizations, civil society is understood as making up the entirety of the society of citizens that flourishes from the activity of such private organizations. In other words, civil society in its broad sense is a citizens' society that consists mainly of private organizations, such as NPOs and NGOs, and is also the realm in which these organizations are active.

At the beginning of this chapter, I cited three conditions under which civil society emerges: the presence of a pluralistic society, respect for the private, and popular awareness of the public interest. Has Japanese society today achieved these conditions?

It may be said that Japanese society has made great progress as far as pluralism is concerned. In any society where modernization has been forcibly initiated from above, state authority grows too strong no matter what political system is adopted. The idea of "respect for authority and contempt for the masses" was fostered in Japan not only by traditional factors but also in response to external crisis and the necessity for modernization initiated from above. When the post–World War II reconstruction drive and rapid economic growth, once again orchestrated by initiative from the top, were complete, a large middle class stretched across the spectrum of Japanese society. While the tendency toward uniformism and groupism can still be found in society and people's attitudes, the social structure is more diverse than it has ever been.

Respect for the private was fully recognized in principle in Japanese society after the end of World War II, but that did not mean that the tradition of authoritarian rule led by the bureaucracy had disappeared. The power of the bureaucracy to issue permissions and certifications, handle matters at its own discretion, and exercise broad monopolies on information continues to prevail. The bureaucracy still holds many of the privileges of a semi-independent kingdom that are beyond the reach of democratic controls. Many officials in the bureaucracy are convinced that their institutions represent the sole legitimate agencies that possess the qualifications and the ability to formulate state policy for the public good.

Today, however, this mentality of bureaucratic superiority has been profoundly shaken. Development-oriented policies planned by the bureaucracy and the immense powers needed to implement them have all but become things of the past. As a result, the sense of mission and the devotion that inspired members of the bureaucracy to work long hours day after day despite meager salaries for the sake of serving the state and the people have eroded. The public has been disillusioned by the recent rash of cases revealing civil servants who took advantage of their positions for personal gain.

The problem is perhaps not so much the moral integrity of individual officials as it is the situation in which the bureaucracy has grown into one huge, unrivaled think tank. What is most urgently needed is a recovery of political leadership capable of using the bureaucracy to best advantage. In order to achieve such a goal, the party system has to be rebuilt, and the process is about halfway through. No less important in the long run is the necessity to expand the work of private think tanks and the development of civil society that assumes responsibility for public issues in general. Both public and private must be equally sturdy wheels of the cart for it to steadily carry the burdens of the public interest, but as society grows more advanced more weight will have to shift from the public to the private. Now that the state has become too big to look after the needs of individuals and too small to deal with the larger, globally related issues, citizens and private organizations endowed with a spirit of self-help and a sense of responsibility for the public good should play a much larger role in its stead.

Is it possible in these times, when even public servants who have lost sight of the public interest are tempted by the pursuit of personal profit, that ordinary citizens might develop a greater consciousness of the public good? Most people would probably say no. Nowadays, one often hears people talk about and decry the changes: Old-style morals have collapsed; everywhere you find people acting selfishly or irresponsibly, taking advantage of the looseness of social rules and constraints.

That tendency is undeniably part of what is changing in Japan, but fortunately it is not the whole story. Quite in the opposite direction, we also find that people today are cultivating a new consciousness that is open-minded and informed and are engaging in more sophisticated forms of activity. Observing the tendencies of university seminar students, for example, one notices that they are less interested in loyal, group-oriented sports-type activity with strict senior-junior distinctions and more inclined to join civic-related activities and groups which are more loosely structured and where members are relatively independent. Nevertheless, one sees almost no irresponsible students of the kind who fail to turn in seminar reports or absent themselves from activities. While their preferences and character have changed, they are no less hard-working than their predecessors. On the contrary, many now take an interest in the environment and international issues and there are now many more women students, for example, who go on for graduate study or choose to study abroad.

Even professional baseball fans seem to have changed. I attended a game recently after not having been to a baseball stadium for a long time. Where once fans had no eyes for any but their own team and would fall silent even when a member of the other team hit a beautiful home run or performed a fine play, I was surprised to find them reacting quite differently. While naturally eager to see their own players do well and their team win, they now actually showed appreciation for and empathy toward skillful plays and home runs executed by the other team. In this way, I believe, people's thinking is becoming relativized as they develop the empathy to understand universalities that transcend in-group norms, local chauvinism, and narrow nationalism.

The earthquake disaster that hit Tokyo and Yokohama in 1923 triggered shocking attacks on Korean residents of the metropolitan area. Following the 1995 Kobe earthquake, no such antiforeign incidents were observed and local Japanese and foreign residents shared the same relief supplies of rice balls offered by volunteers. Suspicions of people of different nationality were overridden by empathy for other human beings caught in the same calamity. In the decades of peace since the end of World War II, Japanese do seem to have lost their former toughness, as often pointed out in their reluctance to perform dull, dirty, and dangerous jobs, but at the same time they have become more thoughtful of others and more broad-minded in their views. The outpouring of some 1.3 million volunteers at the time of the Kobe disaster must be interpreted as evidence not of a decline but of a heightening of care and understanding for others.

Responding to temporary needs out of sympathy for the victims of a terrible disaster is one thing; engaging in ongoing activity for the public good on a routine basis is another. The large number of short-term volunteers represent the fringes of a growing bulwark of civic activists. In order to build that bulwark into a solid civil society through which citizens can move beyond such outer-fringe activities and support the core of public service activities on their own initiative, there is still a need for development of both subjective and objective conditions.

We may celebrate the passage of the NPO Law (officially the Law to Promote Specified Nonprofit Activities), signaling the acceptance in society of the NPO and NGO activities that form the core of civil society. Nevertheless, the shortage and inexperience of leadership for organizations engaged in public-interest activities are chronic. On the one hand, many long-established public-interest organizations have depended on government rules, protection, and financial resources for so long that they do not know how to act independently. On the other hand, the NGOs, many of which grew out of leftist or grass-roots citizens' movements, find it difficult to shed their anti-establishment attitudes. Some members of NGOs, while they possess the activists' devotion to dealing with problems, are sometimes guilty of narrow-minded self-righteousness, and without appreciating the complexity and difficulty of issues they sometimes revert to negative or even destructive acts.

There are many NGO activists in the field of international cooperation, meanwhile, who believe that accepting funds that are part of ODA is tantamount to submitting to government authority and to their own spiritual downfall. Some NGO activists with a strong sense of mission believe that their work can more effectively meet human needs than government programs and assert that part of public funds paid to the government in the form of taxes should be apportioned to them for these activities; however, there are very few NGOs that possess the organizational experience and skills to effectively act on this noble sense of mission. A more enabling environment is needed that will facilitate pluralistic and complementary roles for NGOs to make it possible for them to cooperate with government activities or even to rival them. Japan will attain an advanced civil society when NGOs can sometimes obtain access to government funds for their activities without giving up their autonomy from the government and when they have developed high-caliber skills that will even influence government activities to greater improvement.

As important as and inseparable from these subjective conditions are social and institutional conditions. In the United States and Europe, NGO and NPO activities take place in a culture of giving and traditions of volunteerism and philanthropy that are firmly and widely rooted among the people. Conditions in these countries are immeasurably more favorable to such activities than in Japan. It is only a few years since the flood of 1.3 million volunteers that descended on Kobe to help deal with a disaster finally succeeded in arousing public recognition of volunteer activities. This lack of a deeply rooted tradition of volunteerism and philanthropy makes all the more decisive the role of institutional inducement efforts in order to encourage development of civil society. The framework for tax deductions on donations to organizations engaged in public-interest activities is far more limited in Japan than that in the West, for example.

On the premise that the government alone is best able to judge what is in the public interest, Japan has maintained a long tradition of paying all taxes to the government and leaving it to officialdom to decide how those resources will be divided. On this point as well, some diversification is needed. Whether it is for welfare, for education, or for international cooperation, as long as it is for a purpose in the public interest there should be room for the idea that the use of at least part of tax revenues should be left to the discretion of citizens themselves. By allowing a fixed deduction on income tax for donations to nonprofit public-interest organizations, citizens can assure that part of their tax payments will be spent for a certain purpose they can determine themselves. The same principle should be made to apply to inheritance taxes. It should be made possible to extend to people the freedom to decide on the basis of the value judgments they have developed during their lifetime how a fixed amount of the wealth they have accumulated over a lifetime will be spent in an area of activity they choose. In that sense, the clauses regarding tax deductions on donations which were omitted from the recently approved NPO Law are extremely important in order to foster a culture of giving and civil society in general in Japan. Have we not reached a stage at which we can think of tax not just as something arbitrarily "taken away," but as money we voluntarily invest through the tax deduction system in an area in the public interest that we think particularly important?

Notes

1. Information on this topic is primarily available in the multivolume *Nihon kyōkasho taikei* (Comprehensive series on textbooks in Japan) (Kōdansha 1961–1965). The section titled "Kindai kyōkasho sōsetsu" (Textbooks in the modern period: A general introduction) in volume 1 (Kōdansha 1961) was particularly helpful.

2. On this subject, see the study by Muramatsu, Itō, and Tsujinaka (1986).

3. After the Manchurian Incident of 1931, the military increased its control over political processes in Japan. The military-led government opened hostilities with China in 1937 that continued, and following Germany's military successes in western Europe in the spring of 1940 Tokyo signed the Tripartite Pact with Berlin and Rome. In dire need of oil and other resources, Japan subsequently sent troops to French Indochina and threatened to invade the Dutch colony of Indonesia. In response, the "ABCD" powers—the United States, Britain, China, and the Netherlands—joined forces to contain Japan.

Bibliography

Hayashi Yūjirō. 1997. "Nihonjin no genkachikan to firansuropī" (Basic Japanese values and philanthropy). *Asteion,* no. 45 (Summer): 48–61.

Honma Masaaki and Deguchi Masayuki, eds. 1995. *Borantia kakumei* (The volunteer revolution). Tokyo: Tōyō Keizai Shinpōsha.

Inoguchi Takashi, ed. 1988. "Kokka to kigyō, dantai, kojin" (The state and corporations, organizations, and individuals). *Leviathan* (Spring). Special issue.

Kōdansha, ed. 1961. *Kindai hen* (Moral Training I). Volume 1 of Kōdansha, ed. 1961–1965. *Nihon kyōkasho taikei* (Comprehensive series on textbooks in Japan). Tokyo: Kōdansha.

———. 1961–1965. *Nihon kyōkasho taikei* (Comprehensive series on textbooks in Japan). Tokyo: Kōdansha.

Kōsaka Masataka. 1964. "Kaiyō kokka Nihon no kōsō" (Japan as a maritime nation). *Chūō kōron* (September): 48–80.

———. 1996. *Fushigi no Nichi-Bei kankei shi* (The curious history of Japan-U.S. relations). Tokyo: PHP Kenkyūjo.

Matsuno Osamu. 1996. *Kindai Nihon no kōmin kyōiku* (Public education in modern Japan). Nagoya: Nagoya Daigaku Shuppankai.

Muramatsu Michio, Itō Mitsutoshi, and Tsujinaka Yutaka. 1986. *Sengo Nihon no atsuryoku dantai* (Pressure groups in postwar Japan). Tokyo: Tōyō Keizai Shinpōsha.

Shiba Ryōtarō. 1989. *Meiji to iu kokka* (The state that was Meiji). Tokyo: NHK Shuppan.

CHAPTER THREE

Emergence of Japan's Civil Society and Its Future Challenges

Yamamoto Tadashi

PUBLIC ATTENTION TO CIVIL SOCIETY surged abruptly and dramatically in Japan in the wake of the Great Hanshin-Awaji Earthquake in Kobe in January 1995, which took the lives of over 6,400 people. More than 1.3 million volunteers and a large number of nongovernmental organizations (NGOs) converged on the devastated city to offer relief and assistance to the victims. Their dedicated and impressive work was a bright spot in the otherwise grim scene of disaster. The media reported a number of poignant stories about the critical role played by volunteers and NGOs and nonprofit organizations (NPOs),[1] and belabored the allegedly bureaucratic and inept response of national and local government officials. Though there may have been a lack of balance in portraying the effectiveness of civil society organizations and volunteers in contrast with the ineffectiveness of "bumbling bureaucrats," the intense reportage helped the Japanese public as well as government officials and political and business leaders focus on civil society.

This sudden awareness of the value or utility of volunteers and NPOs prompted the government and political parties to find ways of facilitating their activities. Because as many as 18 government agencies rushed to respond to the new popularity of volunteer activities, they decided to form a Liaison Committee for Related Government Ministries and Agencies Regarding Volunteer Activities. Most of the main political parties started drafting new NPO legislation that would effectively promote and support the activities of Japan's nonprofit sector. For

97

three years following the earthquake, intense debate over the NPO legislation occurred, involving not only NPO leaders but also politicians,
bureaucrats, business leaders, and the media. The so-called NPO Law
(officially the Law to Promote Specified Nonprofit Activities) finally
passed the Diet in March 1998, providing a new impetus for the further
growth of civil society in Japan. Equally significant is that the debate over
the NPO Law fostered a better understanding among leaders and the
public of the ways in which civil society could contribute to the public
good.

But because public attention to civil society swelled so abruptly and
quickly, the debate over civil society development tended to be super-
ficial and even emotional at times. There is a lack of awareness, for example, of the significant growth of NGOs/NPOs in Japan before the
earthquake, and little effort has been made to understand the causes for
the evolution of civil society domestically. Thus, some of the government responses following the earthquake focused on "volunteers" and
overlooked other actors in civil society commonly recognized in many
other countries, such as NGOs/NPOs, private foundations, and independent policy research institutions. Moreover, some bureaucrats (and
conservative politicians who have close ties with them) regarded volunteers as inexpensive subsidiaries to government bureaucrats, as evidenced by some legislative proposals at the time of debate over the NPO
Law that called for limiting the number of paid staff for incorporated
NPOs. It is not surprising, therefore, that recent debate on civil society
in Japan has typically been devoid of sufficient analysis and understanding of the relevance of civil society development for the governance of
society. Nor has there been much effort to relate civil society debate to
the debate over deregulation and downsizing of the government, which
is by far the most critical issue of the day in Japan.

FORCES BEHIND THE DEVELOPMENT
OF CIVIL SOCIETY

The Great Hanshin-Awaji Earthquake clearly was a major turning
point in the development of civil society in Japan. It is generally believed that had the earthquake not highlighted the activities of volunteers and NPOs, it would have taken many more years for government
agencies and the major political parties to act to pass the NPO Law. It
is more accurate, however, to say that the earthquake was an event that

galvanized the forces already at work in Japan to bring about an important leap forward for civil society—namely, enactment of the law. Without the foundation laid in the years preceding the earthquake by dedicated civil society actors, the concerted efforts of many groups and individuals to get the NPO Law passed would not have been successful. Whether the momentum to build a stronger civil society can be sustained and will eventually prevail in Japan's sociopolitical milieu is a critical question to be addressed.

THE GLOBAL TREND
TOWARD CIVIL SOCIETY DEVELOPMENT

Diverse exogenous factors have influenced the development of civil society in Japan. It is widely acknowledged that the United Nations Conference on Environment and Development in 1992 in Rio de Janeiro was a watershed event for Japan's NGO movement. Japan's NGOs gained momentum through successive UN conferences, such as the World Conference on Human Rights in Vienna in 1993, the International Conference on Population and Development in Cairo in 1994, the World Summit for Social Development in Copenhagen in 1995, and the Fourth World Conference on Women in Beijing in 1995. Even prior to the 1992 Rio conference, Japanese NGOs started emerging in response to changing external environments. Several NGOs were established in 1979 to support Indochinese refugees. In the late 1980s, the international NGO movement to address global environmental issues stimulated the founding of many environmental NGOs. The growing number of regional networks among NGOs in Asia encouraged participation by Japanese NGOs, thus stimulating their growth.

"Good corporate citizenship" became an important corporate practice after the extensive exposure of Japanese corporations to American local communities following the surge in Japan's foreign direct investment subsequent to the Plaza Accord in the mid-1980s. Trade tensions and calls for Japan to play a larger international role prompted Japanese corporate giving abroad.[2] The growing interest among Japanese corporations in forming partnerships with NPOs follows a noticeable trend set by multinational corporations in recent years.

The development of think tanks in Japan has also been significantly influenced by the international trend of "track two diplomacy" and the international collaborative networks of independent policy research institutions that are increasingly pursuing common research agendas.

The need to strengthen Japan's representation in such international cooperative networks is stimulating exploration on how to bolster Japan's policy research institutions.

Another recent international phenomenon that has contributed to the development of Japan's civil society is the impressive growth of what has come to be known as "transnational civil society"—the set of collaborative networks of civil society organizations addressing global issues. The International Campaign to Ban Land Mines, which effectively engineered the "Ottawa process" resulting in the treaty to ban antipersonnel land mines in December 1997, is one prominent example. At COP3, the Third Session of the Conference of the Parties to the U.N. Framework Convention on Climate Change, held in Kyoto in December 1997, the Climate Action Networks, consisting of 250 NGOs concerned with the global environment, and the Kiko Forum '97, a group of NGOs organized in Japan to work for the Kyoto conference, played a critical role in giving transparency to the conference proceedings through information dissemination, which greatly influenced participating governments. The emergence of transnational civil society reflects the limits of national security in the post–cold war world, the deepening of economic interdependence worldwide, and the relative lowering of the authority of states. Revolutionary advances in information technology have created a situation in which the state can no longer monopolize information. Under such circumstances, international networks of organizations and people sharing a commitment to a certain set of values or ideas can be expected to play an even greater role in international governance.[3]

As Japanese NPOs became more exposed to the international trend of NPOs playing a bigger role in society and became more conscious of the need for enhancing their infrastructure and social recognition, they grew keenly aware of various factors inhibiting their growth and became motivated to work to remove the serious impediments to the development of the NPO sector in Japan.

GREATER ACCEPTANCE OF CIVIL SOCIETY
AS A CONSTRUCTIVE SOCIAL FORCE

In the early years after the end of World War II, Japan's NGO movement was characterized by its antigovernment and anticorporate position. During that period, Japan was heavily influenced by the ideological conflict between the socialist-communist camp and the democratic–free market camp. Those who worked for the NGO movement, which was sometimes referred to as the "citizens' movement," were labeled as left-wing elements. This image has changed considerably, if not totally, in recent years, particularly with the end of the cold war. Many NGOs, now more commonly called NPOs, were formed to address the issues created by a complex and pluralistic society, such as home care for senior citizens, environmental protection, foreign labor, social welfare, and consumer protection. A pattern of partnership between NPOs and municipal governments to address social issues in their local communities began to emerge. NPOs have been particularly effective in areas where government bureaucracy does not have sufficient flexibility or resources to respond effectively. As social needs and values became more diverse and the government budget became more constrained, the space for NPOs widened.

Significantly, more and more corporations started to find partnership with NPOs to be a useful approach for satisfying the interests of their stakeholders. The sense of good corporate citizenship that corporations acquired through their overseas experience was buttressed by the consciousness that corporations must meet the pluralistic interests of society. The concept of *kyōsei* was introduced by Hiraiwa Gaishi, president of Keidanren (Japan Federation of Economic Organizations), in 1991 as a guiding principle of corporate activities. The word *kyōsei* can be translated as "symbiosis" and refers to the Japanese business concept of interdependence and mutual prosperity—hence, in this context, a need to promote good corporate citizenship. The One Percent Club was established within Keidanren in 1989 to encourage corporations to contribute 1 percent of pretax revenues to worthy social causes, and, along with the Committee on Corporate Philanthropy of the same organization, encourages corporate support and partnership with NPOs. Though corporate support for NPOs is still limited, it has greatly helped recognition of NPOs as a constructive social force.

The media had started paying attention to the importance of civil society even before the Great Hanshin-Awaji Earthquake, and the media coverage raised people's consciousness about the contributions NPOs could make to society. The combined number of articles on NGOs and NPOs in the *Asahi Shimbun,* the *Yomiuri Shimbun,* and the *Mainichi*

Shimbun, three major Japanese dailies, rose from 178 in 1990 to 850 in 1992, and to 1,455 in 1994. After the earthquake, the number jumped to 2,151 in 1995, and it continued to rise thereafter, reaching 2,868 in 1997.

GROWING RECOGNITION OF CIVIL SOCIETY'S ROLE IN GOVERNANCE

Even before the earthquake, a new awareness had emerged among Japanese leaders and the general public that the forces of globalization had brought about a situation where government alone cannot cope with today's increasingly complex socioeconomic issues, leaving a growing space for NGOs to fill. This recognition of government's limits coincided with a global trend of a decline of confidence in government in advanced industrial democracies as well as in developing nations. Joseph Nye of Harvard University, in a 1997 article titled "In Government We Don't Trust," wrote that governments "will share more of the processes of governance with market and nonprofit institutions" into the next century (111). Nye also pointed out that the popularity of the concept reflects the antigovernment mood in many countries, which has led to demands that government's role be reduced and that the nongovernmental sector be relied on to a greater degree. This trend has become pronounced in Japan, where confidence in bureaucracy has plummeted in recent years. Bureaucrats, once regarded as the agents of change in Japan's phenomenal industrialization and modernization process, have come to be seen as a major hindrance to the changes needed in the country today.

The global trend toward more reliance on the nongovernmental sector was clearly identified by a 13-nation (including Japan) study undertaken at the initiative of Johns Hopkins University in 1990–1995 —the Johns Hopkins Comparative Nonprofit Sector Project. On the basis of this study, Lester Salamon, director of the project, concluded that the world is witnessing a global "associational revolution" and argued that it "may prove to be as significant to the latter twentieth century as the rise of the nation-state was to the latter nineteenth." Salamon reported that the upshot of this associational revolution is the emergence of "a massive array of self-governing private organizations, not dedicated to distributing profits to shareholders or directors, pursuing public purposes outside the formal apparatus of the state." He suggested that "the proliferation of these groups may be permanently altering the relationship between states and citizens" (Salamon 1994, 109).

Similarly, a survey project launched in the spring of 1993 by the Japan Center for International Exchange (JCIE) to assess the current state of civil society organizations in 15 countries in Asia Pacific noted the impressive growth of the nonprofit sector in the region in recent years. The results of the study were published jointly by the Singapore-based Institute of Southeast Asian Studies and JCIE in September 1995 under the title *Emerging Civil Society in the Asia Pacific Community*. In addition to an expansion of the size of the sector, the survey pointed to an evolution of the scope and nature of activities. In the "Integrative Summary," this writer, acting as the editor of the book, reported that "many NGOs and philanthropic organizations in these countries have been transforming themselves from traditional organizations that provide charitable contributions and services to the poor, to those that directly involve themselves in the development process or in addressing issues such as the environment and human rights" (Yamamoto 1995, 5).

Indeed, the rise of civil society in Japan before the earthquake was evident in the then new phenomenon of citizens coming together to address new and complex issues, such as caring for the growing number of elderly in many communities, providing support for the large number of foreign laborers migrating into urban as well as rural communities, and protecting the natural environment against industrial pollution. The government's failure to respond effectively to the vast social changes and the pluralization of social values brought about by the forces of globalization and the intensification of interdependence, on the one hand, and a growing interest on the part of citizens in responding to the widening space of social needs, on the other hand, resulted in the emergence of civil society in Japan.

However, the development of civil society in Japan, as is the case with many other countries in the region as portrayed in the Asia Pacific survey report, has been hindered by the continuing tendency of the government to "turn to" the nonprofit sector, spawning a hierarchical relationship where civil society organizations are reduced to mere subsidiaries of government agencies. The debate over the NPO Law reflected the tension between the government bureaucracy and civil society, as will be further analyzed later. It can be argued, then, that the development of civil society itself has become the issue of governance.

IMPETUS TO IMPROVE THE LEGAL
AND REGULATORY CONTEXT OF CIVIL SOCIETY

One prominent aspect of the recent NPO movement in Japan is the tendency for these organizations to form networks among themselves to exchange information and to cooperate to remove the various constraints against their activities. Often these networks are linked with overseas networks. As NPOs tried to help each other and attempted to improve effectiveness through collaborative networks, they became keenly aware of various government controls that impede their activities. Removal of governmental control over NPOs and facilitation of their activities through changes in the incorporation process and the provision of tax incentives for contributions to NPOs became a common cause of those who worked in NPOs and supported NPOs.

Such concerns gave rise to several initiatives to study the possible change of the legal and administrative context of civil society in Japan in the years immediately preceding the Great Hanshin-Awaji Earthquake, particularly between 1993 and 1995.[4] Those study groups established around this time include the Coalition for Legislation to Support Citizens' Organizations (called C's); the Japan Civil Liberties Union; the Study Group on Tax Provisions for Contributions to NGOs, established by the Liberal Human Rights Association; the Committee for Promotion of NGO Activities, established by the People's Forum 2001, an environmental NGO; the NPO Study Forum, set up by a group of scholars led by Professor Honma Masaaki of Osaka University; and the Study Group on Building Infrastructures for Citizens Public Interest Activities, supported by the National Institute for Research Advancement (NIRA). The aforementioned Johns Hopkins Comparative Nonprofit Sector Project gave impetus to such research activities through its study group on the Japanese case organized by JCIE and begun in 1990. The Johns Hopkins study group played an important role in stimulating more intense research activities to deal with what was considered to be an outmoded and deficient legal and administrative context for NPO activities in Japan. This served as the basis for the studies conducted by Professor Amemiya Takako of Shoin College and other experts concerning the legal and regulatory context of civil society in

Japan, which resulted in perhaps the first definitive studies on Japan's civil society published in English (Yamamoto 1998).

Efforts to strengthen independent policy research institutions in Japan and promote more active Japanese participation in policy-oriented intellectual exchange activities were started in the early 1990s. In the late 1980s, NIRA undertook a multipronged research project titled "Agenda for Japan in the 1990s,"[5] and as a part of this project commissioned JCIE to analyze the role of independent research institutions in other advanced industrial democracies in Europe and North America. The Sasakawa Peace Foundation (SPF) started a study project in 1991 on "Think Tanks in Japan—Their Potential and Prospects" with a view to rectifying Japan's policy-making process, which, because it is dominated by the bureaucracy, is devoid of long-term perspective and creative approaches to diverse socioeconomic issues. As a part of this project, a study was commissioned to the Urban Institute in the United States, which produced a report titled *A Japanese Think Tank: Exploring Alternative Models*. On the basis of this project, SPF organized the World Think Tank Forum in Tokyo in February 1995, bringing together representatives of a number of major independent research institutions in Japan. The Global ThinkNet Washington Conference in March 1997 and the Global ThinkNet Tokyo Conference in February 1998 organized by JCIE may be regarded as sequels to the World Think Tank Forum.

The pressures to build more full-fledged independent policy research institutions have grown considerably in the past few years, owing to the increasing inability of government bureaucracy to generate coherent policy directions in diverse issue areas. In the debate over the government-initiated financial restructural law in 1998, the government bureaucracy's role, in particular that of the Ministry of Finance, was substantially reduced, and in a departure from the the traditional legislative process, negotiations occurred between young turks of the governing Liberal Democratic Party (LDP) and the opposition Democratic Party of Japan (DPJ) over the draft bill. Significantly, the government bureaucrats were essentially shut out of the legislative process as the contents of the draft bill were rigorously debated between relatively young politicians on both sides of the political divide. While this episode, as well as the legislative process for the NPO Law, indicated the likely emergence of a new pattern in the legislative process with more active participation by Diet members, defying the traditional pattern of legislators sitting on the sidelines while bureaucrats handle the drafting of bills, it also highlighted the absence of appropriate staff capacity or policy ideas and advice from independent policy research institutions.

EMERGENCE OF PARTNERSHIP
BETWEEN POLITICIANS AND CIVIL SOCIETY LEADERS

In the early 1990s, a number of political parties started showing strong interest in the nonprofit sector. On September 8, 1994, Diet member Hatoyama Yukio and several other representatives of the New Party Sakigake (*sakigake* means harbinger), which would join the LDP and the Social Democratic Party of Japan (SDPJ) in the coalition government in 1994, visited JCIE headquarters for an extended discussion over what is called in the United States a "brown bag dinner." Hatoyama's talk with this writer and senior staff of JCIE continued late into the evening. As a follow-up to this session, JCIE organized a series of five seminars for the members and staff of the New Party Sakigake in October and November of the same year; NPO leaders attended as resource persons to help the party formulate its draft proposal for legislation to promote civil society.

Around that time, other parties were also setting up study teams on the subject of civil society. The SDPJ began to hold discussions with the Japanese Center for International Cooperation (JANIC) and other NPO groups in the summer of 1994 concerning means of enhancing NGOs, including streamlining incorporation procedures and allowing tax-deductible donations. Speaking in the House of Representatives Committee on Finance on November 18, 1994, Dōmoto Akiko of the SDPJ noted, "NPOs and NGOs are now essential as intermediaries in the relationship between the government and the people and in links between local government bodies and their residents and between businesses and consumers." She went on to say, "We already have three or so drafts of proposed bills in our hands," suggesting that the cooperation between legislators and representatives of the nonprofit sector had already reached the stage of work on concrete legal provisions. When the New Frontier Party (NFP) was formed in December 1994, it included "building a private nonprofit sector" as one of its key policy commitments as set forth in its inaugural manifesto.

By this time, citizens' groups, private research and exchange institutions, and private foundations were already actively conducting research and lobbying in connection with the issues of incorporation and taxation for civil society organizations. Of particular significance was the launching in November 1994 of C's, which brought together 24 citizens' groups to work on these issues. They further intensified the dialogue between political parties and NPOs. Reflecting on the developments around this time, Nakamura Keizō, a senior editor of the daily *Mainichi Shimbun*, wrote in the paper on January 23, 1997: "We cannot overlook the fact that research into NPO issues among politial parties, citizen groups, and others has picked up since the start of the 1990s; the groundwork has thus been laid for a wide-ranging debate if the political leaders take an initiative on this issue."

IMPEDIMENTS TO THE DEVELOPMENT OF CIVIL SOCIETY

The rising waves of demand for a more enabling environment to nurture civil society in Japan reflected the heightened frustrations and concerns of civil society leaders over the many constraints against their efforts. The excessive government intervention in the affairs of civil society organizations is symbolic of the traditional Japanese system of state-centric governance, which served the country well when it was trying to pursue rapid industrialization and economic growth. As Japan achieved its earlier development goals, however, the society found itself with many more pluralistic needs than the government alone could deal with. Ironically, when citizens today try to come together to address these issues by themselves in the spirit of "associational revolution," they are confronted with a multitude of governmental regulations, not to speak of the lack of incentives for self-help.

Outside the country, the paucity of Japanese NGOs, independent research institutions, and organized philanthropies has caused a situation that is sometimes referred to as the "underrepresentation" of Japan in many international cooperative ventures and dialogues. It is said that Japanese organizations are little in evidence in places like refugee camps, where NGOs from around the world converge, and only a limited number of Japanese NGOs are taking part in the international NGO networks of the Asia Pacific region. The scarcity of Japanese participation in "track two" exercises, namely, policy research and dialogue concerning international relations among private-sector think tanks and policy thinkers, has become a matter of considerable concern among intellectual leaders around the world.

BUREAUCRATIC CONTROL OVER INCORPORATION AND THE OPERATION OF CIVIL SOCIETY

Under the current system, regulations for granting incorporated status to NPOs are stipulated in Article 34 of the Civil Code, which was adopted in 1898. Article 34 specifies that "an association or foundation . . . relating to public interests and not having for its object the acquisition of gain may be made a juristic person subject to the permission of the competent authorities." "Competent authorities" refers to government ministries with jurisdictional authority over the area of activities of the nonprofit organization in question. The Civil Code, in other words, left it up to bureaucrats to determine whether a particular organization was in fact contributing to the public interest; also, incorporation required explicit permission. Thus, the competent authorities possess discretionary authority to approve or reject applications for incorporated status without regard to objective criteria. Moreover, through mere administrative guidance without any legal basis, government agencies currently require applicants for incorporated status to have a minimum of approximately ¥300 million as an endowment and of approximately ¥30 million as an annual budget. The application process is complex, and it can take one year easily. This situation has resulted in a pervasive pattern of bureaucratic control over public-interest corporations and has led to a trend whereby so-called independent organizations employ former bureaucrats who, because of their connections with government ministries, can expedite the organization's incorporation and secure government subsidies.

The extent of the government subsidies and commissioned work given to incorporated NPOs is an indicator of their degree of dependence on their competent authorities. Of the 26,089 incorporated NPOs and NGOs, in fiscal year 1995 (April 1995 to March 1996) over 5,000 organizations received a total of ¥583.6 billion in subsidies, and 3,781 organizations received commissioned contracts for ¥659.3 billion (Prime Minister's Office 1998).

The limited availability of tax incentives for financial contributions to NPOs makes it extremely difficult for these organizations to maintain their autonomy from government agencies. As of 1996, there were only 906 public-interest corporations under Article 34 with the privilege of tax-deductible contributions. That is a mere 3.4 percent of public-interest corporations. Needless to say, the process of gaining the special tax privilege is even more difficult and cumbersome than the incorporation process. Moreover, the privilege has to be renewed every two years. Most of the recipient organizations, called "Corporations to Promote Specially Designated Public Interest," are those created by government agencies, with staff seconded by these agencies and budgets augmented by subsidies.

The competent authorities exert rigid control over the activities of NPOs under their jurisdiction. The incorporated NPOs must submit budgets and plans of activities for the coming fiscal year, and file a financial report and a report of activities after the end of the fiscal year. This, and the fact that NPOs have to receive approval of their activities from their competent authorities, which are compartmentalized in the bureaucratic system, contributes to the inflexibility of incorporated NPOs in responding to new and complex issues, many of which are interdisciplinary in nature. It is reported that only a limited number of incorporated NPOs could respond to the Kobe disaster, which meant that much of the urgent work was left to the unincorporated NPOs.

GROWING CRITICISM OF GOVERNMENT CONTROL
OVER CIVIL SOCIETY

Because of the formidable complexities of the incorporation process and the cumbersome control of the government agencies, many NPOs prefer to operate without incorporated status. Nonincorporated status means that bank accounts must be opened or vehicles purchased in the name of an individual representing the organization, rather than in the name of the organization itself; when that individual resigns from the organization, new bank accounts must be opened and vehicles must be reregistered. More important, remaining unincorporated deprives an organization of social status. Because of these inconveniences, of the 243 think tanks with some working relationship with NIRA, 108 think tanks (44.4 percent) chose for-profit status largely to avoid the difficult incorporation process and control by government agencies over their activities.

A report published in 1994 by the Ōiso Study Group, made up of leaders of foundations and exchange organizations active in promoting closer cooperative relations between Japan and the United States, fueled public concern about the impediments facing Japan's civil society organizations. The report, titled "Toward More Effective U.S.-Japan Exchanges: Challenges and Opportunities," pointed out the major obstacles faced by many civil society organizations dedicated to promoting Japan-U.S. cooperation and exchange. Most American private foundations, major NGOs, and exchange organizations, for example, cannot incorporate themselves in Japan, and, thus, encounter many inconveniences such as being forced to use individuals' names to set up bank accounts, get telephone numbers, and rent offices. The more than 50 non-Japanese civil society organizations with operational bases in Japan all have to promote their activities under such unfavorable conditions. From its perspective on the plight of these non-Japanese civil society organizations operating in Japan, the report threw new light on the numerous and complex impediments to the activities of unincorporated domestic NPOs.

The heightened concern about civil society among NPO leaders and a growing number of opinion leaders, including those in politics and business, starkly contrasted with the traditional view of a significant number of bureaucrats who believed that they are the sole legitimate arbiters of public interest and, thus, entitled to control civil society organizations. A growing tension became evident between those who believed in the importance of an unfettered civil society and those who believed in the necessity of continued bureaucratic control. When the Center for Global Partnership (CGP) was created in 1991 within the Japan Foundation with Japanese government funding, an inaugural symposium was organized two months prior to its establishment on the theme of "Challenges and Opportunities for U.S.-Japan Exchange in the New Era." Many representatives from major U.S. foundations and research institutions were invited to discuss the future direction of policy-oriented intellectual exchange, in which CGP would play a major role. A high-ranking government official caused an uproar when he stated in his presentation something to the effect that the newly created CGP should be controlled by the government bureaucrats because "the fund is backed by taxpayers' money" and an "overly independent fund might strike out a certain independent, individualistic, unorthodox, or controversial policy unacceptable to the government." Indignant reactions from the audience, particularly from the Japanese participants, were indicative of the growing sentiment in Japan that more autonomous civil society organizations would be critical for Japan's future governance and the country's external relations.

THE EARTHQUAKE AND NPO BILLS

The Great Hanshin-Awaji Earthquake occurred as tensions were rising between the government bureaucracy and civil society leaders over the autonomy of NPOs. Many of the organizations and study groups that had started studying the legal and administrative context of civil society organizations converged on the site of the disaster. They experienced firsthand and in a poignant manner how civil society organizations could make a difference in dealing with the acute suffering of fellow citizens. Within three days of the earthquake, several organizations, such as JANIC, the One Percent Club, and C's, set up field offices to coordinate the rescue work of volunteers and the delivery of food and supplies.

A seminar that JCIE had happened to organize on January 23, 1995, just over one week after the earthquake, to launch the results of the Johns Hopkins Comparative Nonprofit Sector Project turned out to be a timely and emotional event. Several NPO leaders returned from field offices in Kobe to attend the seminar. It was evident that the tragedy of such a huge loss of life provided civil society leaders with the opportunity to push forward their agenda. "Volunteer," spelled out in katakana, a Japanese alphabet, as "*borantia*," suddenly became a household word. A newspaper ran the headline "Have You Been to Kobe Yet?," urging more volunteers to join the rescue work. Aside from the 1.3 million people who aided the earthquake victims in the field, Japanese throughout the nation contributed money and relief supplies. The Red Cross, the Community Chest, media organizations, and NPOs raised ¥160 billion in financial contributions within three months. The One Percent Club alone collected ¥13.2 billion and donations of tons of food and supplies from corporations. One NPO leader commented to this writer around that time that "this tailwind behind our movement is almost scary."

THE NPO BILLS AS A CENTRAL FOCUS OF DEBATE ON CIVIL SOCIETY

That tailwind brought about several legislative initiatives related to volunteer activities and NPOs. "NPO bills" proposed by diverse actors were basically designed to facilitate the application process for NPOs/ NGOs seeking incorporation and to restrict the traditional intervention of government agencies.

Given the aforementioned formidable constraints against the autonomous activities of NPOs, it is understandable that the three-year debate over the NPO bills was extremely intense. There were mainly five contending forces in this debate. One was the ruling coalition of three parties, the LDP, the Social Democratic Party (the former SDPJ), and the New Party Sakigake. Second was the opposition parties, led by the New Frontier Party until its demise in December 1997. The third was the government agencies represented by the aforementioned Liaison Committee. Fourth was the NPO group centered largely around C's and advocates and supporters of NPOs, including Keidanren, a business organization. Fifth, the media played a significant role in the legislative process and was a strong promoter of the NPO bill. Naturally, there were disagreements and conflicts within each of the contending forces. Bureaucrats persistently lobbied the conservative elements within the LDP, whereas the more liberal wing of the party was willing to work with the coalition partners to support NPO positions. The NPO side was divided on some issues, such as tax privilege. The legislative process for the bill represented a major departure from the way normal bills are drafted in that dynamic interactions occurred over different draft bills, including the one proposed by C's representing NPO positions. Normally, legislative bills are drafted by government bureaucrats and passed through the Diet with the support of the ruling party with only minor modifications.

The debate over enactment of legislation to facilitate the incorporation process for NPOs and their tax treatment gained momentum with the interest shown by political leaders. But the political initiative had to await the tragedy of the earthquake. On January 24, 1995, the day after the aforementioned seminar organized by JCIE, Lester Salamon had a breakfast meeting with Katō Kōichi, then chairman of the Policy Affairs Council of the LDP, and they discussed the legislation needed to bring about a more enabling environment for civil society development in Japan. On January 27, 1995, Katō delivered the following remarks during a session of the House of Representatives Budget Committee.

We had been generally conscious of the recent emergence of a new wave of activity involving volunteers, nonprofit groups and organizations, and what are called NGOs in other countries. Our own party had set up a study group in order to explore our position on these entities. It was in this context that the earthquake struck. Within the LDP, the attitude had been that volunteer groups were adversarial toward the government and public sector, but it seems that over the past few years the view has been growing within administrative circles acknowledging the utility of these organizations to take care of matters that the government lacks the resources to handle. . . . In his response just now, the minister of justice expressed the view that legislation should be enacted to provide for the incorporation of these groups. Once this issue of incorporation is accomplished, there is another issue that I realize will be difficult but that should be worked on, even if the progress is only gradual. This is the question of what to do about the tax provisions. I believe that this is a matter for which the office of the chief cabinet secretary should draw up a coordinated action on the part of the government.

Normally, legislative processes are launched with this type of exchange between a representative of the ruling party and a cabinet minister in charge at the Diet interpellations. This was the case with the NPO bill as well, but what followed diverged substantially from the normal pattern.

RESPONSE OF GOVERNMENT BUREAUCRACY

Though some government officials, particularly those in the Economic Planning Agency, had started studying about civil society before the earthquake, most of them were not well informed about the civil society development in Japan or abroad. Because of the new attention given to volunteers and nonprofit organizations, 18 government agencies were keen on getting involved in drafting the new legislation, making it necessary for them to organize the Liaison Committee mentioned earlier. Not all were well prepared to take on the task of drafting new legislation, however. For example, one of the first things the committee did was to contact the American Embassy to inquire which American organizations to contact if the committee were to send an investigation team on civil society to the United States.

The first draft of proposed legislation that came out of the committee met severe criticism from NPO leaders and the media. The draft was aimed primarily at providing for the incorporation of volunteer groups, and it did not consider NPOs in general. Moreover, the draft clearly revealed the government's intention of imposing its control over volunteer groups. Even the revised drafts continued to reveal the traditional bureaucratic views toward NPOs, namely, that they should be subject to government control and be limited to a role supplementary to that of the government. For example, the initial draft provided that consumers' groups and organizations involved in advocacy movements of a political nature not be included among those eligible for incorporation, that organizations be required to report to the authorities the names of executives and other paid staff members, and even that the responsible government agency have the authority to search an organization's premises and, if it so judged, to revoke the organization's incorporated status.

The issue of tax deductibility for contributions to NPOs was a point the government bureaucracy was adamant about from the outset of the legislative process. The bureaucrats' reluctance to extend the range of organizations eligible for tax deductible contributions was predictable given the current situation regarding the tax privileges of NPOs. The bureaucrats see themselves as being the ones most qualified to decide resource allocations, and they fear that the tax privilege would be abused as a route for tax evasion. When the NPO bill was finally passed in March 1998, tax deductibility was not one of its provisions. After a fierce debate, a Diet resolution was attached to the bill to the effect that the issue of tax privilege will be reviewed within two years of promulgation.

At this same time, moves were under way to achieve deregulation and downsize the government. As discussions on the NPO bill blossomed into a debate on the role of bureaucracy in the governance of society and became intermingled with arguments over streamlining government bureaucracy, the government's position was gradually undermined. Moreover, a series of scandals that had tarnished the bureaucrats' reputation caused distrust of their claim—which for many years had been legitimate—that they were the sole guardian of the public good. Meanwhile, in the debate over the NPO bill the issues moved beyond support for volunteers to focus more on the role of civil society organizations in conducting public-interest activities within the context of the enhancement of domestic governance. Thus, though they had initially hoped to take charge of the legislative process, the government bureaucrats gradually became disengaged from the process except for lobbying politicians to support their views. It was the final straw for the government bureaucrats when Katō, who as chairman of the Policy Affairs Council was in a position to coordinate legislative matters, stated, "NPOs are nongovernmental organizations, so it would be peculiar for the government to take the initiative in proposing legislation concerning them. Since it is a matter of putting completely new ideas into law, there will be difficult problems, but I definitely want the bill to be submitted to the Diet by legislators" (quoted in the *Mainichi Shinbun* 23 January 1997).

RESPONSE FROM POLITICAL PARTIES

The political parties sided with the NPO leaders in their reaction against the government-sponsored legislative proposal. The critical political issue of deregulation and downsizing of government reinforced support from the parties for the nonprofit sector's position. As mentioned before, most of the political parties had started working with NPOs before the earthquake. Against this background of readiness, in mid-February of 1995 a special project team on NPOs was launched by the ruling coalition. The opposition New Frontier Party formed a similar group in March. These teams served as the core for drafting the respective legislative proposals. The Japan Communist Party also drafted its own proposal. These study groups worked closely with NPO leaders in drafting their respective bills. The process of drafting the new legislation was a historic breakthrough in the way it was based on close cooperation between legislators and leaders of NPOs, excluding the bureaucrats who ordinarily play the dominant role in drawing up bills.

Certainly there were some politicians, particularly within the LDP, who were skeptical of the greater roles to be played by civil society. Government bureaucrats lobbied hard to retain their long-held control over civil society organizations. Conservative politicians refused to have the word "citizen" appear in the draft title, as the word still connoted leftist activisits in their understanding. Some others questioned the use of the English alphabet in the bill, opposing the use of the acronym "NPO." There were some disagreements among the political parties regarding certain critical elements of the draft bills. The New Frontier Party, for example, insisted that no draft bill without a tax provision should be passed. Nevertheless, politicians across party lines felt civil society development should be encouraged. In the end, the bill was passed with the unanimous support of all the parties.

Such strong support from the political parties could not have been imagined some years ago. Some recent statements by leading political figures indicate that their support for civil society is largely a reflection of their concern about the current state of Japan's governance. For example, at the Global ThinkNet Conference in February 1998, LDP Secretary-General Katō made a speech including the following remarks:

> It was considered to be normal for the politicians, namely, the elected representatives of the state, not to challenge the bureaucrats. Such a tendency persisted even after Japan had gone through the modernization process successfully. Our competent bureaucrats defined the national interest and were its sole guardians; as such, they monopolized resource allocation. That system worked well while Japan was pursuing catch-up development, and was seen to be working well until recently.... As the power balance between bureaucrats on the one hand and politicians, the media, and the general public on the other will continue to shift, the think tanks and their networks can start working with politicians and bureaucrats to generate policy debate in our society, which will then be a broader basis for political decision-making. (Katō 1998, 13, 15)

Similarly, Hatoyama, one of the founding members of the DPJ, referred to the role of civil society in the governance of society in a magazine article considered to be the manifesto of the newly formed political party:

> According to the conventional wisdom of the past century, public affairs were the domain of the "authorities," and those in the private sector could be no more than beneficiaries. But from now on we require a new arrangement, one in which citizens, local governments, businesses, and the national bureaucracy face each other as equals around the table of "public affairs," all undertaking their appropriate roles and engaging in constructive rivalry with each other ... so as to create a locus of public-interest values. This requires holding down the weight of the public sector, which has been too prominent so far, and giving much freer rein to the wisdom and energy of the private sector.

This is an important part of what we mean when we speak of shifting from a "state-centered society" to a "citizen-centered society." (Hatoyama 1996, 122)

Even some of the senior politicians seen as conservative and relatively cool to citizens' involvement have come out with statements in favor of an increased role for civil society. For example, former Prime Minister Miyazawa Kiichi stated in the *Asahi Shimbun* on June 29, 1997, in an article titled "Proposals for the Twenty-first Century": "Our country lacks leadership now that we have finished the process of catching up with the West. Bureaucrats are incapable of setting our goals. At a time when leadership needed to be exercised, Japan's politicians, myself included, failed to provide it. . . . From now on the role of the nongovernmental sector will become greater and greater vis-à-vis that of the government."

Another former prime minister, Nakasone Yasuhiro, offered the following remarks to reporters in the wake of the nuclear tests by India and Pakistan (as reported in the *Asahi Shimbun* on May 30, 1998): "I think we're now at the point where the Japanese government needs to enlist the cooperation of the NGOs in a global movement like the one for the treaty to ban land mines so as to promptly bring the Comprehensive Test Ban Treaty into effect, achieve ratification of START II, and get the nuclear powers to make a no-first-use commitment, particularly toward the nonnuclear states."

RESPONSE FROM NPOS AND NPO SUPPORTERS

When the full debate on the new legislative proposal was launched in early 1995, the NPO side was the best prepared. To seize the new opportunity to advance their cause, a group of NPOs launched the Liaison Group on Systems for Citizens' Activities with the participation of various organizations that had been studying the regulatory and fiscal context of civil society since before the earthquake. The participants in this new liaison body included C's, the Research Group to Consider Support Systems for Citizens' Public-Interest Activities, JANIC, and the NPO Forum, Japan.

One critical point in the legislative process for the NPO bill was the coordinated joint efforts by NPO leaders and supporters of NPOs. Extensive discussions and lobbying activities were carried out in connection with the bill with the participation of NPO leaders, leaders of businesses interested in working in partnership with the nonprofit sector, senior officials of labor unions, academics and researchers studying civil society, and journalists. C's, which was formed as a nationwide coalition of concerned citizens' organizations, acted as a catalyst for this development. In addition, C's held numerous meetings to discuss the specific provisions of the bill, conducted continuing and persistent lobbying activities supplemented with the submission of petitions with thousands of signatures, made direct appeals to key politicians, carried out media briefings, and kept up a stream of faxes informing its members of the state of progress of Diet deliberations on the bill.

Another distinctive feature of the process leading to the enactment of NPO legislation in Japan was the active involvement of business and the media. Keidanren's Committee on Corporate Philanthropy came out with a statement declaring, "NPOs are important partners for corporate philanthropy, and they are an essential part of efforts to build a rich and diverse society." Furthermore, staffers from the One Percent Club joined NPO leaders in virtually camping out in the Diet to conduct lobbying activities.

In October 1997, when prospects for the bill's passage were at the final make-or-break point, Keidanren Chairman Toyoda Shōichirō made a direct appeal to Prime Minister Hashimoto Ryūtarō for his help in getting the bill enacted, and Wakahara Yasuyuki, chairman of the One Percent Club, took on the task of overcoming the strong opposition of Murakami Masakuni, secretary-general of the LDP in the House of Councillors. In addition, Wada Ryukoh, senior managing director of the Keidanren Secretariat, and members of the secretariat staff called on numerous legislators to request their cooperation. Meanwhile, the major newspapers all printed repeated editorials and analysis concerning the proposed legislation, calling for it to be enacted and supporting suggested amendments.

As a fruit of these cooperative ties, the Japan NPO Center was established in November 1996 as a national organization bringing together representatives of prefectural NPO centers, leaders of business groups, representatives of major nonprofit organizations, foundations, and research institutions, and others. In addition, on July 13, 1998, researchers on nonprofit activities and representatives of the sector joined in forming a founding committee dedicated to the establishment of a Japan NPO Research Association (JANPORA). The inauguration of these new organizations has strengthened the networks at both the national and local levels among those directly involved in the work of nonprofit/nongovernmental organizations, people in businesses and local governments that are building cooperative relationships with such organizations, academics, researchers, journalists, and others, all of whom wish from their respective standpoints for the development of Japan's civil society.

PASSAGE OF THE NPO LAW
AND FUTURE CHALLENGES FOR CIVIL SOCIETY

The NPO bill became law on March 19, 1998, was promulgated on March 25, 1998, and enacted on December 1, 1998. The bill's passage through the Diet can be regarded as historic both because of the legislative process and because of its having been passed unanimously by all the political parties. Under the new legislation, NPOs can be incorporated without the approval process, and the governor of the prefecture where the proposed corporations are located (or the Economic Planning Agency in the case of NPOs with offices in at least two prefectures) is required to authenticate establishment of such organizations if they conform with the provisions set forth in the new legislation. The incorporation process will be much quicker under the new legislation because the granting authorities must decide on the certification within two months immediately succeeding the two-month period of public announcement.

It took almost three years from the time the NPO draft legislation was first submitted to the Diet to its final enactment. A variety of factors worked to delay the process, including disagreements among the coalition parties, disagreement between the ruling coalition and the opposition parties, a complex legislative calendar, and the general election in the House of Representatives while the bill was still under consideration. It also indicated the continuing challenges for civil society's full-fledged development. In the course of the debate on the NPO bill, some fundamental questions on the role of civil society were raised: Who is to define the public interest? Who is to maintain and promote the public interest? Who is to respond to the challenges and needs of society? What are the roles of the bureaucracy and the citizens in the governance of society? While these issues are related to the role of civil society in the governance of society, civil society organizations have to improve their performance in order to prove that they can significantly contribute to the ongoing efforts in Japan to improve its system of governance.

PROVING THE ROLE OF CIVIL SOCIETY
IN IMPROVING GOVERNANCE

Whether in developing or industrialized countries, it is an article of faith among those involved in the nonprofit sector that civil society contribute to the improvement of governance. By comparison with the rigid bureaucratic organs of the state, civil society institutions can display greater creativity, be more innovative, and act without hesitating to take on risks in dealing with the varied issues of a pluralistic society, since they themselves are capable of adopting pluralistic responses.

In addition, they can take more humanistic approaches, dealing with many problems in a way that places greater weight on the personal or human dimension. They can also keep a watch over the organs of the state, playing the role of ombudsman. Furthermore, they can promote solutions to problems through greater citizen involvement. Unlike bureaucrats, who are constantly struggling to keep up with the demands of their everyday tasks, the people in civil society organizations can take a longer perspective.

Civil society thus offers a number of advantages, but the key point for those involved in or supporting nonprofit activities in Japan is to demonstrate empirically that these advantages actually apply in Japan's case. It is also essential to consider the potentially negative aspects of nonprofit activities. For example, certain nonprofit organizations undeniably have a tendency to focus on a single issue and pay insufficient attention to the overall picture of the interests of the community or the country as a whole. It is also not uncommon for them to criticize government policies without offering alternatives or considering the actual work involved. There still is a lingering doubt among many Japanese as to whether these NGOs have done away with their earlier ideological orientation. What is therefore essential for civil society organizations is to clearly demonstrate that they can, indeed, effectively deal with the issues facing society in the manner governmental institutions alone cannot. They have to do so with their own track record of their visible contributions to domestic governance as well as international governance. This is the only way to win the trust of the government, businesses, and the people, and build a firm and broad support base for civil society in Japan.

CAPACITY BUILDING
FOR CIVIL SOCIETY ORGANIZATIONS

To demonstrate the effectiveness of civil society, these nonprofit and nongovernmental organizations must enhance their institutional capacity to address the issues they deal with. They have to prove that they can make a difference. This requires greater efforts to develop human resources and improve professional expertise of the organizations. There has not been a clear career path in Japan for those who wish to engage themselves in civil society activities. This is, in large measure, due to a dearth of civil society organizations with financial bases strong enough to allow the payment of adequate salaries to their staff. The fact that Japan has a low level of labor mobility between sectors further impedes the process of professionalization, though this traditional pattern of "lifetime employment" is slowly eroding. While the number of private foundations and independent policy research institutions has increased significantly over the past years, the lack of highly qualified human resources is impeding their development. In most cases, these organizations rely on former bureaucrats and retired businessmen rather than individuals they have groomed internally. The number of nonprofit groups with a full complement of professional staff is minuscule; in most cases they depend on a small number of dedicated individuals without sufficient remuneration.

A similarly important issue in terms of gaining the trust of the government and the public is for these organizations to increase their levels of transparency and accountability. Without such efforts, it will be difficult for them to resist the attempts of the bureaucracy to maintain its controls over them. A challenge for civil society organizations to be incorporated under the NPO Law is their new obligation to file annual financial statements for public record. This requirement places an added burden on the small number of staff they can afford to have.

CONTINUED EFFORTS TO IMPROVE THE LEGAL
AND REGULATORY ENVIRONMENT

As observed earlier, the enactment of the NPO Law represented a major advance in the legal and regulatory environment for nonprofit organizations in Japan. But additional efforts are required for the sake of the further development of civil society as a whole. Efforts must be redoubled to improve the tax system so as to promote contributions to nonprofit organizations. This issue has become a central focus of networks of civil society organizations and their supporters in business and the media.

There is also a fundamental contradiction in the legal structure related to civil society that has to be addressed. The NPO Law has been regarded as "special case" legislation under Article 34 of the Civil Code. As a result, the legal framework applicable to civil society organizations has become two-tiered. The law has created a new category of incorporation on top of the incorporated foundations and associations provided for by the Civil Code. It is not yet clear what implications this will have on the development of the nonprofit sector as a whole. It appears likely that most independent groups will seek incorporation under the NPO Law. And if it becomes clear that the new system allows organizations to operate with less interference from the government, the question will probably arise of whether public-interest corporations incorporated under the old system may be allowed to switch to the new system. These issues show the need for a review of the existing legal framework for civil society as a whole, a task that some legal scholars and nonprofit organization leaders are already addressing.

In addition, there is a need to consider changing the provisions of Article 89 of the Constitution, which reads, "No public money or other property shall be expended or appropriated for the use, benefit, or maintenance of any religious institution or association, or for any charitable, educational or benevolent enterprises not under the control of public authority." If strictly applied, this provision would make it impossible for the government to provide any direct financial support for independent private-sector organizations that are not under direct control of government agencies. This will constitute a significant obstacle to the development of equal partnership between the government and other public institutions and autonomous civil society organizations.

CROSS-SECTORAL PARTNERSHIP
FOR IMPROVED GOVERNANCE

In the context of the domestic drive to deregulate and to streamline the government, it is only natural to consider increased involvement by citizens in governance. The task of governance should be seen as something to be approached on the basis of a partnership across sectoral lines among the government, businesses, and civil society. In order to consider the proper future shape of governance on the basis of such partnership, those in each of the three sectors must redefine their respective roles.

The bureaucracy has come under harsh criticism for a tendency to place its narrow sectional interests ahead of the national interest and for the corrupt behavior of some of its members. Politicians have also complained about bureaucrats' policy blunders and the excessive concentration of power in their hands. This has led conscientious civil servants to undertake a serious reexamination of their future role.

A new awareness is also budding within the world of Japanese business, whose corporations were the engines of the country's remarkable postwar economic development. A considerable number of business leaders are similarly reexamining the role their corporations should play as members of society with responsibilities to a wide range of stakeholders.

What this indicates is that those in diverse sectors will have to reconsider their respective roles for the governance of society. What is most important of all is for citizens to overcome their sense of dependence on the bureaucracy and take responsibility themselves for maintaining and developing the common interests of society. The role of Japan's emerging civil society is to bring about a fundamental transformation of the country's governance. The development of civil society, we may say without exaggeration, will be the basis for Japan's metamorphosis from a state-centric, producer-led, inward-looking society to a more humanistic and democratic society with strong emphasis on people's interest, one that stresses the quality of life and is open and oriented to the rest of the world.

NOTES

1. There is confusion in Japan regarding the semantics for the terms used for NPOs and NGOs. The term NGO has been used in reference to nonprofit organizations in overseas programs, such as development assistance and global environmental issues. The term NPO has come to be used in recent years to encompass nonprofit organizations engaged in domestic as well as international activities.

2. The impact of changing external environments on Japan's philanthropic development is analyzed in Yamamoto (1997).

3. In the fall of 1997, the Japan Center for International Exchange launched a multinational study project to undertake six case studies on transnational civil society. The results will be published in late 1999.

4. This section draws heavily on C's Book Series No. 2 (Coalition for Legislation to Support Citizens' Organizations 1996).

5. The results of this research were reported in National Institute for Research Advancement (1988).

BIBLIOGRAPHY

Coalition for Legislation to Support Citizens' Organizations. 1996. *Kaisetsu: NPO hōan—sono keii to sōten* (Commentary on the NPO bill: Background and issues). Book Series No. 2. Tokyo: Coalition for Legislation to Support Citizens' Organizations.

Hatoyama Yukio. 1996. "Minshutō, watakushi no seiken kōsō" (The Democratic Party of Japan and my political platform). *Bungei Shunju* (November): 112–130.

Katō Kōichi. 1998. "Keynote Speech." *Globalization, Governance, and Civil Society.* Tokyo: Japan Center for International Exchange.

National Institute for Research Advancement. 1988. *Agenda for Japan in the 1990s.* NIRA Research Output No. 1 Vol. 1.

Nye, Joseph S. Jr. 1997. "In Government We Don't Trust." *Foreign Policy* 108 (Fall): 99–111.

Prime Minister's Office. 1998. *Kōeki hōjin hakusho* (White paper on public-interest corporations), 1997 ed. Tokyo: Ministry of Finance Printing Bureau.

Salamon, Lester M. 1994. "The Rise of the Nonprofit Sector." *Foreign Affairs* 74(4): 109–122.

Yamamoto Tadashi, ed. 1995. *Emerging Civil Society in the Asia Pacific Community.* Tokyo: Japan Center for International Exchange and Institute of Southeast Asian Studies.

———. 1997. "The Evolution of Japan in International Giving and Its Future Prospects." *International Grantmaking: A Report on U.S. Foundation Trends.* New York: Foundation Center.

———, ed. 1998. *The Nonprofit Sector in Japan.* Manchester, U.K.: Manchester University Press.

CHAPTER FOUR

Sharing Governance:
Changing Functions of Government,
Business, and NPOs

Ōta Hiroko

INTEREST in nonprofit organizations (NPOs) has recently been rising in Japan, as elsewhere. A number of factors account for this phenomenon, including Japan's rapidly aging society and the visible activities of NPOs and volunteer groups following the Great Hanshin-Awaji Earthquake that hit the Kobe area in January 1995. Another important factor is administrative reform.

The Japanese government has for years intervened directly in markets by means of excessive regulation and the fiscal investment and loan program. Moreover, the function of policy making has actually been exercised not by the legislature, as it should be, but by the central bureaucracy. This bureaucracy-led socioeconomic system was effective during the period when Japan was catching up with developed countries, but recently inefficiencies and various ill effects, such as government-business collusion, have been pointed out. It is also true that markets offering neither companies nor consumers an adequate range of options have been created; government regulations designed to protect producers have hindered the development of new products and services, and the uniform goods and services supplied by the government cannot meet people's diverse needs. All this has created momentum for administrative reform.

In 1996, the Official and Private Sector Activity Allotment Subcommittee of the government's Administrative Reform Committee enunciated three basic principles for administrative involvement: (1) Administrative activities should be minimized, on the principle that tasks which the private sector can perform should be left to the private sector. (2) Administrative services should be tailored to people's needs (the demand side) and should be provided at the lowest possible cost, in the interest of efficient, citizen-centered administration. (3) When administrative involvement is necessary, the organs carrying out administrative activities must be accountable to the people. Together these three principles represent the key criteria for assessing the government's role, and in conjunction with the reorganization of central ministries and agencies the government must review administrative involvement in their light.

The private sector referred to in the first principle does not mean companies alone. Even if they took over all activities that government should not undertake, this would probably not maximize utility for the household sector, because certain goods cannot always be adequately supplied through the workings of the market mechanism, even if those goods are ones that should not be supplied by government. To maximize utility for the household sector, it is essential that the nonprofit sector participate in the market along with government and business and that each of the three function to the fullest. NPOs in Japan, however, are still in their infancy, making it necessary to facilitate their development in tandem with administrative reform.

This chapter will consider the significance and role of NPOs in connection with administrative reform. Part one discusses the theoretical basis for the role of NPOs in economic activities. Part two briefly reviews the major features of the government's role during the period of rapid economic growth. Part three identifies the ill effects of these activities and the factors behind the mounting need for administrative reform. Part four discusses deregulation, decentralization, and other administrative-reform initiatives now under way and assesses the results so far. Finally, part five considers the role NPOs should play following administrative reform.

THE ROLE OF NPOS IN ECONOMIC ACTIVITIES

It is considered necessary for government to supply certain goods, either directly or indirectly, because they cannot be adequately provided by means of market transactions. These goods fall into five categories. Pure public goods—the first category—are characterized by nonexcludable consumption (users who do not bear the cost cannot be excluded) and nonrivalrous consumption (one person's use does not deprive others of use). It is easy to understand these characteristics if we think of such classic public goods as diplomacy and defense. Goods of this kind can neither be valued by means of the price mechanism nor effectively supplied by private enterprises.

Second are goods possessing externalities, which may be either external economies or external diseconomies. Goods with external economies are those whose social benefits outweigh their private benefits, such as public health and education, which benefit not only individuals but also society as a whole by, for example, raising the standard of living. In the case of goods with external diseconomies, conversely, the social costs outweigh the private costs. Examples of these types of goods are polluted water, toxic waste, and automobile exhaust fumes. The market mechanism cannot supply the optimal volume of goods possessing externalities.

Goods characterized by asymmetry in the information available to buyers and sellers constitute the third category. In the case of medical care, for example, prices of goods whose quality consumers cannot adequately determine for themselves are not set based on their differing characteristics; the market mechanism is not fully operational. For goods possessing information asymmetry vis-à-vis market participants, governmental regulations to control quality are often required.

Fourth are goods that generate natural (regional) monopolies. In the case of such industries as electric power and railways, which have huge economies of scale because of such factors as high fixed costs, government involvement is needed because competition among private enterprises would lead to excessive duplication of investment.

The fifth category is those goods best supplied by government from the viewpoint of income redistribution, such as public housing.

Aside from those falling in the first category, all the goods listed above can be supplied by companies, for which reason they are sometimes called quasi-public goods or merit goods (goods meriting government encouragement). It is difficult to work out an appropriate division of labor between the public and private sectors with regard to such goods. In the field of medical care, for example, Japanese hospitals are either publicly operated or organized as nonprofit medical corporations.

Although medical corporations belong to the nonprofit sector, they have a strong profit-oriented character, and the grounds for prohibiting hospitals operated by profit-seeking companies are not altogether clear.

What, then, is the significance of NPOs supplying goods? In terms of economic theory, NPOs can be defined as "nongovernmental organizations so constituted that they cannot distribute net profits (the profits remaining after costs are deducted from receipts) to interested parties" (Yamauchi 1997). The constraint on distributing profits does not arise from an inability to make profits. What net profits there are can be reinvested in the organization. The behavioral principle of a company is to maximize profits, but that of an NPO is to supply services to maximize the benefit to participants to the extent allowed by maintenance of a balance between income and expenditure.

The Johns Hopkins Comparative Nonprofit Sector Project, led by Lester M. Salamon, lists five features shared by NPOs. Such organizations are (1) formally constituted, (2) organizationally separate from government, (3) not profit seeking, (4) self-governing, and (5) voluntary to a significant degree. (To facilitate international comparisons, the project excludes religious and political organizations.)

Let us consider the significance of NPOs in relation to government. First, government activities lead to such "government failures" as bureaucratic bloat and corruption, inefficiency, and inflexible decision making. Of course, it must be borne in mind that inefficiency and bureaucratism can also afflict NPOs, if not to the same degree. Second, goods and services supplied by government are uniform and cannot meet all users' needs. For example, Japan's welfare administration has been described as "administration by measures," "measures" meaning administration on the basis of statutes. Instead of users deciding what kinds of welfare services they require, welfare offices carry out their own surveys and determine what measures to take, an approach that is not based on the idea of providing services to those who need them in accordance with their needs. When a country is poor, government needs to swiftly provide basic, uniform services, but with growing affluence people's needs diversify. To respond to this diversification, it is more efficient for a variety of suppliers to provide a variety of services, putting in place a system that enables users to pick and choose. An NPO can be defined as a group of people with common needs who join forces to supply public services.

Next, let us look at the significance of NPOs in relation to companies. First, by utilizing donations and subsidies NPOs can supply goods that the market mechanism cannot provide for adequately and services whose costs are likely to outweigh receipts. Second, in the case of goods featuring information asymmetry, information about and trust in suppliers are important. The fact that NPOs do not distribute profits can gain them added trust. NPOs also have the advantage of enabling users to feel more directly involved than companies can.

In addition, NPOs are significant in the context of citizen activities: monitoring opinions and conveying them to government and business and supplying information to citizens. As already noted, however, NPOs' activities, like those of government, can become inefficient, and the fact that NPOs do not distribute profits sometimes leads to their being operated in an untransparent manner. NPOs are meant to compensate for market and government failures; they must ensure adequate disclosure to prevent similar failures on their part.

GOVERNMENT'S ROLE IN THE RAPID-GROWTH PERIOD

DIVERSE INCOME-REDISTRIBUTION POLICIES

It is often observed that one role of the government in the post–World War II Japanese economy was to formulate and implement an industrial policy aimed at strengthening the international competitiveness of businesses, known collectively as "Japan Inc." It is true that through the 1950s the Ministry of International Trade and Industry's foreign-exchange quotas exerted a strong influence on businesses and that the Foreign Investment Law's restrictions on inward direct investment protected domestic industries. From the 1960s onward, however, economic growth was driven mainly by the private sector; the government's industrial policy did not play that great a role.

More important during the rapid-growth period of the 1960s and early 1970s were the government's income-redistribution policies. In general, productivity widens regional and industrial disparities. In Japan, a variety of steps were taken to minimize such disparities. Revenue from national taxes (local allocation and transfer taxes) was redistributed to regions, and resources were distributed through public works, while unproductive industries were protected by means of subsidies and regulations. Income-redistribution policies usually target individuals, but Japan's were aimed at collectivities—regions and industries.

These policy measures created a society with unusually small economic disparities despite the nation's rapid growth. Social stability was maintained, and a "virtuous circle" was generated whereby rising income boosted saving and consumption, which encouraged further growth.

In politics, generally there is conflict between pro-growth conservative parties and liberal parties more concerned with income distribution. During Japan's rapid-growth period, however, there were no marked differences in parties' attitudes toward the government's income-redistribution policies. All favored supports for unproductive industries, such as agriculture, and for small business and regions. These policies came to be regarded as entitlements, and a political structure was created whereby vested interests (beneficiaries) influenced politics. As a result, income-redistribution policies were retained even after rapid growth gave way to slower growth. There is still no political party representing the interests of consumers and city dwellers.

THE GOVERNMENT AS RISK MANAGER

Another salient feature of the postwar Japanese government was its role in managing market risks by means of regulation. Generally, there are deemed to be valid grounds for regulation in the case of fields that generate natural (regional) monopolies, that feature information asymmetry, and that involve values that deserve to be upheld, such as the environment and security. But in Japan even fields in which these grounds do not pertain were regulated, as evinced by measures to protect producers and small business.

A classic example was the limitation of new entrants to markets to balance supply against demand as projected by the government. There were myriad regulations of this kind, such as those restricting the size of aircraft, bus, and taxi fleets, the authorization of large retailers, the issuing of business licenses for banks, the approval of new telecommunications carriers, the issuing of liquor-manufacture licenses, and so on. One reason given for regulations aimed at adjusting supply and demand was that excessive competition would be to the disadvantage of consumers, but in fact such regulations led to the protection of existing companies and was used as a pretext for excluding applicants who were actually turned away for other reasons. Government discretion in this area sheltered existing companies from the risk of supply-demand fluctuations.

Excessive regulations were also implemented to shield consumers and investors from risk. For example, for many years corporate bonds had to be backed by collateral. Even after the introduction of unsecured bonds in 1979, criteria for issuing bonds and determining financial soundness were stringent, which meant that in reality only safe, blue-chip companies could issue bonds. The government managed risk even in the bond market, where the assessment of risks and returns is of crucial importance, so that for a long time neither those procuring funds nor those investing in them were exposed to risk. (All regulations on corporate bond issues have now been scrapped.)

Companies and consumers also became strongly dependent on the bureaucracy. As a result, whenever there is any market disruption, the government is immediately accused of inept management. That is why there has been little criticism of excessive regulation. Only pharmacies, for example, are allowed to sell even nonprescription preparations. These include over-the-counter drugs, as well as vitamin- and mineral-enriched drinks that are akin to food products. Prohibiting ordinary retail outlets from selling such products in effect protects pharmacies, but there is little protest from consumers.

In short, a climate has been created in Japan in which companies, consumers, and investors alike look to the government, relinquishing the growth of profits based on self-responsibility in return for avoiding risk.

THE ACTUAL POLICYMAKERS

In Japan, the task of policy making, which is supposed to belong to the legislature, has been taken over by the central bureaucracy. Legislation based on bills sponsored by members of the Diet is extremely rare, and there is little Diet debate on bills. And whereas executive power ostensibly rests in the cabinet, it is actually exercised by the central bureaucracy; by custom only matters agreed on at conferences of administrative vice-ministers, who are career bureaucrats, are put on the agenda of cabinet meetings, and when ministers are questioned in the Diet, bureaucrats known as "government delegates" very often answer in their stead.

A system of advisory councils has been set up to enable citizens to participate directly in government administration, but council proceedings are orchestrated by the relevant ministry or agency and are frequently used as a cover for the bureaucracy's own agenda. If the reports issued by advisory councils offered a range of policy options, including minority as well as majority views, which were then debated in the Diet, all would be well; but in the majority of cases central bureaucrats actually write a council's scenario, draft legislation on the basis of the council's seal of approval, then sound out politicians and arrange to get the bill passed.

The central bureaucracy also has broad discretionary powers in regard to the application of legislation. Some improvement was finally seen with the enforcement of the Administrative Procedures Law in 1994, but the operational criteria for licensing and certification remain extremely vague. Applications are often shelved for long periods, and many decisions are made on the basis of extralegal "administrative guidance." Partly because there is still no freedom of information law, almost no information on administrative decision making is available to ordinary citizens.

The executive branch, which is to say the central bureaucracy, has also exercised some of the functions of the judicial branch. The bureaucracy has created market rules through its discretion in relation to the imposition of most ex ante regulations and to the application of regulations. When there are market disruptions, the bureaucracy addresses them before they are taken to court. That is why ex post facto regulations, such as the Antimonopoly Law, the Product Liability Law, and information disclosure criteria, which should serve as market rules, are so underdeveloped. The handling of failed *jūsen* housing-loan companies a few years ago provides a good example of the bureaucracy's preemption of the judiciary's role. Since the *jūsen* were ordinary companies, not financial institutions, bankruptcy proceedings should have been left to the courts, but instead the bureaucracy wrote the scenario for dealing with the problem. The judiciary itself is not fully functional. It has been dubbed the "20 percent judiciary" because it fulfills only 20 percent or so of its role, and Japanese trials are notorious for being expensive, slow, and "user unfriendly."

Ill Effects of a Bureaucracy-Led System

the central bureaucracy's enormous powers

The type of government described above functioned effectively in the period of rapid economic growth. While Japan was quickly catching up with developed countries, it was efficient for the government to manage markets and minimize disruption. And income transfers to unproductive industries and to regions contributed considerably to social stability. But the bloated bureaucracy was not reformed once the rapid-growth period had ended, and recently its ill effects have become blatantly obvious.

One ill effect is that the central bureaucracy's great powers have resulted in extremely inflexible policy decision making. The vertically integrated bureaucratic apparatus has led to vertically integrated policy decision making. In other words, the "iron triangle" of the central bureaucracy, industry, and Diet cliques associated with specific industries and the government agencies having jurisdiction over them has dictated the framework of policy decision making. This kind of iron triangle is not unique to Japan, but its influence is especially strong and wide ranging there because of the plethora of licenses and certifications and because the bureaucracy is effectively in charge of policy making. The bureaucracy's tight grip is obvious if we look at how inflexible public-works budget allocations to various government agencies have become over more than 30 years.

Another ill effect is that the central bureaucracy dominates local governments' policy decisions through the use of subsidies and regulations. Partly because of the large scale of fiscal adjustments among regions, local governments are heavily dependent on the central government. Generally, government's role changes as the population structure ages. The emphasis shifts from services targeting the nation as a whole, such as diplomacy and defense, to those affecting citizens' daily lives, such as welfare. With this shift, local governments assume a more important role than the central government. Because of Japan's highly centralized system, however, even government services affecting daily life tend to be uniform nationwide and often do not respond to individual regions' needs. Meanwhile, when residents complain to their local government, it hides behind the skirts of the central government, evading responsibility on the grounds that it cannot do anything because it is simply following Tokyo's orders.

LACK OF TRANSPARENCY
IN MARKETS AND GOVERNMENT DECISION MAKING

The bureaucracy's sweeping powers and discretion have resulted in inadequate and vague market rules. For example, when it was revealed in 1990 that securities companies had been reimbursing important clients for market losses, less attention was focused on whether the judiciary would rule these activities legal or illegal than on whether Ministry of Finance officials had verbally approved such behavior before the fact. All too often in Japan, decisions on the legality or otherwise of actions are left to the discretion of the bureaucracy. This has resulted in what can only be called collusion between government agencies and companies. Whereas they share information, too little is disclosed to markets.

Earlier I observed that the government has taken charge of risk management. Risk and information are closely intertwined, and it is the risk managers that possess information. Information on a given company has been held mainly by the government agency having jurisdiction over its industry and by the company's main bank. Because they have together managed the company's risks and watched over it, insufficient information has been disclosed to investors and other market participants, whose trusting nature meant there was little need to disclose information. A number of financial institutions have recently collapsed under the weight of nonperforming loans, but the full extent of their bad debts has still not been disclosed. This is a holdover of the bureaucracy's traditional administration of financial institutions. One reason for the anxiety over the financial system that has gripped Japan since the autumn of 1997 is the lack of transparency of Japanese markets.

Inadequate disclosure has discouraged consumers and investors from making choices on the basis of self-responsibility. As things stand, they neither take responsibility nor are made to do so. For example, although under the deposit insurance system there is a ceiling of ¥10 million for payouts to individual depositors in failed financial institutions, all deposits are insured in full until 2001; the reason is insufficient disclosure on the part of financial institutions.

Government policy decision making itself lacks transparency. The iron triangle referred to earlier has resulted in a policy decision-making system dictated by the supply side; consumers have no say, nor are they provided with information. The absence of a freedom of information law and the lack of effective checks on the bureaucracy are serious problems. Cases like the revelation in 1997 that the Ministry of Health and Welfare had concealed information that people had been infected with HIV because of the ministry-sanctioned use of contaminated blood products are merely the tip of the iceberg. Not enough information on either budgets or balance sheets is made available, so that at present it is difficult for outsiders to evaluate policy decisions.

CITIZENS' LACK OF RESPONSIBILITY TOWARD POLICY AND EXCESSIVE EGALITARIANISM

I have noted that a variety of income-redistribution policies led to the creation of a society with small economic disparities. On the down side, however, these policies also cultivated an excessive egalitarianism. As seen in the proliferation of Shinkansen high-speed train lines, most people take it for granted that their own region should be equipped with whatever amenities other regions possess. The big problem here is that people tend to make such demands without any consideration of the costs. In other words, the public works allocated to various regions are not chosen by residents on the basis of cost consciousness. Of course, people will make excessive demands if they can receive benefits at no cost to themselves.

This dissociation of costs and benefits has led taxpayers to abdicate responsibility for policy decisions. I have stated that all market disruptions are laid at the government's door. There is also a tendency to regard fiscal matters as totally the government's responsibility. Although taxpayers foot the bill for everything the government does, that tends to be forgotten. At present, there is a structural gap between revenue and expenditure. As things stand, the revenue shortfall can be covered only by constantly issuing deficit-financing bonds. The dissociation of costs and benefits is partly to blame for this situation.

One underlying factor is that the system followed so far has turned beneficiaries into political vested interests. Another is the government's inadequate disclosure of information. In regard to public pension systems, for example, for many years benefits exceeding premiums have been guaranteed. As a result, it is highly probable that future generations will have to bear an unrealistically heavy burden, but too little information on projections regarding pension systems has been made available, and reform has been put off. Only very recently has the Health and Welfare Ministry taken a more forward-looking attitude toward disclosure. A third factor is that because of centralization the unit citizens have to monitor and evaluate is too large. If the unit were reduced to a regional bloc at most, the way policies were assessed would probably change significantly.

ADMINISTRATIVE REFORM INITIATIVES
SUCCESSIVE WAVES OF ADMINISTRATIVE REFORM

The need for reform is obvious from the foregoing discussion of the ill effects of a bureaucratic society. The aims of administrative reform can be summed up in the following four points: (1) government accountability for all policies and transparent policy decision making; (2) abolition of unnecessary regulations and creation of markets in which economic actors can exercise choice to the fullest; (3) minimization of bureaucratic discretion and creation of transparent markets; and (4) creation of lean, efficient government and reduction of the costs of an aging society. Administrative and fiscal reform toward these ends is now in progress.

The first wave of administrative reform was marked by the formation of the First Provisional Commission on Administrative Reform in 1964, which focused on streamlining the bureaucratic apparatus. Next came the Second Provisional Commission on Administrative Reform, formed in 1981 (known popularly as the Doko Commission after its chair, Doko Toshiwo, then chair of Keidanren [Japan Federation of Economic Organizations]), which addressed the division of labor between the public and private sectors. This was followed by three Provisional Councils for the Promotion of Administrative Reform between 1983 and 1993, which concentrated on the same issue. During that period, the Japanese National Railways and the domestic telecommunications monopoly, Nippon Telephone and Telegraph, were privatized (Namikawa 1997).

This was the background for the present wave of administrative reform, which has been pursued on three fronts. The first is the Administrative Reform Committee, established in 1994 with a three-year mandate. It had three subcommittees: the Administrative Information Disclosure Subcommittee, charged with drafting the major provisions of a freedom of information law; the Deregulation Subcommittee; and the Official and Private Sector Activity Allotment Subcommittee. The second is the Committee for the Promotion of Decentralization, formed in 1995. And the third is the Administrative Reform Council, set up in 1996, which has drawn up a blueprint for reorganization of the central ministries and agencies. In addition to issues inherited from the earlier waves of administrative reform, such as the division of labor between the public and private sectors, deregulation, and decentralization, the present wave is addressing the way in which policy decisions are made, including examination of the bureaucratic system itself.

THE STATUS OF DEREGULATION AND DECENTRALIZATION

Let us now evaluate the progress so far in two areas of administrative reform regarded as closely related to the future role of NPOs, deregulation and decentralization.

Deregulation

Deregulation has been addressed chiefly by the Administrative Reform Committee's Deregulation Subcommittee. For three years, from 1994 to 1997, the subcommittee submitted to the prime minister an annual opinion paper concerning areas for deregulation, on the basis of which the government drew up deregulation promotion plans whose implementation was monitored by the subcommittee. A fair amount of progress has been seen. A schedule has been drawn up for sweeping financial liberalization, the so-called Japanese Big Bang advocated by the prime minister. In transport, relaxation of regulations aimed at adjusting supply and demand with regard to aircraft, buses, taxis, and so on is under way. In labor, restrictions on commercial employment agencies have been loosened. Timetables for deregulation in many other fields have also been set (Administrative Reform Committee 1995, 1996, 1997).

Nevertheless, many fields remain heavily regulated, notably agriculture, insurance, and postal services, which are represented by strong political interests. Of course, a degree of regulation is necessary in regard to medical care, welfare, and other fields involving public health and security, but some controls that are designed to protect producers remain and have not been adequately scrutinized. Another thorny area, as might be expected because the interests of the mass media are at stake, has to do with controls on the resale price of publications and other copyrighted materials. Newspapers have taken the ethically problematic approach of using news pages to campaign against deregulation.

Judicial deregulation is also an important issue. I have already noted that Japanese trials are notoriously expensive, slow, and user unfriendly. One reason for this state of affairs is that from the 1960s until 1990 only some 500 people a year were allowed to pass the state judicial examination (only those passing this exam are qualified to become attorneys, public prosecutors, and judges). It has finally been agreed to increase the number of passes to 1,000 a year, but this is still not enough. Judicial functions, which constitute an important basis for administrative reform, are in urgent need of improvement.

In addition to the relaxation or abolition of ex ante regulation, ex post facto regulation by means of the Antimonopoly Law and financial services legislation need to be strengthened. Because the Administrative Reform Committee was dissolved in December 1997, a new neutral organization was established in its place in 1998.

Decentralization

The Committee for the Promotion of Decentralization has issued four sets of recommendations so far. Among the measures it advocates are abolition of the system whereby certain functions are delegated by the central government to local governments and streamlining of subsidies (Committee for the Promotion of Decentralization 1996, 1997). A fifth recommendation, to be issued in 1998, advocates transferring powers regarding public works projects from the central government to local governments.

If decentralization is tackled in earnest, it will lead to a fundamental change in the vertically integrated, top-down decision-making system that has prevailed so far. For governors and mayors to be invested with stronger powers than central-government leaders would enable "horizontal" policy decision making; decentralization would break down the hierarchy that places the central government above local governments. Despite the importance of this reform, however, debate has been muted at best. It is far from clear who wants decentralization and is prepared to promote it. With few exceptions, local governments themselves have expressed little enthusiasm. Some feel that it is not necessary to change the present centralized system, that it would be enough if the central government allocated local governments funds that could be used freely instead of providing subsidies earmarked for specific uses. Local residents have had little to say about decentralization and seem to regard it as a tussle between the central bureaucracy and local bureaucracies.

The reason the debate on decentralization is so lackluster is that the issue of revenue sources has not been addressed head on. This should actually be the most important subject of debate, since the basis of government is the provision of services to residents and the collection of taxes to pay for them. Some degree of fiscal coordination is necessary to maintain a national minimum, but there can be no real decentralization when the greater part of local governments' revenue comes from central-government allocations (income redistribution), as at present. For example, part of the consumption tax on goods and services, raised from 3 percent to 5 percent in April 1997, is levied by local governments, but did residents attack them when the tax was raised? The central government was the butt of criticism; local governments were let off the hook. Local governments' levying of taxes needs to be exposed to residents' assessment. And if residents do not pay for local services with taxes, they will not develop cost consciousness and will make excessive demands.

If the ill effects of centralization are to be alleviated and taxpayers enabled to exercise the functions of assessment and choice, it is crucial that local governments create a fiscally autonomous framework. In addition to transferring the source of taxation to local governments and empowering them to levy taxes on their own initiative, the central government must drastically reduce the redistribution to local governments of national-tax revenue. From the viewpoint of fiscal autonomy, debate on the optimal scale of local governments, including consideration of merging municipalities or introducing a regional-bloc system, is also necessary. If some such framework could be created, local governments would become civil societies in their own right.

The Infrastructure of Administrative Reform

In advancing administrative reform, we must take a number of steps to create a climate conducive to diminishing the central government's functions. First, market rules must be improved. So far the government has played the major role as market manager, but it is now necessary to enhance the fair-trade rules of the Antimonopoly Law and financial services legislation to enable markets themselves to deal with market disruptions. Greater accountability must also be demanded of companies. Second, judicial functions need to be reinforced to enable market disruptions to be dealt with by law. This requires deregulating and otherwise reforming the legal world.

Third, conditions to facilitate NPO activities must be put in place. In the field of welfare, for example, if the government's role were restricted to guaranteeing a national minimum, companies and NPOs could take up the slack. As discussed in the first section of this chapter, NPO activities are especially important in supplying diversified rather than uniform services that the market mechanism cannot provide for adequately. Social welfare councils and some other NPOs are already supplying certain welfare services, but these organizations have close ties to local governments. It is hoped that a large number of more diverse NPOs will emerge to offer such services. Costs could be covered by reducing taxes and allowing people to direct the savings toward dues and donations to NPOs. This would enable users to choose for themselves the public goods with which they wished to be supplied.

NPOs' FUTURE ROLE:
TOWARD A NEW FORM OF GOVERNANCE

AN ALTERNATIVE TO A BUREAUCRACY-LED SOCIETY

Japan's economic system is facing a major transition. Relations between the public and private sectors, between companies, and between companies and their employees are likely to change rapidly, and the bureaucracy-led system will perforce shift to a market-led system. How will all this change governance? What kind of socioeconomic system should we envisage, and how should we prepare for it? I believe that the kind of system we should aspire to will include the following characteristics.

First, consumers, companies, residents, investors, and other economic actors will be accorded a diverse range of options and will exercise them to the full. The kinds of choices made through consumption and business management will in themselves constitute expressions of opinion regarding governance.

Second, the demand side will monitor the supply side and assess the services supplied. Oversight and assessment are predicated on supply-side accountability. The supply side includes the nonprofit sector as well as government and business. The government must be accountable for its full range of policies, not just its supply of public services.

Third, top-down decision making, with the public sector above the private sector and the central government above local governments, will give way to horizontal, citizen-participatory decision making.

In the kind of society outlined above, both the supply side and the demand side, both government and taxpayers, will participate in governance, the demand side through the exercise of choice, taxpayers through oversight, assessment, and the expression of opinion. This type of governance cannot exist without the involvement of NPOs. They will have an immeasurably more important role than at present—as suppliers of services, as users, and as key actors in community development. Let us examine what will be expected of NPOs.

As important participants in governance, NPOs will need to contribute in three major ways: as suppliers of diverse services, as participants in community development, and as forces exercising the functions of oversight, assessment, and advocacy.

Suppliers of Diverse Services

I have already alluded several times to NPOs' role as service providers. What is important is that they not simply supplement government services but provide different services. As the Japanese term *minkatsu* (utilization of the private sector) indicates, the private sector, including the nonprofit sector, has been regarded primarily as augmenting the public sector. But as stated at the beginning of this chapter, unless government, business, and the nonprofit sector function as separate systems, utility for the household sector will not be maximized.

I have noted that new types of NPOs are important even in the field of welfare, where the nonprofit sector is already a major supplier. In this connection, Kansai Inter-Discipline Studies Inc. has carried out a most interesting survey (Kansai Inter-Discipline Studies Inc. 1996).[1] The institute surveyed the activities and other aspects of citizen-participatory welfare service organizations,[2] which were divided into the "government-backup type" (organizations like social welfare councils and welfare public corporations, which local governments helped set up and provide backup for) and "local welfare NPOs" (organizations based on voluntary, autonomous citizen activities and operating independently of government and business). The survey results reveal various differences between the two types, even though both belong to the nonprofit sector. For example, as table 1 shows, when questioned about the circumstances leading up to the inauguration of their activities, 17.5 percent of "citizen mutual-aid type" organizations replied that they had been unable to leave things to local government, while 2.0 percent of social welfare councils said so.

The emergence of diverse NPOs as independent service providers will probably change the present tendency to consider NPOs as synonymous with volunteer groups. In Japan, volunteer activities are in the

Table 1. *Circumstances Behind Inauguration of Activities (Multiple responses) (%)*

	No. of organizations	Needs that public services cannot meet	Easily accessed services	Services commissioned by local government	Unable to leave things to local government	Other	No response
			Local welfare NPOs				
Citizen mutual-aid type	80	55.0	27.5	0.0	17.5	21.3	2.5
Cooperatives	38	47.4	31.6	0.0	7.9	34.2	0.0
Consumer cooperatives	8	37.5	50.0	0.0	0.0	12.5	0.0
Workers' collectives, etc.	30	50.0	26.7	0.0	10.0	40.0	0.0
Subtotal	118	52.5	28.8	0.0	14.4	25.4	1.7
			Government-backup type				
Social welfare council–administered type	49	67.3	28.6	22.4	2.0	6.1	0.0
Government-participation type	26	57.7	7.7	30.8	0.0	11.5	0.0
Subtotal	75	64.0	21.3	25.3	1.3	8.0	0.0
Total	193	57.0	25.9	9.8	9.3	18.7	1.0

SOURCE: Kansai Inter-Discipline Studies Inc. (1996).

forefront of the voluntary, independent nonprofit sector, which has led people to take it for granted that the kinds of services provided by this sector cost little or nothing. But NPOs differ from volunteer groups and supply distinctive services. Another important characteristic of NPO service providers is that they act as critics of government services.

Participants in Community Development

Private-sector, nonprofit groups known as neighborhood associations have long been involved in a variety of community activities. Recently, however, many NPOs addressing community development from different perspectives have sprung up. Neighborhood associations include all residents, take the household as the basic unit, and have a close relationship with local government. The new NPOs, by contrast, feature voluntary membership, take the individual as the basic unit, and are independent of local government (21st Century Hyogo Project Association 1995).

To improve their communities, these NPOs engage in a variety of advocacy activities as well as activities to preserve historical townscapes and scenic areas. Not only are they independent of local government,

in many cases they have persuaded the authorities to support commu-
nity-development efforts. In Nanao, Ishikawa Prefecture, for example, a
group of citizens concerned over the city's decline formed a council to
address the problem. After much discussion and firsthand investigation
of conditions in other countries, the council undertook development of
the city's waterfront, including construction of a fisherman's wharf by
means of a so-called third-sector (joint public- and private-sector) project. There have been a number of fisherman's-wharf projects in other
parts of Japan, but Nanao's is one of the very few that has proved an
economic success. The council enabled members, including local bureaucrats taking part in a private capacity, to use their professional expertise more freely than they could have otherwise.

In Japan, residents tend to take a passive approach to community
development, which is usually spearheaded by local government and a
handful of vocal interests. The appearance of NPOs approaching community development in diverse ways is slowly but surely raising awareness that the community belongs to its residents.

Forces of Oversight, Assessment, and Advocacy
Recently, citizen ombudsmen in various parts of Japan have been in-
vestigating illegal spending by local governments and other issues. It
has been said that Japanese taxpayers have a keen interest in their own
tax burden but little interest in how tax revenue is used, but the activities of NPOs are gradually increasing people's interest in this area, as
well.

Many consumer groups monitor and assess the activities of companies, and consumer cooperatives serve as critics of business by directly
involving themselves in the production and distribution of goods. But
the Japanese consumer movement still does not represent the mass of
consumers. Various problems have been identified—failure to make
use of experts, positions that differ from those of consumers in general, the high average age of participants, the extreme paucity of male
participants. It is hoped that consumer NPOs with diverse aims and
with activities going beyond those of traditional consumer groups will
emerge.

In addition to oversight and assessment, advocacy is part of the
NPOs' brief. The need for neutral policy-oriented think tanks has long
been pointed out. Groups of scholars that issue proposals on their own
initiative do exist, but they are far too few. In a country like Japan, where

policy making is effectively monopolized by the central bureaucracy and politicians are unable to support adequate specialized staffs, the existence of NPOs functioning as think tanks is extremely important.

ENCOURAGEMENT OF COMPETITION AMONG NPOS

If NPOs are to perform the roles outlined above, numerous and diverse NPOs are required, and they must compete with one another. Just as with companies, it stands to reason that NPOs that cannot respond to society's needs or are managed inefficiently will fall by the wayside.

To encourage healthy competition, disclosure by NPOs is important; they must be accountable. Strict disclosure should be required, especially of NPOs that enjoy tax breaks or receive support from public funds. Under Japan's taxation system, so-called charitable corporations (foundations, charitable trusts, and some other categories of NPOs with corporate status)—that is, nonprofit corporations serving the public interest—receive preferential treatment with regard to corporate tax. Individuals can claim tax deductions for donations to only an extremely limited range of NPOs, but all corporate donations, whatever their use or destination, can be registered as losses, just like political donations. In short, tax breaks are not determined in accordance with consistent criteria of "public interest." NPOs should be reclassified in accordance with clear-cut criteria so that only those organizations that meet the criteria receive preferential tax treatment, and rigorous disclosure should be required (Honma 1993).

Creating a framework enabling residents and consumers to choose among NPOs is also important. Revising the taxation system to encourage individual donations to NPOs, such as by permitting tax deductions on donations to a wider range of NPOs and doing away with the requirement that a donation must total at least ¥10,000 before a tax deduction can be claimed, will lead people to choose more actively among public services. The government grants subsidies to selected NPOs, but if those funds were used to enhance the taxation system with regard to donations along the lines suggested above, taxpayers could decide for themselves which NPOs' services they wished to support. While the selection of NPOs eligible for tax deductions on donations must not be excessively rigid, eligibility must be determined on the basis of set criteria emphasizing NPOs' character as organizations serving the public interest. At present, deductions can be claimed on donations to NPOs designated by the government as "certain public organizations established by special law and listed in cabinet orders," but ill effects arise from the fact that every such organization is chartered and subject to oversight by one or more government agency; moreover, the criteria applied by different agencies are not consistent. A neutral third-party chartering body is needed.

In addition to donations, in the case of welfare services choice could be exercised through the introduction of a voucher system. If users were issued vouchers for home-care services, for example, they could make their own choice of service providers. This would encourage competition not only among NPOs but also among the government, NPOs, and companies. It is a pity that the Long-Term Care Insurance Law enacted in 1997 does not provide for the use of vouchers.

In creating a framework enabling residents and consumers to choose among NPOs, it is important that the bureaucracy not arbitrarily select the NPOs to be included. As I have said repeatedly, the raison d'être of NPOs lies not in their supplementing the efforts of government but in their providing different services from government and exercising functions that go beyond those of government. This indeed is why sharply curtailing government's scope of action and reducing the tax burden, allowing people to use the savings for membership dues and donations to NPOs, will help maximize utility for the household sector.

The bureaucracy-led socioeconomic system was the product of Japan's single-minded pursuit of economic growth. The society of the future, however, must be based on pluralism, which affirms the coexistence of diverse values. The public sector does not stand above the private sector; each has its own functions and complements the other. What is desirable is market participation by economic actors that have differing values and aims, along with markets that fully guarantee economic actors freedom of choice. If this way of thinking takes hold, Japan will see the emergence of many superb NPOs and the creation of a new form of governance.

NOTES

1. This questionnaire survey, conducted in 1995, targeted 413 citizen-participatory welfare organizations in the Kansai and Kantō regions of Japan (roughly, the western and eastern regions of central Honshu).

2. The National Social Welfare Council defines citizen-participatory welfare services as "home welfare services that are not profit seeking but aim to

supplement residents' mutual aid and are centered on help with household tasks on a paid basis."

BIBLIOGRAPHY

Administrative Reform Committee. 1995, 1996, 1997. *Kisei kanwa no suishin ni kansuru iken* (Opinions regarding the promotion of deregulation).Three reports.

Administrative Reform Committee. 1996. *Gyōsei kan'yo no arikata ni kansuru kijun* (Criteria for administrative involvement).

Committee for the Promotion of Decentralization. 1996, 1997. *Chihō Bunken Suishin Iinkai daichiji kara daiyoji kankoku* (Reports one through four of the Committee for the Promotion of Decentralization). Four sets of recommendations.

Honma Masaaki, ed. 1993. *Firansuropī no shakai keizaigaku* (The socioeconomics of philanthropy).Tokyo:Tōyō Keizai Shinpōsha.

Kansai Inter-Discipline Studies Inc. 1996. *Chiiki fukushi ni okeru NPO shien, ikusei hōsaku no teigen* (Proposals for policy measures to support and foster NPOs in local welfare). National Institute for Research Advancement research report.

Namikawa Shino. 1997. *Gyōsei kaikaku no shikumi* (The administrative-reform system).Tokyo:Tōyō Keizai Shinpōsha.

Tokyo Metropolitan Government. 1996. *Gyōsei to minkan hieiri dantai (NPO)* (Government administration and nonprofit organizations [NPOs]). Tokyo:Tokyo Metropolitan Government.

21st Century Hyogo Project Association. 1995. *Chiiki shakai ni okeru minkan hieiri soshiki (NPO) no yakuwari to sono kanōsei ni kansuru kenkyū* (Research on the role and potential of private nonprofit organizations [NPOs] in the community). Kobe: 21st Century Hyogo Project Association.

Yamauchi Naoto. 1997. *Nonpurofitto ekonomī* (The nonprofit economy).Tokyo: Nihon Hyōronsha.

CHAPTER FIVE

Nonstate Actors
as Forces of Globalization

Iriye Akira

NONSTATE ACTORS have been playing increasingly important roles in international relations. In discussing the growth of civil societies throughout the world, we may wish to pay particular attention to the ways in which these societies interact across national boundaries, thus constituting a vital aspect of the phenomenon of globalization. While it is customary to discuss the phenomenon as a post–cold war development, in fact cross-national exchanges among nonstate actors have been going on for quite some time; indeed, there are writers who contend that interactions among nonstate actors were characteristic of the prestate (i.e., premodern) period of history. Even if we confine ourselves to the history of the 20th century, when state power has tended to extend itself to cover more and more aspects of human life, we can see a trend to preserve the autonomy of individuals, private groups, and various organizations and communities, both within the territorial state and across national boundaries.

Although nonstate actors and civil societies engage in a myriad of activities, this chapter will focus on one of them, intellectual exchange, and discuss how the promotion of intellectual exchange programs among nations has fostered, and been in turn fostered by, the growth of nonstate organizations, together contributing to the emerging process of globalization. The integrative forces drawing national societies into a global community have of late converged with domestic forces in Japan (many of which are discussed in the other chapters of this volume) to ignite momentous change in the country's private sector. It is hoped that a historical view of the development of nonstate actors through intellectual exchange will provide clues to how Japan's civil society can respond to the challenges of globalization.

EARLY INTERNATIONALIST CULTURAL ACTIVITIES

Intellectual exchange is part of the broad phenomenon known as cultural exchange: interactions at the cultural level among individuals and groups across national boundaries. In a book entitled *Cultural Internationalism and World Order* (Iriye 1997), I argued that the movement for promoting cross-national understanding through the sharing of information, the holding of world fairs and international conferences, and, quite simply, the coming together of scholars, students, artists, journalists, tourists, and many others was a notable aspect of international relations at the turn of the 20th century—the very moment when the "great powers" were amassing arms and colonies to turn themselves into even greater powers. Their (presumably) constant struggle for power was taken for granted by strategists, politicians, and publicists alike. Conflict, as Alfred Thayer Mahan, the U.S. naval strategist who exemplified this type of thinking, asserted, was and would continue to remain the basic law of national and international affairs. Such being the case, all states, and all people whose identity was primarily defined by them, had to struggle to be strong—stronger than their neighbors and the neighbors of their neighbors; otherwise, they were destined to "decline," since all nations either "rose or fell."

Against this sort of geopolitical determinism, thinkers, mostly in Europe and North America, began a movement, which they called "internationalism," to overcome such fatalism and to organize the world differently, to internationalize it so that people everywhere would develope a sense of shared destiny. Even those who did not articulate such a vision self-consciously—businesspeople, travelers, even characters in fiction—became part of the movement by meeting with their counterparts in other countries, thereby developing connections, friendships, and networks that did not coincide with the territorial definition of loyalty and human association. At that time, intellectual exchange was particularly conspicuous because intellectuals—scholars, artists, journalists—were in a better position to try to practice what they preached; they not only talked about international understanding but sought to promote it by organizing international professional associations and holding conferences that brought their members together every few years.

Already by the first decade of the century there had been organized scores of such organizations, including, for instance, the International Union of Ethical Societies, the International Musical Society, and the International Society of Intellectuals. These organizations held their meetings periodically; examples would include the International Art Congress, the International Congress of Historians, and the International Congress of Geographical Sciences. Some of the international conferences were of really grand scale, the World Congress of Arts and Science held in St. Louis in 1904 being a conspicuous example. Scores of distinguished scholars of the natural sciences, philosophy, politics, economics, history, linguistics, literature, art history, religion, medicine, and other fields came to discuss recent achievements and future prospects. These organizations and conferences dedicated themselves to the proposition that intellectual and cultural endeavors must be promoted internationally and that their internationalization would be conducive to friendship and understanding among nations. It must be admitted, though, that at this time the vast majority of participants came from Europe and North America.

These were notable beginnings, indicating not only the emergence of an internationalist cultural movement but also the development of nongovernmental organizations (NGOs). According to Johan Galtung (1975), in 1910 there were already 135 internationally oriented nongovernmental organizations. F. L. S. Lyons (1963) notes that 466 international NGOs were established between 1815 and 1914. Whichever figure we choose, it is noteworthy that the vast majority of these organizations were created toward the end of the 19th century and at the beginning of the 20th, and that a significant portion of them were concerned with the promotion of intellectual exchange broadly defined. It is not too much to say that both nongovernmental organizations and intellectual exchange activities had their initial and promising start in the years preceding the Great War.

That the Great War came despite such activities suggests, of course, that a handful of organizations of intellectuals was powerless against the far more formidable tides of nationalism and militarism that were enveloping the world. As is well known, most, if not all, of the European internationalists subordinated their faith to their respective loyalties to nationalistic causes during the war. The war was waged on foreign soil and on the domestic front against foreigners and against foreign cultural influences. For the duration of the war, there was no room for cross-national intellectual exchanges or for internationally oriented NGOs except for those considered useful for war purposes.

That sad story, however, proved to be the catalyst for significant developments in the history of intellectual exchange and of international NGOs, for those who witnessed the wartime erosion of internationalist cultural activities and those fortunate enough to have survived the war redoubled their efforts so as never again to repeat the tragedy. The fact that, according to Galtung's figures, the number of international NGOs increased from 135 in 1910 to 375 in 1930 tells the story. The increase took place in the immediate aftermath of the war as intellectuals, artists, and now even government officials were determined to expand internationalist cultural activities and eagerly established new organizations to realize their goal. There is little doubt that the growth of international NGOs and of intellectual exchange took place in an environment where strong reaction against geopolitically defined international affairs was developing. To be sure, geopolitics, exclusionary nationalism, and militarism never disappeared, and they would return with even greater force in the 1930s. But the point is that there was a moment, in the wake of the Great War, when it seemed possible to replace power politics and armaments as determinants of international relations with nonmilitary instrumentalities, including cross-national cultural undertakings.

These undertakings would include, as earlier, international conferences, exchanges of students and scholars, and the like, but now their scope was much wider, and the participants in these programs more diverse, than before the war. Thus, whereas earlier Europeans and North Americans had predominated the scene, after the war individuals and groups from Asia, the Middle East, and Latin America became eager promoters of the movement. To cite but one example, the International Research Council, established in 1919 by associations of scientists, geographers, and others to serve as the headquarters for scientific data and coordinator of conferences, included members from all over the world, even from former enemy nations such as Germany and Austria. International congresses that used to be held almost entirely in Europe or North America were now organized in other parts of the globe;

international congresses of geography, for instance, were convened in Cairo and Buenos Aires.

Nowhere was international intellectual exchange promoted more vigorously or systematically than by the new League of Nations' Intellectual Cooperation Organization, which was established in 1921 in the belief that "no association of nations can hope to exist without the spirit of reciprocal intellectual activity between its members." This was, of course, not a nongovernmental organization but rather an intergovernmental organization. (The growth of intergovernmental organizations was also an important phenomenon of the interwar years, paralleling that of the international NGOs.) But private individuals and groups contributed enormously to the working of the Intellectual Cooperation Organization. In many countries, prominent scholars organized national committees on intellectual cooperation as a liaison between their local cultural institutions and the Geneva organization, often with the support of their respective governments. The fact that by the end of the 1920s more than 40 countries had established national committees on intellectual cooperation suggests that for the first time in modern history nations were giving official recognition to the importance of intellectual and cultural exchange. Still, governmental support, moral or financial, was rather limited, and the initiatives behind the formation and functioning of these committees lay in the hands of private individuals and the organizations they represented.

In all these initiatives, an internationalist ethos, "the international spirit," was manifest. What the term meant was not simply the assertion that the nations of the world must cooperate to preserve the peace through collective-security arrangements; far more important was the proposition that peace and order in the world must be based on cross-national exchanges in such areas as health, education, scholarship, and the arts. These were by definition nonmilitary, nongeopolitical activities, so that the stress on exchange programs was tantamount to a search for an alternative to the traditional international system in which sovereign states and power considerations had been uppermost. International relations, in a sense, were being conceptualized as less great-power oriented and more nonstate driven.

Woodrow Wilson, the preeminent exponent of the postwar international order, was convinced that this must be built upon "world public opinion." Although the term was rather vague, it would not be too far-fetched to say that the many international NGOs as well as the League and several other intergovernmental organizations that emerged in the aftermath of the war came close to representing world public opinion. Contemporary observers were aware that organization was the key to modern life, both national and international. As Mary Follette, one of the most astute students of political affairs in the United States, wrote as early as 1918, "group organization is to be the new method in politics, the basis of our future industrial system, the foundation of international order" (1918, 345). That was precisely the significance of the new international NGOs and other organizations. This was nowhere more evident in cultural and intellectual exchanges. In the words of Follette, "the old-fashioned hero went out to conquer his enemy; the modern hero goes out to disarm his enemy through creating a mutual understanding," with the result that the world would witness the creation of "a group culture which shall be broader than the culture of one nation alone" (346). Such a vision was behind the countless exchange programs undertaken by so many organizations in the postwar years.

The momentum would never quite dissipate even during the dark decade of the 1930s. It is interesting to note, for instance, that the number of international NGOs actually increased between 1930 and 1940, from 375 to 427, according to Galtung. Why could this have been the case when Germany, Italy, Japan, the Soviet Union, Spain, and so many other countries were becoming narrowly nationalistic, forsaking internationalism for nationalism? Totalitarian, militaristic states allowed little room for free organizations at home, not to mention free international exchanges. Still, even they at times encouraged the creation of cross-national institutions, "friendship associations" between Germany and Japan, and between Italy and Japan, being examples. Some of the international NGOs founded during the 1930s specifically aimed at mitigating the effects of totalitarianism and war, such as the International Rescue Committee and the Save the Children Foundation. In addition, new student exchange programs were launched, such as the Experiment in International Living (U.S.) and the U.S.-Japan Student Conference, to continue what had begun in the 1920s even in the midst of a world depression and mounting international tensions. Precisely because of these tragic circumstances, thoughtful individuals in many countries, including nondemocratic ones, were determined to promote exchange programs to keep alive the spirit of international understanding. (It is interesting to note that the Ford Foundation in the United

States, the British Council, and Japan's Society for International Cultural Relations were all established in the mid-1930s.) While none of these organizations or activities prevented the coming of war in Asia and Europe, we should note that most of them survived the war and became part of the phenomenon of globalization.

WORLD COMMUNITY DURING THE COLD WAR

If the growth of international NGOs and of intellectual exchange programs was quite notable after the First World War, the story was nothing less than spectacular after the Second World War. There is all too persistent a tendency to view post-1945 world affairs solely in the framework of the cold war. The fact that we tend to call the recent years the "post–cold war" world is an indication of our inability to conceptualize the second half of the 20th century in any other way than through the framework of the cold war. But the cold war, like all wars, is a geopolitical phenomenon; there is nothing particularly unique about it, and to focus on it as the key theme of recent world affairs is to lose sight of the very significant transformation that has taken place in international relations. And one important key to that transformation is the phenomenal growth of internationally oriented NGOs. From a little over 400, their number almost doubled by 1950, tripled by 1960, and reached 2,000 by 1970, a fivefold increase in 30 years—this at the very time when cold war tensions are said to have characterized international affairs. One cannot, of course, ignore the confrontation between the two nuclear superpowers during those decades, but even while they, together with their allies, were busily preparing for (or trying to prevent, through nuclear deterrence) a Third World War, a very significant movement was afoot in all parts of the globe. Part of this was in response to the very gravity of the cold war confrontation; private individuals and organizations, not content to resign themselves to living in fear of nuclear war, launched their own, often modest, endeavors to restrain the arms race and to keep open the channels of communication across the great divide that separated one side in the cold war from the other.

But the fear of war was only one factor behind the expansion of international NGOs. Many cross-national organizations were created to concern themselves with such matters as refugee relief and settlement, alternative energy development, economic and technical assistance, human rights, and the protection of the natural environment. Most of these issues were new; at least they became objects of cross-national concern on a massive scale only after the Second World War. The sheer facts, for instance, that over 30 million Europeans became "displaced persons" or that 25 million Russians were homeless in the wake of the war required massive relief work by international agencies. The development of nuclear energy attracted the attention of scientists all over the world who saw it as a solution to the vexing problems of poverty in most parts of the globe. Likewise, the decolonization of so many former colonies and "nation-building" endeavors by the newly independent nations called for technical assistance, capital investment, and educational reforms for which international NGOs would provide private funds and services where governments could not. But economic development, as well as rapid economic growth on the part of advanced countries, created environmental problems which, perhaps more than anything else after the war, mandated international solution. In the meantime, the experiences of the 1930s and the war seemed to reveal that abuses of children, women, minorities, prisoners, and other marginalized groups in various countries should never be seen as merely domestic phenomena but should be viewed as objects of shared concern by the whole world. Here again, international organizations, both governmental and nongovernmental, would play key roles in identifying and trying to mitigate these abuses.

It should be noted that most of these issues and the efforts to cope with them existed in the early postwar years; that is why so many intergovernmental organizations and international NGOs were created during the quarter century after the Second World War. CARE (Cooperative for American Remittances to Europe) was established in 1946, the Church World Service also opened in 1946, private voluntary organizations replaced the U.S. government as funders for UNRRA (United Nations Relief and Rehabilitation Administration) in 1947, Direct Relief International's establishment followed in 1948, in 1949 the United Nations sponsored a conference of scientific experts on utilization of resources, and in 1950 the International Confederation of Catholic Charities was created. The eruption of the Korean War and, throughout the 1950s, of other international crises did not halt the momentum. In addition to agencies primarily concerned with relief work, such as the International Voluntary Service and the Medical Assistance Program International, organized in 1953 and 1954, respectively, new ones came into being that were concerned with energy and

environmenal questions. Various organizations represented at the first
Geneva conference on atomic energy held in 1955 were an example of
the former, and Human Earth, established in Switzerland in 1960, is an
example of the latter.

These initiatives would be followed in the 1960s and the 1970s by
international NGOs with a mission to assist development and eradicate
poverty in Third World countries, as well as, increasingly, to protect the
rights of women, children, and dissidents there and elsewhere. Among
the most famous of such organizations were the Pan-American Development Foundation (1962), the Protestant Association for Cooperation
in Development (1962), Terre des Hommes France (1963), the International Association for Rural Development (1964), the Interchurch
Coordinating Committee for Development Projects (1964), Comité
Catholique contre la Faim et pour le Développement (1965), the Pan-
African Institute for Development (1965), the Australian Council for
Overseas Aid (1965), and Les Hommes pour les Hommes (1968). The
list can be extended almost indefinitely, especially after around 1972
when the number of international NGOs began to grow even more phe-
nomenally than earlier. Suffice it to note that during the quarter century after 1945, the geopolitics of the cold war described only one layer
of world affairs, and that underneath the surface drama grave problems
of demography, migration, decolonization, democratization, and environmental protection constituted additional layers, impelling private individuals and groups in many lands to organize themselves, since their
states appeared less willing to commit their attention to these matters
than to national security or armament. (It should also be recognized that
there was, from time to time, cooperation between the United States
and the Soviet Union in some of these areas, most notably in alternative
energy development.)

The spirit of these nongovernmental organizations went back to
Wilsonian internationalism. At a meeting of the United Nations' Human Rights Commission in 1951, for instance, a spokesman for the
World Jewish Congress, one of the prominent international NGOs,
stated, "nongovernmental organizations represent elements and aspi-
rations in international public opinion which must play a significant
role in the development and consolidation of a genuine world community." Every part of this sentence echoed the internationalist spirit of the
1920s, but the spirit now confronted an even graver challenge because
of the rise of the new issues claiming world attention. It is not too much

to say that thanks to the strength of such conviction and to the growth of international NGOs that embodied it, the world community survived the cold war; indeed, the very concept of world community would have been incompatible with the cold war confrontation, and it is to the great credit of the international NGOs as well as of the United Nations and other intergovernmental organizations that the concept survived the nuclear fear. In 1940, on the eve of the German spring offensive, Leonard Woolf had written, "If, when this war is over, we continue to live under the threat of yet another war . . . the black-out of civilised life will be permanent" (1944, 36–37). The cold war did continue to force people to "live under the threat of yet another war," but we can also say that in most parts of the globe a "black-out" of civilization did not occur. Woolf's prophesy proved inaccurate to that degree because he underestimated the growing strength of nongovernmental organizations. (Ironically, he had been one writer who had stressed the importance of such organizations in the world after the First World War.)

Because the post-1945 international NGOs were concerned with so many issues, they were no longer synonymous with cultural and intellectual exchanges as earlier. Humanitarian, economic, and politically oriented NGOs were often far more conspicuous than more traditional exchange programs across nations. There was even a tendency for intellectual exchange programs to become politicized when intellectuals from many countries cooperated, not primarily in exchanging information or coordinating their research activities, but in pursuing political objectives or ideological agendas. Perhaps this was inescapable, given their widely shared alarm over the possibility of a nuclear war or their eagerness to promote dialogue across the Iron Curtain. Such examples as the Pugwash Conferences, where scientists from many countries came together and called for nuclear arms control, and the Committee of Scholarly Exchange with the People's Republic of China, organized in Washington long before the establishment of diplomatic relations between the two countries, come to mind. Moreover, the participation of more and more intellectuals from outside Europe and North America in exchange activities inevitably gave rise to some serious questioning about the alleged universalism of certain values and principles. Cultural and intellectual exchange, many of them came to assert, had too often meant the transmission of Western ideas and standards to the non-West. It was time, they argued, that there developed a more equal exchange. Instead of universalism, they would stress cultural diversity.

There was a danger that such a clash between different perspectives could stifle cross-national exchange programs, as happened most graphically when the United States and Great Britain withdrew from UNESCO (United Nations Educational, Scientific, and Cultural Organization), the major international organization dedicated to intellectual exchange, accusing it of having succumbed to parochial agendas of Third World countries.

Nevertheless, intellectual exchange programs, now as part of the wider phenomenon of various types of cross-national, nonstate activities, did their part in promoting an alternative to the cold war. Students, scholars, artists, and many others crossed national borders and developed what would later come to be called cultural "borderlands"— shared spaces that belonged to no particular country but where individuals and groups from a number of nations exchanged, shared, and molded their own ideas and agendas. Besides, although often heated argument took place between universalists and particularists, between the exponents of universal values and of cultural diversity, a number of nongovernmental organizations (such as the Hazen Foundation of New Haven) quietly undertook the task to search for a framework of intellectual cooperation encompassing a variety of cultural perspectives. Despite the often harsh rhetoric of Third Worldism, Orientalism, and the like, in reality there was a great deal of engagement among intellectuals of all countries. Even a phenomenon like the "counter-cultural" movements of the 1960s in many parts of the world may be understood in the same context of global cultural exchange. This was a significant phenomenon in that nonstate actors were asserting a role to determine individual and social destinies. They were preserving and strengthening the vision of a world community at a time when adherents to the cold war definition of international affairs were dividing the globe.

INTERNATIONAL NGOs AND GLOBALIZATION

In some such fashion, international NGOs in general and intellectual exchange programs in particular may be said to have contributed to the globalization of human affairs. Clearly, globalization did not arise all of a sudden in the wake of the cold war; it had emerged long before there was a cold war, but it also developed as a reaction against the cold war. By the 1980s, the number of international NGOs had increased to over 10,000, with some 80,000 national branches. They, combined with intergovernmental organizations (now numbering over 1,500) and multinational business enterprises, were overshadowing the states whose traditional roles as providers of security and welfare for their citizens were also in need of redefinition in view of such globalizing tendencies.

The phenomenon is the most significant aspect of the so-called post–cold war world order. As noted already, the end of the cold war is not a particularly notable landmark in the long history of international NGOs, but to the extent that a geopolitically defined international system collapsed in 1989, it is easy to see that the international NGOs have become all the more important. Of course, geopolitics has not gone away, nor have armaments, war plans, and such. But that does not mean that we have to continue to conceptualize international affairs solely or primarily in the geopolitical framework. The widespread preoccupation with the emergence of China as the next superpower suggests an inability to go beyond the geopolitical mode of thinking. Whatever the merits of the geopolitical imagination, it is totally inadequate as a guide to understanding the contemporary world, a world in which 200 or so states are competing with 20,000 or 30,000 international nongovernmental organizations for people's loyalty, and in which nongeopolitical issues such as human rights and environmental protection are daily gaining importance. International NGOs as gathering places of those who have tended to be excluded from positions of influence in a geopolitically defined world—women, minorities, the disabled, the disenfranchised—are also likely to continue to grow.

That various international NGOs, together with intergovernmental organizations, have already made a difference may be seen in such recent examples as the successful negotiation for a treaty to ban the use of antipersonnel land mines, the Kyoto agreement on limiting carbon dioxide emissions, or the prospective drafting of an international convention on crimes against humanity. Changes in the international system, generations of theorists have insisted, are possible only through force or the threat of use of force. Ian Clark, for instance, notes in a widely used textbook, "the major deficiency of the international system is its inability to devise any universally acceptable means for promoting peaceful change" (1989, 28). Such truisms can no longer be taken for granted in a world in which a large number of voluntary organizations are working together to bring about peaceful change.

The numerical growth of international NGOs has, it is true, created some serious problems. One concerns the issue of accountability. To whom are the international NGOs accountable when their officers are not usually elected by their members and come from several countries? Is there any guarantee that they will not disregard laws and interests of sovereign nations? A founder of Médecins sans Frontières has even asserted that all international NGOs are by definition subversive of state authority, that in serving the interests of the whole of humanity, these organizations cannot be constrained by any government. But who determines what constitutes the interests of humanity? One way of coping with such criticism would be to say that the international NGOs are accountable to "international public opinion," but unlike domestic public opinion, world public opinion is not institutionalized and is impossible to measure. Moreover, if some international NGO mismanages its affairs, what sanctions can be applied, and by whom? A super-international NGO, an umbrella organization, may then become necessary to maintain some order among the proliferating organizations, but the question of accountability will remain. The matter becomes complicated because, although international NGOs have been spreading all over the world, funds, leadership personnel, and initiatives for issue-oriented movements are still predominantly concentrated in Western Europe and North America. Can it be said that what Europeans and Americans undertake reflects the wishes of people elsewhere?

These are serious questions that will grow even more so as the number of international NGOs continues to increase. But they cannot be satisfactorily discussed except cross-nationally; to deal with them within the framework of sovereign states will be unrealistic for the very reason that the international NGOs have mushroomed precisely because the states have failed to cope with many of the world's acute problems. At the same time, it will be naive to expect that an easy solution will be found to the question of the governance of international NGOs. As a modest beginning, may we not say that this is where intellectual exchange becomes of such critical importance? Intellectuals from various countries would seem to have a duty to try to understand and respond to the urgent problems that have resulted from the very successes of the international NGOs. It is often said that what the world needs is "confidence-building." Mutual understanding and confidence must be built not simply among nations and among international NGOs but also between the states, on one hand, and the international NGOs, on the other. For this reason alone, the significance of intellectual exchange will remain.

There is, however, another way in which we can understand today's international NGOs in general and intellectual exchange programs in particular. It may very well be that they can serve to provide links to traditional values such as justice, freedom, and compassion, which are said to be eroding in the rapidly changing technological environment of today's world. If globalization is pushing for a more interdependent world in terms of commerce, investment, migration, and especially transportation and communication, it has also undermined the sense of community among people who feel themselves to be adrift in a sea of technology that they cannot control. They may vaguely feel they are part of an interdependent world community, but that community has not yet defined its own moral or spiritual basis. The stress on individual acquisitiveness in a materialistic world tends to erode any sense of community. Perhaps to overcome this tendency, religious, ethnic, and other groups have asserted their role as definers of a new loyalty, as foundations for a new culture. The result has been that globalization has produced its antitheses: localism, ethnocentrism, and cultural chauvinism.

In such a situation, may we not say that cross-national associations of individuals such as international NGOs serve to preserve a sense of community and provide a moral basis for human interactions? David Hollinger (1995), one of the most perceptive observers of the contemporary American scene, has noted that there has emerged a tension between "cosmopolitanism" and "pluralism" in the United States and (by extension) elsewhere, the former favoring voluntary associations and the latter stressing segmented identities. By definition, NGOs belong in the former category, but they may also serve to provide a sense of identity. The American philosopher Richard Rorty has argued that in today's changing world, "private clubs" of like-minded individuals may be the only institutions giving people their identity and sense of community. NGOs are like private clubs, bringing together individuals who share similar concerns and values. But these individuals need not be members of the same national, ethnic, or religious community. There can be cross-national private clubs that provide a sense of identity, loyalty, and purpose to individuals who otherwise feel lost in an uncertain world.

Intellectual exchanges from the beginning involved the creation and development of "private clubs," consisting of educated men and women who shared similar interests and goals. They have developed their own networks which, combined with countless other networks built by international NGOs, are now enveloping the world. They have not replaced, nor will they replace, other institutions (including states) in the governance of people. But to the extent that globalization requires some semblance of order and a measure of accountability, here is a critical role to be played by those international NGOs that are engaged in intellectual exchange programs. Their challenge in the next century will be to try to be more successful than states, churches, or business enterprises have thus far been in providing the world community with sensible balance between globalization and diversity, between modern technology and traditional values, and between freedom and order.

BIBLIOGRAPHY

Caldwell, Lynton K. 1996. *International Environmental Policy*. Durham, N.C.: Duke University Press.

Clark, Ian. 1989. *The Hierarchy of States*. Cambridge: Cambridge University Press.

Condamines, Charles. 1989. *L'aide humanitaire entre la politique et les affairs*. Paris: L'Harmattan.

Diehl, Paul. 1977. *The Politics of Global Governance*. Boulder, Colo.: Lynne Rienner.

Follette, Mary. 1918. *The New State*. New York: Longmans, Green.

Galtung, Johan. 1975. "Nonterritorial Actors and the Problem of Peace." In Saul H. Mendlovitz, ed. *On the Creation of a Just World Order*. New York: Free Press.

Hollinger, David. 1995. *Postethnic America*. New York: Basic Books.

Iriye Akira. 1997. *Cultural Internationalism and World Order*. Baltimore: Johns Hopkins University Press.

Jacobson, Harold. 1984. *Networks of Interdependence*. New York: Knopf.

Luard, Evan. 1977. *International Agencies*. London: Macmillan, for the Royal Institute of International Affairs.

Lyons, F. L. S. 1963. *Internationalism in Europe*. Leiden: A. W. Sythoff.

Mendlovitz, Saul H., ed. 1975. *On the Creation of a Just World Order*. New York: Free Press.

Mitchell, J. M. 1986. *International Cultural Relations*. London: Allen & Unwin.

United Nations Commission on Human Rights. "Proceedings" (1951–). Unpublished.

Weindling, Paul. 1995. *International Health Organisations and Movements,*
   1918–1939. Cambridge: Cambridge University Press.
Woolf, Leonard. 1944. *The War for Peace.* London: George Routledge and Sons.
Yamamoto Tadashi. 1995. *The Role of Non-State Actors in International Affairs.*
   Tokyo: Japan Center for International Exchange.
————, ed. 1995. *Emerging Civil Society in the Asia Pacific Community.* Tokyo:
   Japan Center for International Exchange and Institute of Southeast Asian
   Studies.

CHAPTER SIX

Civil Society in Japan
through Print and Statistical Data

Wada Jun

JAPAN TODAY FACES the highly practical questions of how to foster civil society and change the nature of governance in a tangible way. The body of literature published in Japan addressing these questions is growing, and it is the purpose of this chapter to introduce specific titles while also offering a brief review of the basic statistical data pertaining to the nonprofit sector.*

I have focused as much as possible on materials with a practical and empirical approach, rather than on theoretical works. Specifically, I have concentrated on materials relating to the private nonprofit sector, which is expected to play the key role in Japan's civil society of the future (indeed, the term *shibiru sosaetī* often denotes the sector itself). In this way, we can begin to make out the contours, as seen in Japan, of the great groundswell which Lester M. Salamon, in "The Rise of the Nonprofit Sector" (1994), called the "associational revolution," and for which Jessica Mathews coined the term "power shift" in her 1997 article of the same name.

The list of publications in this chapter is by no means exhaustive. I chose those publications that can serve as guides for further exploration

*In the preparation of this chapter, I received a great deal of advice from my colleagues at the Japan Center for International Exchange. In particular, I would like to extend my thanks to Katsumata Hideko and Menju Toshihiro for suggesting many references, and to Suzuki Tomoko and Furuya Ryōta for their assistance in collecting and sorting the materials.

of a particular field, as well as those that contain important perspectives or basic data not available elsewhere. Priority has been given to difficult-to-obtain unpublished materials, usually referred to as "grey literature" (such as surveys and research reports), rather than to publications available in general bookstores, and wherever possible I have cited the most up-to-date sources (mainly those published since the mid-1990s). Where related information has been published on the World Wide Web, the URL is included in the bibliography entry.

Most of the publications introduced here are written in Japanese. English-language translations of the titles are given in the body of the chapter; the original Japanese-language titles are recorded in the bibliography under the authors' names. A supplementary list of URLs for those organizations mentioned with Websites follows the bibliography.

For convenience, I have divided the discussion into seven topics. Because publications differ greatly in their approach, however, their contents do not always fit neatly under one heading. In particular, there is much confusion over such terminology as "private nonprofit sector," "nonprofit organization (NPO)," "nongovernmental organization (NGO)," "citizens' activity group," and "volunteer group"; the boundaries of these terms in the Japanese context are very unclear, and the variations in usage can be said to reflect the diversity of authors' viewpoints. A further problem is that, owing to the lack of exact Japanese equivalents for English expressions such as "civil society," "governance," or "philanthropy," there may be considerable differences in nuance when the available Japanese terms are used. Accordingly, in reading this chapter, it should be understood that the section headings are intended merely for the sake of convenience, and that the contents overlap and interrelate in a complex way.

There is not a large body of work in Japan that directly addresses the relationship between civil society and governance. This book may be seen as one step in this direction. Before discussing titles falling under the aforementioned seven topics, I would like to suggest some books that are of value in considering the relationship between civil society and governance in the Japanese context: *The End of Americanism: Toward Rediscovering the Spirit of Civic Liberalism* (Saeki 1993); *Japan's Foreign Relations Strategy: Creating a Post–Cold War Vision* (Funabashi 1993); *Local Self-Government and Devolution in Japan* (Matsushita 1996); *Liberalism in Modern Japan* (Saeki 1996); *The Pathology of Modern Democracy: How Should We View Postwar Japan?* (Saeki 1997a.); *Who*

Is "the Citizen"?: Reexamining Postwar Democracy (Saeki 1997b); *The Age of Relativization* (Sakamoto 1997); *"Asian-Style Leadership" and the Formation of the State* (Iokibe 1998); and *What Are "Asian Values"?* (Aoki and Saeki 1998).

AN OVERVIEW OF CIVIL SOCIETY

It is not easy to gain an overview or to grasp the actual state of Japan's private nonprofit sector. Reliable comprehensive studies and statistics remain limited in number, as the concept of civil society itself is new, it is viewed and defined in various ways, and there is a lack of existing data that can be applied. In recent years, however, efforts to obtain an overall picture have begun to make rapid progress.

The first real advance toward mapping Japan's civil society took the form of two surveys of public-interest corporations by the Sasakawa Peace Foundation. The results of the first were published in two volumes, *Public-Interest Corporations in Japan* (Sasakawa Peace Foundation 1992) and *Japan's Foundations and Associations as Seen in a Questionnaire Survey of Public-Interest Corporations* (Hayashi and Katayama 1995). The findings of the first survey formed the basis of the second, whose results were analyzed in *The Reality of Public-Interest Corporations* (Hayashi and Iriyama 1997), while the full statistics were published in *Nonprofit Corporations in Japan Today* (Hayashi 1997).

Although restricted in scope to incorporated foundations and associations, these studies were a landmark event—a private-sector effort to survey the scene despite the dearth of public information. Moreover, they made valuable contributions by pointing out the very broad range of entities that are grouped together as public-interest corporations, establishing that these entities can be divided into two types, those created by private-sector initiative and those which supplement the work of government agencies, and analyzing the properties and problems specific to each type.

According to Hayashi and Iriyama, there are about 18,000 corporations of the private-sector initiative type. Their main types of work are as follows: public education, 61.9 percent; research, 45.0 percent; promoting goodwill, 45.6 percent; grant-making and awards, 42.0 percent. They are active in diverse fields, with the category "other activities" ranking alongside education, welfare, and environmental and wildlife protection. Although highly independent (membership dues and investment income are their principal revenue sources), they tend to be small in scale, with 44.1 percent having annual revenues of less than ¥30 million.

Approximately 7,000 corporations supplement the work of government agencies. Their main types of work are public education, 45.8 percent; operation of facilities and equipment, 43.7 percent; and implementation of projects, 37.7 percent. To a great extent they depend on local governments for their revenues, with 60.6 percent receiving promotional budget allocations, subsidies, and donations, and 50.6 percent carrying out government contracts. The typical corporation of this type is medium-sized, with annual revenues of ¥100 to ¥300 million.

As an overall trend, the studies note that while corporations with revenues of ¥500 million or more represent only about 13 percent of the total number, they account for about 75 percent of total revenues. In particular, those with revenues of ¥10 billion or more, which make up only about 1 percent of the total, have enormous influence, but their activities are not made public.

Of equal significance as this groundbreaking research is another private-sector study, *An Overview of the Private Public-Interest Sector* (Minkan Kōeki Sekutā Kenkyūjo 1997). As the title suggests, this study sought to cover the private public-interest sector to the broadest possible extent, defining it as that sector whose activities (a) are undertaken from an autonomous and independent standpoint, (b) are not profit-seeking, (c) aim for the betterment of society, and (d) are conducted by private-sector organizations.

After discussing this concept, the report divides the sector into the following types of organizations: Civil Code corporations (incorporated foundations and associations), private school corporations, social welfare corporations, medical corporations, religious corporations, consumer cooperatives, other nonprofit corporations, unincorporated associations, and private overseas cooperation groups. For each category, it sets out information including the relevant legislation, classification, history, tax status, scale, state of information disclosure, and basic data. Next, it examines the sector's financial support, providing an outline, summary of operations, and basic data under each of the following headings: individual donations; corporate donations; charitable trusts; private grant-making bodies; government-affiliated grant-making bodies (special public corporations of the financial assistance type; auxiliary agencies responsible for publicly operated racing sports and lotteries; community chests; and international volunteer savings deposits); local government grants; and volunteer activities. Lastly, the report points to the need for greater freedom of information as a step toward clarifying the overall situation.

As indicated by the words "preliminary study" in its subtitle, the report presents as full a picture of the system and its workings as could be compiled at the time, while including the available information sources and basic data. It thus not only lays the groundwork for further research but, in view of the slow pace of information disclosure, will also be valuable as a concise guide for those seeking an overview of the private public-interest sector.

As if following the lead of the private sector, the national government gradually began to make information available in the mid-1990s. Before this time, the Prime Minister's Office had conducted surveys of public-interest corporations, starting in 1986, but had not published the results. Even directories had been scarce: The first to be made public was the *Directory of Public-Interest Corporations* (Management Office of Minister's Secretariat 1993). At the ministry level, directories or other data on the corporate bodies under their jurisdiction were issued by only eight ministries (Transport; International Trade and Industry; Health and Welfare; Posts and Telecommunications; Education; Agriculture, Forestry and Fisheries; Construction; and Labor).

The first white paper devoted to public-interest corporations was *1997 White Paper on Public-Interest Corporations* (Prime Minister's Office 1998). This marks the first release of government materials giving an overall view of the incorporated associations and foundations established under Article 34 of the Civil Code ("Article 34 corporations"). Amid the movement toward administrative reform, one factor underlying publication of the white paper was the mounting criticism of such practices as the profit-making activities of public-interest corporations and the sale of dormant corporations. More importantly, the rising interest of the Japanese general public in the nonprofit sector was undoubtedly a key factor.

The white paper bases its concept of a public-interest corporation on three criteria: (a) it conducts works for the public good; (b) it is not profit-seeking; (c) it has the permission of the competent authorities. There follows an outline of the system (definition of public-interest corporations, legislation, guidance and oversight, accounting procedures, and taxation) and a discussion of their administrative history, recent policies, and the present situation. A reference section containing various agreements among government authorities concerning public-interest corporations and statistics is also included.

According to the white paper, as of October 1, 1996, there was a national total of 12,618 incorporated associations and 13,471 incorporated foundations, for a combined total of 26,089. Of these, 6,815 were under the jurisdiction of the national government and 19,366 were under prefectural jurisdiction. In fiscal 1995, their annual revenues totaled ¥24.3507 trillion and expenditures totaled ¥21.6961 trillion (4.4 percent of GDP, or the equivalent of 12.4 percent of gross general government expenditure; the figure includes ¥15.1404 trillion for direct expenditures for projects). Their total work force of 524,000 (0.8 percent of total industrial employment) was larger than that of the banking industry and comparable to that of the life insurance industry. While 0.5 percent of the corporations date from before World War II, about 70 percent were established since 1965.

Their purposes of establishment fall into the following fields: general living standards, 52.1 percent; education and research, 39.7 percent; industry, 28.2 percent; government and administration, 11.7 percent. The types of work they perform are promotion and encouragement, 47.8 percent; guidance and development, 57.5 percent; research, 43.8 percent; public education and public affairs, 30.1 percent; operation of facilities, 25.3 percent; inspections and examinations, 3.5 percent; exchanges, 9.8 percent; mutual aid, 3.7 percent; others, 7.6 percent. Among the incorporated foundations, 32.1 percent had endowments of at least ¥100 million but less than ¥1 billion, while 7.0 percent had endowments of ¥1 billion or more, and 60.9 percent had endowments of less than ¥100 million. The national government granted subsidies totaling about ¥246.0 billion to 411 corporations and made contract payments totaling about ¥145.0 billion to 592 corporations. The prefectural governments granted subsidies totaling about ¥337.4 billion to approximately 4,800 corporations and made contract payments totaling about ¥514.0 billion to an estimated 3,200 corporations. The report also notes the high proportion of former and seconded government officials among the full-time executive directors of public-interest corporations: 24.6 percent in those under national government jurisdiction, and 24.5 percent in those under prefectural jurisdiction.

While one cannot help feeling that it should have appeared earlier, the report is valuable not only for its official status as a white paper but also for the amount of statistical data it makes available for the first time. It can thus be regarded as a basic resource for studying the administration of public-interest corporations.

A study by the Social Policy Bureau (1998a) of the Economic Planning Agency examines private nonprofit organizations as a whole under the title *The Economic Scale of Japan's NPOs*. In addition to the public-interest corporations covered by the white paper, it also deals with private school corporations, social welfare corporations, religious corporations, relief and rehabilitation corporations, labor unions, chambers of industry and commerce, political parties and organizations, community groups, and medical corporations, together with the citizens' activity groups that are studied in the *Citizens' Activities Report* (Social Policy Bureau 1997b), which will be discussed in detail in the third section of the chapter.

The Economic Scale of Japan's NPOs provides macroeconomic estimates of the added value and output of private nonprofit organizations, and attempts to assign a monetary value to volunteer activities. The first study of its kind, it discusses (a) the range of private nonprofit groups covered; (b) methods and results in the estimation of the scale of activities on a funds basis; (c) methods and results in the assignment of a monetary value to volunteer activities; and (d) future issues. Four criteria are used to define private nonprofit groups: their non-profit-seeking nature, creation of economic value, nongovernmental nature, and voluntary nature. The study thus differs in scope from both the System of National Accounts (SNA) and the Johns Hopkins Comparative Nonprofit Sector Project, which will be discussed in the following section.

According to the report, private nonprofit groups have a total economic scale of about ¥15 trillion (3.1 percent of GDP) in terms of added value and about ¥27 trillion (2.9 percent of GDP) in terms of output. When general medical corporations are excluded, the total added value amounts to about ¥11 trillion (2.3 percent of GDP) and total output to about ¥20 trillion (2.2. percent of GDP). By subsector, the total added value breaks down as follows: general medical corporations, 25 percent; medical care, 21 percent; education, 28 percent; social insurance and social welfare, 13 percent; religion, 5 percent; others, 8 percent.

Further, citizens' activity groups as defined in the *Citizens' Activities Report* have an added value of about ¥30 billion and an output of about

¥120 billion.The monetary value assigned to the voluntary activities of these groups, based on questionnaire surveys, amounts to about ¥650 billion.

While these findings do not go beyond the level of estimates, reflecting the lack of existing data and a social consensus as to definitions, the study is nevertheless worthy of attention in that it provides one model of economic scale.

It should also be noted that a system of special public-interest-promoting corporations, which introduced tax incentives for donations, was launched in 1988. For corporations whose activities meet one of 34 requirements for eligibility (as of April 1, 1997), preferential tax treatment lasting in principle for two years was authorized, subject to administrative discretion. A total of 17,026 corporations have received this authorization (Ministry of Finance data as of April 1, 1996). However, when we exclude 26 special corporations, 1,125 private school corporations, 14,832 social welfare corporations, 163 relief and rehabilitation corporations, and 58 specified Civil Code corporations, we find that only 822 "Article 34 corporations," or just over 3 percent of the total number of such corporations, have been granted preferential tax treatment under this system. A list of special public-interest-promoting corporations can be found in *List of Special Public-Interest-Promoting Corporations* (Japan Association of Charitable Organizations, annual).

For the terminology regarding public-interest corporations, the *Public-Interest Corporation Glossary* (Japan Association of Charitable Organizations 1992) provides a handy guide, while *Taxation of Public-Interest Corporations* (Japan Association of Charitable Organizations 1995) is a useful reference on their tax status. Another valuable work is the *Bibliography Relating to Public-Interest Corporations* (Japan Association of Charitable Organizations 1988); this is a compendium of related publications from before World War II to 1988. It also contains an index to the contents of the association's monthly journal, *Public-Interest Corporations*, from 1972 to 1988.This journal continues to be an important resource, carrying a wealth of information in every issue. For an overview of the taxation of public-interest corporations, a further useful reference is *An Agenda for the Taxation of Philanthropy* (Research Group on Taxation of Public-Interest Corporations and Charitable Trusts 1990).

We can expect to see a growing volume of commercial publications on the private nonprofit sector in the future. A first-rate summary is provided by *What Are NPOs?* (Dentsū Institute for Human Studies

1996). There are also a number of more specialized works focusing on a particular field, such as *NPOs and the New Cooperatives* (Japan Institute of Cooperative Research 1996); *Theory and Practice of the Nonprofit and Cooperative Sectors* (Tomizawa and Kawaguchi 1997); *The Nonprofit Economy: The Economics of NPOs and Philanthropy* (Yamauchi 1997); and *The Potential of a New Social Sector: NPOs and Labor Unions* (Hayashi and JTUC–RIALS 1997).

Basic Course on NPOs (Yamaoka 1997) identifies issues in the future development of Japan's civil society in relation to NPOs. This volume was the first project of the Japan NPO Center, established in November 1996. It is divided into chapters on the significance and present state of NPOs, NPOs in relation to voluntarism, corporate philanthropy, grant-making foundations, and local government, and the laws and taxation as they affect NPOs; it also includes a bibliography. In addition to publishing the periodical *NPO Plaza*, the Japan NPO Center is due to publish a second volume of *Basic Course on NPOs* and an NPO yearbook.

The Law to Promote Specified Nonprofit Activities, or the NPO Law, was promulgated in March 1998 and took effect in December 1998.* For a practical explanation of the new law in a question-and-answer format, see *The Work of NPOs and Volunteers: Legal, Accounting, and Taxation Issues* (NPO-Borantia Kenkyūkai 1998). This deals with the issues under debate, the interpretation of the law, and its practical implications, and contains the full text of the law and supplementary resolution together with an index.

With the establishment of the Non-Profit Policy Association, implementation of the SCOPE (Study Center on Philanthropy) project to promote academic studies on philanthropy, and the scheduled launching of the Japan NPO Research Association in 1999, research on the private nonprofit sector is expected to become increasingly active in the future.

THE PRIVATE NONPROFIT SECTOR IN ASIA PACIFIC

An in-depth international comparison of the private nonprofit sector is provided by the Comparative Nonprofit Sector Project, which was carried out jointly by the Institute for Policy Studies, Johns Hopkins

*See <http://www.epa.go.jp/98/c/19980319c-npo.html> for the full text in Japanese. For an unofficial English translation, see the *Civil Society Monitor* (Japan Center for International Exchange 1998b) and <http://www.jcie.or.jp>.

University, in the United States and the Japan Center for International Exchange (JCIE). The project compared the nonprofit sector's activities and their economic effects in 12 countries between 1990 and 1995. The results generated a series of publications from the Johns Hopkins University Institute for Policy Studies: "In Search of the Nonprofit Sector: The Question of Definitions" (Salamon and Anheier 1992); *The Emerging Sector: The Nonprofit Sector in Comparative Perspective—An Overview* (Salamon and Anheier 1996a); and "Social Origins of Civil Society: Explaining the Nonprofit Sector Cross-Nationally" (Salamon and Anheier 1996b). The results were published in final form as *Defining the Nonprofit Sector: A Cross-National Analysis* (Salamon and Anheier 1997).

The project marked the first attempt to define the nonprofit sector in Japan and determine its economic scale. A chapter of *Defining the Nonprofit Sector* ("Japan," by Amenomori Takeyoshi) was devoted to the findings, which were later published in full as *The Nonprofit Sector in Japan* (Yamamoto 1998). The six chapters of this volume cover the history, legal background, scale, relationship with the state, and current issues of the nonprofit sector in Japan, together with the data sources and methods for estimating the size of the sector. It represents the first attempt to gain an overview of Japan's nonprofit sector from the viewpoint of its members, and also is the first such comprehensive English-language study in book form.

Japan had, however, been included in a number of earlier international comparisons of the private nonprofit sector. The main titles are *Philanthropy and the Dynamics of Change in East and Southeast Asia* (Baron 1991); *Evolving Patterns of Asia-Pacific Philanthropy* (Jung 1994); and *The Nonprofit Sector in the Global Community: Voices from Many Nations* (McCarthy, Hodgkinson, and Sumariwalla and Associates 1992).

Whereas these works are collections of papers on individual countries, *Emerging Civil Society in the Asia Pacific Community* (Yamamoto 1995) is an integrated study of the present state of civil society and the private nonprofit sector in Asia Pacific, carried out with the cooperation of each country in the region. The first such comprehensive study, this massive volume of some 700 pages examines the status and issues of NGOs, policy research institutions, and philanthropy in 15 countries and regions of Asia Pacific on a country-by-country basis. The integrative summary on NGOs in 15 countries and regions of Asia, North America, and Oceania has since been updated and published in Japanese as *NGOs in Asia Pacific* (Japan Center for International Exchange [JCIE] 1998a).

NPOs in Asia (GAP 1997) could be called a companion volume to *NGOs in Asia Pacific*. It describes the present situation of nonprofit organizations (mainly foundations) engaged in international activities in ten countries or regions of Asia, excluding Japan.

CITIZENS' PUBLIC-INTEREST ACTIVITY GROUPS AND VOLUNTEER GROUPS

In Japan, the term "NPO" denotes "citizens' activity group," and often refers to voluntarily established groups not included in the legal framework that governs public-interest corporations—in other words, those groups that are the object of the new NPO Law. Citizens' activity groups are in fact only one type of nonprofit organization in the original sense of the term, but in Japanese usage "NPO" often takes on this more restricted meaning. This is partly due to the influence of the NPO Law, which was enacted without clarifying the relationship of public-interest corporations and citizens' activity groups.

"Volunteer group" is another very loosely defined term, sometimes equated with "NPO" in the sense of a group formed through the voluntary initiative of citizens. Yet volunteer groups—that is, groups in which volunteers participate—are also just one type of NPO, in which professional staff should play a central role. There is much food for thought regarding these points in "Special Feature: Volunteers and NPOs" (Osaka Volunteer Association 1998). In addition to the journal in which this article appears, *Volunteer Activity Studies*, the Osaka Volunteer Association publishes many materials related to voluntarism.

While the concept is still surrounded by much confusion, public attention has been focused on those groups commonly known as NPOs in Japan, that is, citizens' public-interest activity groups (including volunteer groups), as a result of the active role played by volunteers in the Great Hanshin-Awaji Earthquake, together with the campaign for enactment of the NPO Law. A pioneering study in this area was *Study on the Consolidation of Infrastructure for Citizens' Public-Interest Activities* (National Institute for Research Advancement [NIRA] 1994). This study defined citizens' public-interest activities as one area of private nonprofit activities, especially those independent public-interest activities carried on with the autonomous participation and support of many citizens. It examined the social significance of citizens' public-interest activities while analyzing their history, present system, support structure, contents and state of activities, issues, and comparable systems overseas. The study recommended (a) improvement of the support structure; (b) expansion of financial support and encouragement of donations; (c) review of the existing public-interest corporation system and establishment of a new nonprofit corporation system; and (d) enactment of a basic law governing private-sector activities in the public interest.

In the second stage of this research, further results were published as *The Proper Form of Legislation and the System for Promotion of Citizens' Public-Interest Activities* (NIRA 1996b). This report discusses the need for incorporation of citizens' public-interest activities and the appropriate corporation system, then goes on to propose a number of concrete revisions to existing laws and the general outline of a special law. As basic conditions, the proposed system is designed to (a) cover a broad range of fields by doing away with the existing compartmentalization, in which many government departments exercise jurisdiction separately; (b) bring incorporation under a set of legal standards not subject to administrative discretion; (c) use public disclosure, not government supervision, to ensure that activities are non-profit-seeking; (d) treat incorporated and unincorporated associations equally for taxation purposes, but establish separate preferential measures according to such criteria as the social significance of an organization's activities and the extent of its public disclosure of information.

Also published in the same year was the *Comprehensive Study on Support Measures for Volunteers* (NIRA 1996a). This study by legal scholars defines volunteer groups as those which fulfill the criteria of spontaneity, absence of financial compensation (nonprofit nature), and social contribution (objectives in the public interest). After comparing the relevant laws in several other countries, the authors make a series of recommendations. These include setting up a new corporation system to simplify the acquisition of corporate status; having an independent third-party institution screen applications; making corporate status public through corporate registration; placing activities and accounts under the supervision of the competent authorities; and introducing preferential tax measures for those authorized corporations that benefit the public interest to a particularly high degree.

Researchers who were themselves involved in voluntary activities incorporated the views of those in the field into *Nonprofit Groups and the Social Infrastructure* (Japan Networkers Conference 1995). Their report reviews the present state of activities, the problems involved, the availability of support and related issues, and the situation in the United States, and recommends the creation of a support system consisting of a "civil society development framework" and a "civil society development fund." Other publications by the Japan Networkers Conference include *What Are NPOs?* (1992).

There are many other surveys dealing with the situation of NPOs in Japan. To name just a few: *Research on the Consolidation of Infrastructure for Citizens' Public-Interest Activities* (Nara Machizukuri Center 1993); "Discussion of Volunteer Activities in Japan" (Life Design Institute 1994); *Report of a Fact-Finding Survey of Support for Citizens' Activities* (NLI Research Institute 1994); *Research on the Form of Assistance for Development of Citizens' Activities* (STB Research Institute 1994); *Study of Social Participation Activity Groups* (Zenkoku Yoka Gyōsei Kenkyū Kyōgikai 1994); *Study of the System to Promote Social Participation* (Institute for Social Development Research 1995); *Fact-Finding Study of the Activities of Support Groups (NPOs, NGOs) for Foreign Residents of Japan* (Kansai Inter-Disciplinary Studies, Inc. 1995); *Fact-Finding Survey of Citizens' Public-Interest Groups* (STB Research Institute 1996b; commissioned by the Economic Planning Agency); *The Outlook for NPOs to Build a Flexible, Mature Society* (STB Research Institute 1996a).

A number of factors were behind this flood of studies appearing in the early to mid-1990s, and especially between 1993 and 1996. Among them were the deep-rooted campaign for an NPO law by citizens' public-interest groups, changes in attitude among the agencies concerned, and a renewed recognition of the role of NPOs, accelerated by the January 1995 earthquake disaster. Some advocates of an NPO law made appeals in plain language such as *Courage to You: NPOs for Creating One's Own Life* (Grassroots Democracy Group and NPO Promotion Policy Commission 1997). Also active in the campaign were political parties such as the New Party Sakigake, which issued *The Citizens' Activities Corporation Law of Sakigake* (1995). In 1994, activists across the board united to form the Coalition for Legislation to Support Citizens' Organizations (known as C's). The debate over the NPO Law can be followed in a series of publications by C's, including *Commentary on the NPO Bill: Background and Issues* (1996a), *The Law to*

Promote Citizens' Activities: Draft Incorporation System and Discussion Materials (1996b), and *Understanding the "Citizens' Activities Promotion Bill"* (1997). The coalition has also published a handbook for groups aiming to incorporate under the new law, *NPO Incorporation Handbook* (1998b).

If NPOs are to expand, there must be a system to provide them with the backing and support of society. In this regard, two helpful references are *The Support System for the Nonprofit Sector* (C's 1998a), which takes a particular support system in the United States as a practical example, and *Study of Regional Support for Citizens' Activities, Part 3: The Support Sector in Japan* (Study Group on Regional Support for Citizens' Activities 1998). The latter is based on the experience gained in creating the Community Support Center Kobe, and also draws on a fact-finding survey of 1,093 citizens' activity groups in Nara, Hiroshima, Miyagi, and Hyogo prefectures, the results of which can be found in *Study of Regional Support for Citizens' Activities, Part 2: Citizens' Activities and Support Centers in Japan* (Study Group on Regional Support for Citizens' Activities 1997). The 1998 report provides a very concrete account of regional support in general, activities in Kobe, the process of establishing the support center, its programs and plans for stepping up activities, and the ideal form of the center. Similar support centers are now being set up in many parts of Japan, and they are also starting to form a network.

Another major topic of discussion has been the relationship between the community or local authority, on the one hand, and NPOs or volunteer activities on the other. One substantive study in this area is *Research on the Role and Potential of Private Nonprofit Organizations (NPOs) in the Community* (21st Century Hyogo Project Association 1995). The authors examine NPOs' role and productivity in a pluralistic society, viewing their functions in terms of the individual's relationship with society, and offer proposals for the creation and promotion of NPOs in the local community. Also included are the results of an opinion poll of community residents on volunteer activities, and a questionnaire survey on community development and the work of community-based mutual help organizations.

A study focusing on support by local authorities for volunteer activities is *Fiscal 1995 Study on the Proper Form of Social Support Measures for Volunteer Activities* (National Volunteer Activity Promotion Centre 1996). This volume presents the results of a fact-finding survey of 334 local authorities, an opinion survey of 185 experts, and hearings conducted by five agencies. It sets forth basic principles for local authorities as they work with and support volunteers and NPOs, and makes a number of proposals regarding the ideal form and operation of a support system. The discussion is organized under such topics as accommodating plurality and diversity, taking a long-term view, indirect support, the importance of the decision-making process for support measures, providing infrastructure and an enabling environment, the cost burden, and drawing up a charter. The findings of a questionnaire sent to 150 experts on the proper form of social support measures for NPO activities are also presented.

A further related study is *Administration and Voluntarism in the Age of Hollowing-Out of the Regions* (Ogasawara 1996).

Local authorities have conducted their own fact-finding surveys of NPOs. One very substantial study of this type is *The Administration and NPOs: Concerning NPOs in Tokyo* (Bureau of Policy and Information, Tokyo Metropolitan Government 1996). The bureau sent a questionnaire to 1,507 citizens' activity groups based in Tokyo and received 670 responses. The analysis of the data shows that 552 of these groups (82 percent) were unincorporated associations, 45 percent were established within the last 10 years, the majority (64 percent) were "locally oriented" groups active in such areas as "the community and human relations," "the living environment," and "community welfare," and only 30 percent had full-time paid staff. With regard to their financial scale, 49 percent of the unincorporated associations had annual revenues of not more than ¥500,000; in contrast, 92 percent of the public-interest corporations had annual revenues of ¥10 million or more. In light of these findings, the study calls for a more positive evaluation of the functions of NPOs and proposes concrete steps for forming partnerships between NPOs and the administration.

The Tokyo Volunteer Center of the Tokyo Council of Social Welfare has conducted a study on expanding the support provided by government-directed service agencies to include citizens' activities. Both the present situation and a vision for the future are discussed in *Report of the Committee on the Form of Promotion of Volunteer Activities in Tokyo* (Tokyo Volunteer Center 1997). The report emphasizes the importance of a realistic outlook, background support, equal relationships, coordination and teamwork, and maintaining human networks. A second report by the Tokyo Volunteer Center, *Report of the Committee on the Form of Support of Volunteer Activities* (1998), focuses on support for citizens' activities. This interesting report, which deals with referral services and networking, consultation services, gathering and providing information, research, training, and public education, gives an idea of the exploratory efforts being made by agencies in an intermediate position between the administration and citizens' groups.

Citizens' Activities Report, cited in the first section of this chapter, was the first comprehensive survey of citizens' activity groups by the national government. Conducted by the Social Policy Bureau of the Economic Planning Agency (EPA) (1997b), the survey defines citizens' activity groups as nonprofit groups engaged in social activities on an ongoing, voluntary basis, excluding public-interest corporations (such as incorporated associations and foundations). A questionnaire was sent to a random sample of 10,000 such groups out of the national total of 85,786, and 4,152 responses were received. The report presents the statistical results and analyzes them under five headings: the state of activities, finances, organization, city size, and whether groups have ever felt the need to incorporate.

The fields of activity were found to be as follows: social welfare, 37.4 percent; community, 16.9 percent; education, culture, and sports, 16.8 percent; environment, 10.0 percent; health care, 4.7 percent; international exchange and cooperation, 4.6 percent; others, 5.7 percent. The following forms of activity were reported: friendship and exchange, 57.8 percent; training, study, and guidance, 43.5 percent; provision of services, 31.6 percent; public education campaigns, 26.5 percent; publication of newsletters, etc., 21.5 percent. Almost half of the groups had been launched since 1986. The activities of 67.6 percent were located within a ward or municipality, while only 7.3 percent were active outside their home prefecture (including other countries). Groups with annual expenditures under ¥100,000 made up 21.2 percent of the total, and those with annual expenditures under ¥300,000 accounted for 34.5 percent. Fewer than 7 percent of the groups had their own office, while 23.0 percent had full-time paid staff. Over 80 percent felt that government support was necessary, and slightly more than 10 percent had felt the need to incorporate.

As mentioned earlier, when citizens' activity groups as defined above were included in macroeconomic measurements, their added value was estimated at ¥30 billion, their output at ¥120 billion, and the monetary value of their voluntary activities at ¥650 billion.

Further studies by the Social Policy Bureau include *Citizens'Activities Seen through Citizens'Eyes* (1998d), and *Toward Open NPOs:For the Effective Transmission of Information* (1998b).

Citizens'Activities Seen through Citizens'Eyes is based on two surveys, one of members of the general public and one of people involved in civic activities. Among its findings were the following points: there are widely varying interpretations of "citizens' activities"; about 20 percent of the general public currently participate in such activities, while about 80 percent of those not yet participating wish to do so in the future; those who participate are actively involved with their local community, and their reasons for participating are equally divided between an emphasis on society (e.g., "creating a better community") and an emphasis on self-improvement (e.g., "fully utilizing my abilities").The study offers proposals with a view to developing initiators with leadership qualities and expanding the pool of participants.

Toward Open NPOs is a fact-finding study of citizens' activity groups that addresses their policies related to accountability and how they circulate information about their work. While nearly 80 percent of the groups surveyed felt a need to pass on information, fewer than 20 percent thought they were doing enough. In particular, information channels to nonmembers were poorly developed; shortages of staff, funds, technology, and know-how were cited as problems. The study pointed to a number of ongoing issues with regard to accountability, including the need for objective decision-making criteria and ensuring the reliability of information released to the public. It proposed providing a "guide to communicating information on citizens' activities" in order to promote the accumulation and sharing of a minimum level of knowledge and technical expertise common to all groups, together with a stronger "information center function" to offer support and serve as an intermediary in the circulation of information.

A further study by the Social Policy Bureau, commissioned to the Marketing Intelligence Corporation, is *Study on the Status and Problems of Remunerated Projects by Citizens' Activity Groups* (1998c). A remunerated project is defined as any project conducted by a citizens' activity group which receives financial compensation from the beneficiary. Such compensation includes revenues from business activities, payments under government contracts, government subsidies, and private and other grants. Compensation for remunerated projects was found to make up 45.2 percent of the total revenues of the groups surveyed. Government subsidies comprised the largest proportion, at 25 percent, while revenues from business activities and payment for government contracts accounted for a combined figure of 12.5 percent. Most remunerated projects were found to be "projects based on the purpose of establishment"; only 5.6 percent were "projects to generate funds for activities." In two-thirds of all cases, payments for remunerated projects were less than ¥1 million; the payment levels corresponded to direct costs incurred, such as transportation expenses, and only about 10 percent of the groups surveyed stated that they had surplus money to cover indirect expenses. Thus, the study concludes, remunerated projects cannot be said to make a significant contribution to the strength and stability of the financial base of these groups, and they are not in competition with either the private for-profit sector or the public sector; rather, the relationship is one in which cooperation can be expected.

As training material, the Social Policy Bureau of the EPA has published *For Leaders of Citizens' Activities* (1997a). *White Paper on the National Life*, published annually by the EPA, is another important source of information.

The *White Paper on Voluntarism* (Japan Youth Volunteers Association 1997) is also of interest. The 1996–1997 edition, which looks at trends in voluntarism since the Great Hanshin-Awaji Earthquake, presents an analysis suggesting that the number of persons wishing to volunteer may not have increased after the earthquake, together with a discussion of social trends, extracts from recent studies of volunteer activities, and a list of organizations. Further references include: *Volunteer Handbook: 3,000 Volunteer Groups, NGOs, and Civic Groups, '95* (Masukomi Jōhō Sentā 1995); *Introductory Guide to Voluntarism* (PHP Institute 1995); and *The Age of Voluntarism: NPOs Will Change Society* (Tanaka 1998). For a detailed discussion of volunteer activities in the aftermath of the 1995 earthquake, see *The Volunteer Revolution: Reflecting the Experience of the Great Hanshin-Awaji Earthquake in Citizens' Activities* (Honma and Deguchi 1996).

There have been a number of nationwide opinion surveys on aspects of voluntarism. These are discussed in: *Opinion Poll on Lifelong Learning and Volunteer Activities* (Prime Minister's Office 1993); *Attitude Survey on Community Chests and Volunteer Activities* (Central Community Chest of Japan 1995); "Detailed Report of National Opinion Poll: Anxiety about the 'Nontransparent Age'; NGO Opinion Poll"

(Asahi Shimbun 1997); and "Women in Their Thirties Positive Toward NGOs and NPOs: From the Asahi Shimbun National Opinion Poll" (Numajiri 1997).

Citizens' Groups
for International Cooperation

The term "NGO" was originally used in Article 71 of the United Nations Charter. Since the organizations it denotes are presumed to be nonprofit as well as nongovernmental, it is almost equivalent in concept to "NPO" in the proper sense, that is, "a private, nonprofit organization." In Japan, however, since the first groups to adopt the term "NGO" were primarily involved in international cooperation or exchange, it tends to be used with the more restricted meaning of "a group active in international relations," or, even more specifically, "a civic group active in international development cooperation." (They are thus distinguished from civic groups active mainly within Japan, which are called "NPOs" in the narrow sense.)

NGOs that fit the definition "citizens' organizations for international cooperation" and that are mainly active in such fields as development, the environment, human rights, or peace are listed in the *NGO Directory* (JANIC, biennial). In addition to detailed entries on the NGOs, this very useful volume introduces related private organizations of various types and also has contact information for government offices, a bibliography, a directory listed by prefecture, a general index, and indexes of projects arranged by field or type and by country of location. The latest edition (1998) has entries for 368 organizations. Of these, 217 were founded before October 1995, have substantial project budgets (over ¥3 million for NGOs of the development cooperation type, or over ¥1 million for NGOs of the education and proposal type, or over ¥500,000 for NGOs of the network type), and derive at least 25 percent of their funds from their own revenue sources. These 217 organizations have revenues totaling approximately ¥19.6 billion, are active in over 100 countries altogether, and have a total of about 340,000 members and over 3,000 active volunteers, while 120 of their number employ a total of 1,239 paid staff. However, 191 (88.0 percent) are unincorporated associations, and although the average revenue of the 217 organizations is about ¥90.36 million, in practice about 44 percent carry out their activities on an annual budget of ¥20 million or less.

A companion volume, also published biennially by the Japanese NGO Center for International Cooperation (JANIC), analyzes the situation of these NGOs in greater detail. *NGO Data Book* is organized under such headings as origin and aims of activities, project characteristics, countries and regions of activity, bases in Japan, citizen participation, finances, organization, and staff. It also contains a chronology of trends among Japanese NGOs and a comparison with the data in the previous edition, thus serving as an invaluable resource for an overview of NGOs in the field of international cooperation.

Environmental NGOs are the subject of *Comprehensive List of Environmental NGOs* (Japan Environment Corporation [JEC] 1998). The fiscal 1998 edition updates that of fiscal 1995 and provides data on 4,227 groups. The Japan Environment Corporation also commissioned a study from the Japan Environment Association that analyzes the state of 510 of these groups, including 371 unincorporated associations; this was published as *Questionnaire Survey on the Actual Operation of Environmental NGOs* (JEC 1996).

The total amount of self-funded development aid provided by Japanese NGOs is quite difficult to determine, but figures for the previous fiscal year are published annually in *Japan's Official Development Assistance: White Paper on ODA* (Economic Cooperation Bureau, Ministry of Foreign Affairs). They cover those NGOs that meet the definition "private public-interest groups active in social and economic development cooperation in developing nations," and are based on a survey conducted for the Ministry of Foreign Affairs by the Association for Promotion of International Cooperation (APIC), which is published as *Survey of Results of Development Aid by Japan's NGOs* (APIC, annual). The latest edition (fiscal 1997) gives the following findings for a total of 306 NGOs: funding assistance, ¥7.94194 billion; technical assistance, ¥2.05752 billion; material assistance, ¥935.37 million; development education, ¥837.15 million; total, ¥16.99052 billion. The scale of aid breaks down as follows: less than ¥10 million, 203 NGOs (66.3 percent); ¥10 to ¥50 million, 71 NGOs (23.2 percent); ¥50 to ¥100 million, 13 NGOs (4.2 percent); over ¥100 million, 19 NGOs (6.2 percent). The average sum per NGO is ¥55.26 million, but in reality a mere 19 NGOs (6.2 percent) account for 83 percent of the total volume of aid.

Survey of the Support System for Japan's NGOs (APIC 1995) summarizes support programs and results in each of the following categories: the national government and quasi-governmental agencies, regional public bodies, private grant-making groups, companies, and international agencies. It also presents the findings of a survey on how NGOs themselves view this support system, together with the issues and future outlook. APIC continues to carry out surveys relating to NGOs. Another study in this connection is *Study for the Formulation of a Basic Concept for the Promotion of Volunteer Activities Which Make an International Contribution* (Research Institute for Hi-life 1996). This volume covers the present state of volunteer activities that make an international contribution, as well as the present state of support by the national government, affiliated agencies, and prefectural governments. The latest information on funding assistance by NGOs from public fund sources can be found in the "Government Agency Information" section of the monthly journal of the Japan Association of Charitable Organizations, *Public-Interest Corporations*.

In recent years, local governments have assigned a rapidly growing role to cooperation in their international programs. An interesting study of these changes, with actual examples of activities in Asia, is *Japan and Asia Linked at the Local Level* (CLAIR 1998). The report suggests the efforts being made at the regional level to keep pace with new developments, and the possibility of cooperation among local authorities, NGOs, and NPOs.

Another area in which studies have begun is the linking of Japanese ODA funds to the work of international NGOs or NGOs based in the recipient country, rather than in Japan. One such study, with an environmental focus, is *Beyond Grass-roots Grant Assistance: New Adventures of ODA and NGO Cooperation* (Foundation for Advanced Studies on International Development 1998).

There are numerous reports on the overseas activities of Japanese NGOs. Materials concerning ODA and NGOs can be accessed at APIC's home page, which also provides many links to NGOs.

PHILANTHROPY, PRIVATE GRANT-MAKING FOUNDATIONS, AND CHARITABLE TRUSTS

There are surprisingly few works on the social role of philanthropy in Japan. Especially in recent years, the tendency has been to discuss the subject within the broader framework of the private nonprofit sector as a whole (see the first section of this chapter). However, as sources of funding are likely to become a major focus of future debate on the

nonprofit sector in Japan, the nature of philanthropy is a topic that
deserves more attention than it has yet received.

A pioneering work on the history of philanthropy in Japan is *Foundations in Japan* (Hayashi and Yamaoka 1984). More recent studies
include *Philanthropy and Society:The Issues Involved in Japan* (Hayashi
and Yamaoka 1993), which deals with contemporary issues as well as
the historical background, and *Philanthropy:The Social Contribution of
Companies and Individuals* (Deguchi 1993), which is based on a comparison with the United States.

Foundations as a Social Phenomenon (Iriyama 1992) breaks new
ground as a theoretical study by an author who is actually involved in the
management of a private grant-making foundation, and offers many
valuable insights into the nature of foundations' work.

A full picture of the activities of private grant-making foundations
can be obtained from *Directory of Grant-making Foundations: Guide to
Private-Sector Grants*, which has been published biennially since 1988
by the Japan Foundation Center (JFC). (It was preceded by *Directory
of Foundations of the Grant-making Type,* 1985 edition, which was published by the Japan Association of Charitable Organizations to mark
the inception of the Foundation Library Center of Japan, the forerunner of JFC.)

The 1998 edition of the *Directory of Grant-making Foundations* lists
a total of 736 organizations—698 incorporated foundations or similar
bodies, and 38 other organizations that have grant-making programs,
including special public corporations, charitable trusts, and foreign
legal persons. Each entry consists of an organizational and financial
profile, details of regular publications, and details of grant programs
(types of program, funding criteria, eligibility, application period, number of grants, range of grant amounts, etc.). The 698 foundations listed
in the current directory represent a striking increase over the 213 that
appeared ten years ago in the first edition.

JFC also publishes the *Directory of Grant-making Foundations: Calls
for Grant Applications* in April each year. This contains guidelines for
grant, scholarship, and award applications to each grant-making foundation; the 1998 edition has entries for 186 foundations. Details of grant
awards are then published each October in *Directory of Grant-making
Foundations: Grant Awards*; the most recent edition (1997) lists 148
foundations and 7,300 grants. JFC also puts out a series of occasional
publications in English, *Directory of Grant-making Foundations in Japan.*

In the past, each edition of this directory was accompanied by an analysis of grant-making trends in the form of *Special Issue of the Directory of Grant-making Foundations: The Present State of Grant-making Bodies in Japan*, but this has been discontinued; instead, a brief analysis is provided in the center's periodical, *JFC Views*.

Under the system of charitable trusts, the first of which was launched in 1977, assets are placed in trust by an individual or legal person for a given purpose that serves the public good, and are managed in order to realize that purpose by the trust bank which acts as trustee. According to the home page of the Trust Companies Association of Japan, as of March 31, 1997, there were 513 charitable trusts with a total asset value of ¥53.5 billion; they were responsible for 49,590 grants with a total value of ¥15.8 billion. Jurisdiction over 174 of the trusts lay with the national government, while 339 were under prefectural jurisdiction; in other words, regionally based trusts outnumbered nationally based trusts by a ratio of two to one. About 40 percent of all trusts had assets of less than ¥30 million. The purposes of the trusts broke down as follows: scholarships, 29 percent; research grants in the natural sciences, 17 percent; promotion of education, 16 percent; international cooperation and exchange, 12 percent; arts and culture, 7 percent; social welfare, 6 percent; improvement of the urban environment, 5 percent.

CORPORATE PHILANTHROPY

Corporate donation figures, which come under the donation framework of the taxation system, can be obtained from the annual publication *Report on Results of Company Sampling Surveys* (National Tax Administration Agency). Nevertheless, it is not easy to determine the state of corporate philanthropy. The only available basic reference is the *White Paper on Philanthropy* (Keidanren 1992 and 1996). This white paper, which has been published in only two editions, is based on the "Survey of the Results of Philanthropic and International Cultural Exchange Activities," which consists of an annual expenditure survey and a triennial opinion survey conducted by Keidanren (Japan Federation of Economic Organizations) with regard to its member companies and the corporate members of its One Percent Club.

According to the 1996 edition, the 404 companies surveyed reported a total expenditure on philanthropic activities of ¥154.2 billion, or an average of ¥382.00 million per company (3.25 percent of ordinary

income). The expenditure breaks down into donations, averaging
¥281.00 million per company, and own projects, averaging ¥115.00
million per company. Expenditure related to the Great Hanshin-Awaji
Earthquake averaged ¥34.00 million per company. The average rate of
utilization of the tax-deductible limit amount was about 49 percent. A
system to support social contributions by employees existed in 257
companies. In the opinion survey, about 40 percent of the 391 companies that responded stated as a self-evaluation that they actively engage
in philanthropy. The reason for contributions cited by most respond-
ents (about 86 percent) was "responsibility as a corporate citizen."
Ninety-one companies had a department or section dedicated to social
contributions, and 54 maintained an annual budget for their spending
on such programs.

In addition to the detailed survey results, the white paper gives
an account of Keidanren's own philanthropic activities. It reviews the
work of the Committee on Corporate Philanthropy (237 member companies), the One Percent Club (268 corporate and 998 individual
members), the Council for Better Corporate Citizenship (CBCC), the
Keidanren Nature Conservation Fund (41 grants worth about ¥350
million), fund-raising from the business community (48 items, totaling
¥6.6 billion), scholarships, and other programs. It also presents and analyzes the results of a questionnaire on corporate relief work following
the Great Hanshin-Awaji Earthquake, and lists the philanthropic activities of individual companies in fiscal 1993.

Keidanren has also published the *Handbook of Corporate Philanthropy* (1994). This is a concise introduction for companies, written by
staff in charge of corporate philanthropic programs. It explains how
companies view philanthropy, the systems used, donations, company
projects, employee participation, and fields of activity, and also contains
a question-and-answer section, case studies, a glossary, and a list of
agencies. As a field guide that forms a companion volume to the *White
Paper on Philanthropy*, it offers interesting insights into the attitudes of
Japanese companies to philanthropy in actual practice.

The Association for Corporate Support of the Arts has published
the *White Paper on Corporate Support of the Arts* annually since 1991.
The latest edition (1997) reports the findings of a fact-finding survey
to which 325 companies responded, as follows: 230 (70.8 percent)
were active in support of the arts; the total value of their support was
¥17.55527 billion and the average per company was ¥99.75 million.

About 32 percent of the companies had a specialized department, about 60 percent allocated funds in their budget, and donations and sponsorship were about equally prominent as forms of funding. The average number of projects per company was six; financial support for concerts, exhibitions, and stage productions played the central role. In addition to reporting on this annual survey, the *White Paper on Corporate Support of the Arts* also lists support activities by company, national and local government support for the arts, support activities of corporate foundations, related press articles, and the year's events. Each edition carries a special feature on a different topic.

Corporate foundations are the subject of a publication by the Japan Association of Charitable Organizations, *Japanese Corporate Foundations*. This was issued in 1988 and 1992, but there is no more recent edition. In addition to a directory of foundations, each volume contains an analysis of trends.

A publication focusing on forms of corporate philanthropy that have close ties with the local community is the *Fukuoka White Paper on Philanthropy* (Fukuoka Industrial Promotion Council and Fukuoka City Council of Social Welfare 1996).

While there are many books that deal with the philanthropic activities of companies, they tend to mention the subject in relation to corporate governance, or to take an anecdotal approach. Only a few studies provide a complete overview of the field. The most comprehensive is *Japanese Corporate Philanthropy* (London 1991), which has also been published in Japanese. Other titles include: *Corporate Citizenship: Corporate Philosophy for the 21st Century* (Tabuchi 1990); *Philanthropy Blossoms: Asking the True Value of Japanese Corporations* (Shimada 1993); and a collection of case studies, *Introduction to Philanthropy* (Takahashi 1997). On Japanese corporate philanthropy overseas, titles include: *Travels in American Philanthropy: The Social Contribution Activities of Japanese Companies* (Shikata 1992) and *Survey of Philanthropic Activities of Japanese Companies in the United States* (Japan External Trade Organization 1993, 1995), as well as a large number of cross-national comparative studies.

POLICY RESEARCH INSTITUTIONS (THINK TANKS)

A major problem with regard to the development of civil society in Japan is the existing structure in which the drafting of policy is monopolized by the administrative branch at the national and local levels. While it hardly needs to be said that politicians themselves must increase their capacity to develop policy, it is equally vital to ensure that society as a whole has a mechanism for broad policy debate and the presentation of an array of policy options.

In considering this need, we must ask whether independent policy research institutions exist in the private sector. In the United States, especially, these are also known as "think tanks," but the Japanese term *shinku tanku* generally refers to government-affiliated institutions (in light of their funding and staffing, a better description might be "government-controlled"), or else to commercial affiliates sensitive to a parent company's interest. In fact, it must be said that "think tanks" in the sense of independent, private, nonprofit policy research institutions are almost nonexistent in Japan.

With this important proviso, materials on policy research institutions have been included here since those that are truly private and independent are key players in the development of civil society in Japan. The term "think tank," though not strictly equivalent, is used below as a translation of *shinku tanku*.

An overview of think tanks in Japan is provided by *Almanac of Think Tanks in Japan* (NIRA, annual). This presents the results of research by Japanese think tanks in four parts: "Introduction of Research Results," "List of Topics by Field," "NIRA's Research Results," and "Trends among Think Tanks."

The latest edition (1997) lists a total of 243 institutions (108 joint-stock companies, 109 incorporated foundations, and 26 incorporated associations). About 50 percent are located in Tokyo or adjacent prefectures. Of their 24,428 employees, 83.4 percent are employees of joint-stock companies. Research positions are held by 30.6 percent of the total employees, but 24.8 percent of these are seconded from a parent company or government agency, and as many as 54.2 percent of the institutions have research staff seconded to them. The 126 foreign researchers account for a mere 1.7 percent of the total, and are employed in only 15.3 percent of the institutions. The majority of the institutions were small to medium in size, with 43.6 percent having up to nine researchers and 70.4 percent having up to 19. But there was also a clear polarization in terms of size, with 13.1 percent having at least 50 researchers, 6.5 percent having at least 100, and 1.6 percent having at least

300. The think tanks with 50 or more researchers were nearly all joint-stock companies; very few public-interest corporations were numbered among them.

Total revenues amounted to approximately ¥404.6 billion, of which some ¥127.9 billion was generated by research. The income from profit-making activities of think tanks organized as joint-stock companies accounted for 80.1 percent of total revenues and 79.6 percent of revenues from research. The ten top-ranking companies earned 54.0 percent of all research revenues. Contracts from business corporations generated 51.4 percent of research revenues. Contracts from the government or special public corporations accounted for 39.9 percent, while the combined total of contracts from private research institutions, private grant-making bodies, and overseas clients accounted for less than 10 percent.

Almost half the total of 6,892 research projects fell into three fields: "utilization of the national land," 18.1 percent; "the economy," 14.8 percent; and "industry," 14.7 percent. "International issues" made up just 5.0 percent and "politics and government" a mere 4.1 percent of the total. There were only 34 joint research projects with overseas partners, and in only about 20 percent of the total number of cases were the results available to the public. According to the 1996 edition, when the research institutions were asked about their own future direction, the most frequent answer was "strengthening independent policy-drafting functions," a response that can be seen as reflecting their low level of independence under present conditions.

The triennial *Directory of Think Tanks in Japan* (NIRA) summarizes the organization of institutions of this type; the latest edition (1996) covers 413 think tanks. Also, the 1996 edition of the annual *Guide to Members of the Japan Association of Independent Research Institutes (JAIRI)* gives an outline of 51 member institutions, their current and future research topics, and related information.

Japanese universities conduct only a very limited amount of what could be called policy research. The results can be accessed on the science information databases of the National Center for Science Information Systems (NACSIS-IR), but this service is not available to the general public. As for policy research by government agencies, partial results have begun to be published on the home pages of some agencies, but with limited public disclosure it remains impossible to grasp the overall picture. The results of policy research by think tanks can be obtained only by approaching them directly (some publish results on their Websites) or using a library such as that of the National Institute for Research Advancement.

Against this background, the need for independent policy research institutions in the private sector has long been pointed out, for example, by Takenaka and Ishii in *The Japan-U.S. Economic Debate: The Age of "Excuses" Is Over* (1988). Since the early 1990s, these calls have clearly been gathering momentum. The lead was taken by a project supported by the Sasakawa Peace Foundation, "Think Tanks in Japan: Exploring New Options." This gave rise to the proposals published in *A Japanese Think Tank: Exploring Alternative Models* (Struyk, Ueno, and Suzuki 1993).

An event that had a major impact was the "Global Think Tank Forum" held in 1995 at the initiative of, among others, the Japan Ship-building Industry Foundation (Nippon Foundation). The results were published as *The Creation of Policy-making: Think Tanks in Civil Society* (Shimokōbe 1996).

The interest in private policy research institutions has not waned; indeed, amid a growing distrust of the bureaucratic system, it is now stronger than ever. Yet, in reality, there are many obstacles on the road to creating and strengthening private policy research institutions that are independent, nonprofit, nongovernmental entities. Perhaps the situation can best be summed up by saying that there is a new awareness of policy research institutions and think tanks as a key element of the private nonprofit sector, and of the importance of recognizing their need for NPO status.

Further, the role of independent policy research institutions is growing in importance not only in Japan but also internationally. Such a role is often played by international NPOs which specialize in the environment or disarmament, for example. Another increasingly significant area is the "track two" intellectual exchange or dialogue that occurs when independent policy research institutions establish a joint policy agenda and discuss topics that cannot be handled at the government level (track one), or topics with a medium- to long-range time frame. References concerning such trends include: *Survey of the Present Status of Japan-U.S. Intellectual Exchange* (JCIE 1991); "The Role of the Private Sector in International Exchange" (Yamamoto 1995a); "The Role of the Private Sector Is Growing" (Yamamoto

1995b); "Experience-Based Theory of Intellectual Exchange: From the Shimoda Conference to 'Track Two'" (Yamamoto 1996); *Cultural Internationalism and World Order* (Iriye 1997); and "Applying Track Two to China-Japan-U.S. Relations" (Wada 1998).

BIBLIOGRAPHY

Aoki Tamotsu and Saeki Keishi, eds. 1998. *"Ajiateki kachi" to wa nani ka* (What are "Asian values"?). Tokyo: TBS-Britannica.

Asahi Shimbun Opinion Poll Department, ed. 1997. "Zenkoku yoron chōsa shōhō: 'Futōmei na jidai' e no fuankan, NGO yoron chōsa" (Detailed report of national opinion poll: Anxiety about the "nontransparent age"; NGO opinion poll). *Asahi Sōken Repōto*, no. 125 (April): 110–127.

Association for Corporate Support of the Arts, ed. Annual. *Mesena hakusho* (White paper on corporate support of the arts). Tokyo: Diamond.

Association for Promotion of International Cooperation, ed. 1995. *Wagakuni NGO ni taisuru shien taisei chōsa* (Survey of the support system for Japan's NGOs). Tokyo: Association for Promotion of International Cooperation.

———, ed. Annual. *Nihon no NGO ni yoru kaihatsu enjo no jisseki chōsa* (Survey of results of development aid by Japan's NGOs). Tokyo: Association for Promotion of International Cooperation.

Baron, Barnett F., ed. 1991. *Philanthropy and the Dynamics of Change in East and Southeast Asia.* Occasional Papers of the East Asian Institute. New York: The East Asian Institute, Columbia University.

Bureau of Policy and Information, Tokyo Metropolitan Government, ed. 1996. *Gyōsei to NPO: Tōkyō no NPO o megutte* (The administration and NPOs: Concerning NPOs in Tokyo). Tokyo: Bureau of Policy and Information, Tokyo Metropolitan Government. <http://www.wnn.or.jp/wnn-v/book/index.html> (20 October 1998).

Central Community Chest of Japan, ed. 1995. *Kyōdō bokin to borantia katsudō ni kansuru ishiki chōsa* (Attitude survey on community chests and volunteer activities). Tokyo: Central Community Chest of Japan.

CLAIR (Council of Local Authorities for International Relations). 1998. *Chiiki ga tsunagu Nihon to Ajia: Jichitai kokusai kyōryoku chōsa jigyō hōkokusho* (Japan and Asia linked at the local level: Report on the survey project on international cooperation by local authorities). Tokyo: Council of Local Authorities for International Relations.

C's (Coalition for Legislation to Support Citizens' Organizations), ed. 1996a. *Kaisetsu: NPO hōan—sono keii to sōten* (Commentary on the NPO bill: Background and issues). Tokyo: Coalition for Legislation to Support Citizens' Organizations.

———. 1996b. *Shimin katsudō suishinhō, shian (hōjin seido) & tōgiyō shiryō*

(The law to promote citizens' activities: Draft incorporation system and discussion materials). Tokyo: Coalition for Legislation to Support Citizens' Organizations.

———. 1997. *Yoku wakaru "shimin katsudō sokushin hōan"* (Understanding the "citizens' activities promotion bill"). Tokyo: Coalition for Legislation to Support Citizens' Organizations.

———. 1998a. *Hieiri sekutā o sasaeru shikumi to wa: San Furanshisuko no sapōto sentā ni manabu* (The support system for the nonprofit sector: Learning from San Francisco's Support Center). Tokyo: Coalition for Legislation to Support Citizens' Organizations.

———. 1998b. *NPO hōjin handobukku: Tokutei hieiri katsudō hōjin setsuritsu no tame no kentō jikō* (NPO incorporation handbook: Study items for the establishment of specified nonprofit corporations). Tokyo: Coalition for Legislation to Support Citizens' Organizations.

Deguchi Masayuki. 1993. *Firansuropī: Kigyō to hito no shakai kōken* (Philanthropy: The social contribution of companies and individuals). Tokyo: Maruzen.

Dentsū Institute for Human Studies, ed. 1996. *NPO to wa nani ka: Shakai sābisu no atarashii arikata* (What are NPOs?: A new form of social services). Tokyo: Nihon Keizai Shimbun.

Economic Cooperation Bureau, Ministry of Foreign Affairs, ed. Annual. *Wagakuni no seifu kaihatsu enjo: ODA hakusho* (Japan's Official Development Assistance: White paper on ODA). Tokyo: Association for Promotion of International Cooperation.

Economic Planning Agency, ed. Annual. *Kokumin seikatsu hakusho* (White paper on the national life). Tokyo: Ministry of Finance Printing Bureau. <http://www.epa.go.jp/j-j/doc/s9honbun-j-j.html> (20 October 1998).

Foundation for Advanced Studies on International Development, ed. 1998. *Kusa-no-ne mushō enjo o koete: ODA to NGO no renkei no arikata kiso chōsa. Wagakuni seifu kaihatsu enjo to genchi oyobi kokusaiteki NGO no renkei no kyōka ni mukete no teigen* (Beyond grass-roots grant assistance: New adventures of ODA and NGO cooperation. Proposals for strengthening the linkage between Japan's Official Development Assistance and local and international NGOs). Tokyo: Foundation for Advanced Studies on International Development.

Fukuoka Industrial Promotion Council and Fukuoka City Council of Social Welfare, eds. 1996. *Fukuoka firansuropī hakusho* (Fukuoka white paper on philanthropy). Fukuoka: Fukuoka Industrial Promotion Council and Fukuoka City Council of Social Welfare.

Funabashi Yōichi. 1993. *Nihon no taigai kōsō: Reisen go no bijon wo kaku* (Japan's foreign relations strategy: Creating a post–cold war vision). Tokyo: Iwanami Shoten.

GAP (Group Action Planning for International Philanthropy). 1997. *Ajia no NPO* (NPOs in Asia). Tokyo: ALC Press.

Grassroots Democracy Group and NPO Promotion Policy Commission, eds. 1997. *Yūki wo kimi ni: Jibun no kurashi wo jibun de tsukuru NPO* (Courage to you: NPOs for creating one's own life). Tokyo: Japan Junior Chamber.

Hayashi Chikio, ed. 1997. *Genzai Nihon no hieiri hōjin: Nihon no zaidan, shadan no jittai chōsa wo chūshin toshite* (Nonprofit corporations in Japan today: With special reference to a fact-finding survey of Japan's foundations and associations). Tokyo: Sasakawa Peace Foundation.

Hayashi Chikio and Iriyama Akira. 1997. *Kōeki hōjin no jitsuzō: Tōkei kara mita zaidan, shadan* (The reality of public-interest corporations: Foundations and associations as seen in statistics). Tokyo: Diamond.

Hayashi Chikio and Katayama Shōichi. 1995. *Kōeki hōjin ankēto chōsa kara mita Nihon no zaidan to shadan: Sono kōzō, katsudō, keiei* (Japan's foundations and associations as seen in a questionnaire survey of public-interest corporations: Their structure, activities, and management). Tokyo: Sasakawa Peace Foundation.

Hayashi Yūjirō and Research Institute for Advancement of Living Standards (JTUC–RIALS), ed. 1997. *Atarashii shakai sekutā no kanōsei: NPO to rōdō kumiai* (The potential of a new social sector: NPOs and labor unions). Tokyo: Daiichi Shorin.

Hayashi Yūjirō and Yamaoka Yoshinori, eds. 1993. *Firansuropī to shakai: Sono Nihonteki kadai* (Philanthropy and society: The issues involved in Japan). Tokyo: Diamond.

———. 1984. *Nihon no zaidan* (Foundations in Japan). Tokyo: Chūō Kōronsha.

Honma Masaaki and Deguchi Masayuki, eds. 1996. *Borantia kakumei: Daishinsai de no keiken wo shimin katsudō e* (The volunteer revolution: Reflecting the experience of the Great Hanshin-Awaji Earthquake in citizens' activities). Tokyo: Tōyō Keizai Shinpōsha.

Institute for Social Development Research, ed. 1995. *Shakai sanka suishin shisutemu ni tsuite no chōsa* (Study of the system to promote social participation). Tokyo: Institute for Social Development Research.

Iokibe Makoto, ed. 1998. *"Ajiagata rīdāshippu" to kokka keisei* ("Asian-style leadership" and the formation of the state). Tokyo: TBS-Britannica.

Iriyama Akira. 1992. *Shakai genshō toshite no zaidan* (Foundations as a social phenomenon). Tokyo: Japan Broadcast Publishing Company.

Iriye Akira. 1997. *Cultural Internationalism and World Order*. Baltimore: Johns Hopkins University Press.

JANIC (Japanese NGO Center for International Cooperation). Biennial. *NGO dairekutorī: Kokusai kyōryoku ni tazusawaru Nihon no shimin soshiki yōran* (NGO directory: Directory of Japanese civic organizations involved in international cooperation). Tokyo: Japanese NGO Center for International Cooperation.

———. Biennial. *NGO dētabukku: Sūji de miru Nihon no NGO* (NGO data book: Japanese NGOs seen through statistics). Tokyo: Japanese NGO Center for International Cooperation.

Japan Association of Charitable Organizations, ed. 1985. *Nihon no joseigata zaidan yōran, 1985-nenban* (Directory of foundations of the grant-making type, 1985 edition) Tokyo: Japan Association of Charitable Organizations.

———. 1988. *Kōeki hōjin ni kansuru kakushu bunken mokuroku* (Bibliography relating to public-interest corporations). Tokyo: Japan Association of Charitable Organizations.

———. 1988, 1992. *Nihon no kigyō zaidan* (Japanese corporate foundations). Tokyo: Japan Association of Charitable Organizations.

———. 1992. *Kōeki hōjin yōgo jiten* (Public-interest corporation glossary). Tokyo: Japan Association of Charitable Organizations.

———. 1995. *Kōeki hōjin no zeimu* (Taxation of public-interest corporations). Tokyo: Japan Association of Charitable Organizations.

———. Monthly. *Kōeki Hōjin* (Public-interest corporations). Tokyo: Japan Association of Charitable Organizations.

———. Annual. *Tokutei kōeki zōshin hōjin ichiran* (List of special public-interest-promoting corporations). Tokyo: Japan Association of Charitable Organizations.

Japan Association of Independent Research Institutes, ed. Annual. *Nihon Shinku Tanku Kyōgikai: JAIRI kaiin gaido* (Guide to members of the Japan Association of Independent Research Institutes [JAIRI]). Tokyo: Japan Association of Independent Research Institutes.

Japan Center for International Exchange, ed. 1991. *Nichibei chiteki kōryū no genjō chōsa* (Survey of the present status of Japan-U.S. intellectual exchange). Tokyo: National Institute for Research Advancement.

———, ed. 1998a. *Ajia Taiheiyō no NGO* (NGOs in Asia Pacific). Tokyo: ALC Press.

———, ed. 1998b. *Civil Society Monitor*, no. 4 (April).

Japan Environment Corporation, ed. 1996. *Kankyō NGO soshiki un'ei jittai tō ankēto chōsa* (Questionnaire survey on the actual operation of environmental NGOs). Tokyo: Japan Environment Corporation.

———. 1998. *Kankyō NGO no sōran* (Comprehensive list of environmental NGOs). Tokyo: Japan Environment Corporation.

Japan External Trade Organization, ed. 1993, 1995. *Zaibei Nikkei kigyō no firansuropī katsudō ni kansuru chōsa* (Survey of philanthropic activities of Japanese companies in the United States). Tokyo: Japan External Trade Organization. <http://www.jetro.go.jp/top-j/index.html> (20 October 1998).

Japan Foundation Center, ed. Annual. *Josei zaidan: Boshū yōran* (Directory of grant-making foundations: Calls for grant applications). Tokyo: Japan Foundation Center.

———. Annual. *Josei zaidan: Kettei yōran* (Directory of grant-making foundations: Grant awards). Tokyo: Japan Foundation Center.

———. 1988– (biennial). *Josei zaidan yōran: Minkan joseikin gaido* (Directory of grant-making foundations: Guide to private-sector grants). Tokyo: Japan Foundation Center.

———. Monthly. *JFC Views*. Tokyo: Japan Foundation Center.

———. Occasional. *Directory of Grant-making Foundations in Japan*. Tokyo: Japan Foundation Center.

Japan Institute of Cooperative Research, ed. 1996. *NPO to atarashii kyōdō kumiai* (NPOs and the new cooperatives). Tokyo: C & C Publishers.

Japan Networkers Conference, ed. 1992. *NPO to wa nani ka: Sono rikai no tame ni* (What are NPOs?: A guide to understanding NPOs). Tokyo: Japan Networkers Conference.

———. 1995. *Hieiri dantai to shakai kiban: Borantarī katsudō suishin no tame no shikumizukuri ni kansuru chōsa kenkyū hōkokusho* (Nonprofit groups and the social infrastructure: Survey report on the creation of a system to promote voluntary activities). Tokyo: Japan Networkers Conference.

Japan NPO Center. Occasional. *NPO no Hiroba* (NPO plaza). Tokyo: Japan NPO Center.

Japan Youth Volunteers Association, ed. 1997. *Borantia hakusho* (White paper on voluntarism). Tokyo: Japan Youth Volunteers Association.

Jung Ku-Hyun, ed. 1994. *Evolving Patterns of Asia-Pacific Philanthropy*. East and West Studies Series 31. Seoul: The Institute of East and West Studies, Yonsei University.

Kansai Inter-Disciplinary Studies, Inc., ed. 1995. *Zainichi gaikokujin shien dantai (NPO, NGO) no katsudō jittai ni kansuru chōsa kenkyū* (Fact-finding study of the activities of support groups [NPOs, NGOs] for foreign residents of Japan). Osaka: Kansai Inter-Disciplinary Studies, Inc.

Keidanren (Japan Federation of Economic Organizations), ed. 1992 and 1996. *Shakai kōken hakusho: Kigyō to shakai no pātonāshippu* (White paper on philanthropy: The partnership between corporations and society). 2 vols. Tokyo: Japan Industrial Journal.

———. 1994. *Kigyō no shakai kōken handobukku: Kinmirai no kigyōzō* (Handbook of corporate philanthropy: The image of the company in the near future). Tokyo: Japan Industrial Journal.

Life Design Institute, ed. 1994. "Wagakuni ni okeru borantia katsudō no kōsatsu" (Discussion of volunteer activities in Japan). Special issue. *LDI Repōto* (December).

London, Nancy R. 1991. *Japanese Corporate Philanthropy*. New York and Oxford: Oxford University Press.

McCarthy, Kathleen D., Virginia A. Hodgkinson, and Russy D. Sumariwalla and Associates, eds. 1992. *The Nonprofit Sector in the Global Community: Voices from Many Nations*. San Francisco: Jossey-Bass.

Management Office of Minister's Secretariat, Prime Minister's Office, ed. 1993. *Kōeki hōjin meibo* (Directory of public-interest corporations). Tokyo: Japan Association of Charitable Organizations.

Masukomi Jōhō Sentā (Mass Media Information Center), ed. 1995. *Borantia benrichō: Borantia, NGO, shimin dantai 3000 '95* (Volunteer handbook: 3,000 volunteer groups, NGOs, and civic groups, '95). Tokyo: Asahi Shimbun.

Mathews, Jessica T. 1997. "Power Shift." *Foreign Affairs* 76 (1): 50–66.

Matsushita Keiichi. 1996. *Nihon no jichi, bunken* (Local self-government and devolution in Japan). Tokyo: Iwanami Shoten.

Minkan Kōeki Sekutā Kenkyūjo (Private Public-Interest Sector Research Institute), ed. 1997. *Minkan kōeki sekutā no zentaizō: Minkan kōeki sekutā zentaizō no haaku no tame no yobi kenkyū hōkokusho.* (An overview of the private public-interest sector: Report of a preliminary study for an overview of the private public-interest sector). Tokyo: Japan Association of Charitable Organizations.

Nara Machizukuri Center, Inc., ed. 1993. *Shimin kōeki katsudō kiban seibi ni kansuru kenkyū* (Research on the consolidation of infrastructure for citizens' public-interest activities). Nakanoshima-chō, Nara Pref.: Nara Machizukuri Center.

National Institute for Research Advancement, ed. 1994. *Shimin kōeki katsudō kiban seibi ni kansuru chōsa kenkyū* (Study on the consolidation of infrastructure for citizens' public-interest activities). Tokyo: National Institute for Research Advancement. <http://www.nira.go.jp/pubj/output/2813 .html> (20 October 1998).

———. 1996a. *Borantia tō no shien hōsaku ni kansuru sōgōteki kenkyū* (Comprehensive study on support measures for volunteers). Tokyo: National Institute for Research Advancement. <http://www.nira.go.jp/pubj/ houkoku/h950069.html> (20 October 1998).

———. 1996b. *Shimin kōeki katsudō no sokushin ni kansuru hō to seido no arikata* (The proper form of legislation and the system for promotion of citizens' public-interest activities). Tokyo: National Institute for Research Advancement. <http://www.nira.go.jp/pubj/houkoku/h960075.html> (20 October 1998).

———. Annual. *Shinku tanku nenpō* (Almanac of think tanks in Japan). Tokyo: National Institute for Research Advancement. <http://www.nira.go.jp/icj/ index.html> (20 October 1998)

———. Triennial. *Shinku tanku yōran* (Directory of think tanks in Japan). Tokyo: National Institute for Research Advancement. <http://www.nira.go .jp/icj/tt-info/you96/index.html> (20 October 1998).

National Tax Administration Agency, ed. Annual. *Kaisha hyōhon chōsa kekka hōkoku* (Report on results of company sampling surveys). Tokyo: National Tax Administration Agency.

National Volunteer Activity Promotion Centre, Japanese Council of Social Welfare, ed. 1996. *Heisei 7-nendō: Borantia katsudō ni taisuru shakaiteki shiensaku no arikata ni kansuru chōsa, kenkyū* (Fiscal 1995 study on the proper form of social support measures for volunteer activities). Tokyo: National Volunteer Activity Promotion Centre, Japanese Council of Social Welfare.

New Party Sakigake, ed. 1995. *Sakigake no shimin katsudō hōjinhō: NGO/NPO no suishin wo mezashite* (The citizens' activities corporation law of Sakigake: Toward promotion of NGOs/NPOs). Tokyo: New Party Sakigake.

NLI Research Institute, ed. 1994. *Shimin katsudō ni taisuru shien jittai ni kansuru chōsa kenkyū hōkokusho* (Report of a fact-finding survey of support for citizens' activities). Tokyo: NLI Research Institute.

NPO-Borantia Kenkyūkai (NPO-Volunteer Study Group), ed. 1998. *NPO to borantia no jitsumu: Hōritsu, kaikei, zeimu* (The work of NPOs and volunteers: Legal, accounting, and taxation issues). Nagoya: Shin Nihon Hōki.

Numajiri Tsutomu. 1997. "NGO, NPO ni sekkyokuteki na sanjūdai josei: Asahi Shimbun zenkoku yoron chōsa kara" (Women in their thirties positive toward NGOs and NPOs: From the Asahi Shimbun national opinion poll). *Asahi Sōken Repōto*, no. 125 (April): 109–110.

Ogasawara Kōichi, ed. 1996. *Chiiki kūdōka jidai ni okeru gyōsei to borantia* (Administration and voluntarism in the age of hollowing-out of the regions). Tokyo: Chūō Hōki Shuppan.

Osaka Volunteer Association, ed. 1998. "Tokushū: Borantia to NPO" (Special feature: Volunteers and NPOs). *Borantia Katsudō Kenkyū* 9 (March).

PHP Institute, Jōhō Kaihatsu Shitsu (Information Development Section), ed. 1995. *Borantia nyūmon gaido* (Introductory guide to voluntarism). Tokyo: PHP Institute.

Prime Minister's Office, ed. 1993. *Shōgai gakushū to borantia katsudō ni kansuru yoron chōsa* (Opinion poll on lifelong learning and volunteer activities). Tokyo: Prime Minister's Office.

———. 1998. *Heisei 9-nenban kōeki hōjin hakusho: Kōeki hōjin ni kansuru nenji hōkoku* (1997 white paper on public-interest corporations: Annual report on public-interest corporations). Tokyo: Ministry of Finance Printing Bureau. <http://www.sorifu.go.jp/whitepaper/kanri/koekihojin> (20 October 1998).

Research Group on Taxation of Public-Interest Corporations and Charitable Trusts, ed. 1990. *Firansuropī zeisei no kihonteki kadai: Genjō bunseki to teigen* (An agenda for the taxation of philanthropy: Analysis of the present situation and proposals). Tokyo: Japan Association of Charitable Organizations.

Research Institute for Hi-life, ed. 1996. *Kokusai kōken borantia katsudō tō sokushin kihon kōsō sakutei chōsa* (Study for the formulation of a basic concept for the promotion of volunteer activities which make an international contribution). Tokyo: Research Institute for Hi-life.

Saeki Keishi. 1993. *"Amerikanizumu" no shūen: Shibikku riberarizumu seishin no saihakken e* (The end of Americanism: Toward rediscovering the spirit of civic liberalism). Tokyo: TBS-Britannica.

———. 1996. *Gendai Nihon no riberarizumu* (Liberalism in modern Japan). Tokyo: Kōdansha.

———. 1997a. *Gendai minshushugi no byōri: Sengo Nihon wo dō miru ka* (The pathology of modern democracy: How should we view postwar Japan?). Tokyo: Japan Broadcast Publishing Company.

———. 1997b. *"Shimin" to wa dare ka: Sengo minshushugi wo toinaosu* (Who is "the citizen"?: Reexamining postwar democracy). Tokyo: PHP Institute.

Sakamoto Yoshikazu. 1997. *Sōtaika no jidai* (The age of relativization). Tokyo: Iwanami Shoten.

Salamon, Lester M. 1994. "The Rise of the Nonprofit Sector." *Foreign Affairs* 74(4): 109–122.

Salamon, Lester M., and Helmut K. Anheier. 1992. "In Search of the Nonprofit Sector: The Question of Definitions." *Working Papers of the Johns Hopkins Comparative Nonprofit Sector Project*, No. 2. Baltimore: The Johns Hopkins Institute for Policy Studies.

———. 1996a. *The Emerging Sector: The Nonprofit Sector in Comparative Perspective—An Overview.* Baltimore: The Johns Hopkins Institute for Policy Studies.

———. 1996b. "Social Origins of Civil Society: Explaining the Nonprofit Sector Cross-Nationally." *Working Papers of the Johns Hopkins Comparative Nonprofit Sector Project*, No. 22. Baltimore: The Johns Hopkins Institute for Policy Studies.

———, eds. 1997. *Defining the Nonprofit Sector: A Cross-National Analysis.* Manchester and New York: Manchester University Press.

Sasakawa Peace Foundation, ed. 1992. *Nihon no kōeki hōjin: Zenkoku ankēto chōsa ni yoru genjō bunseki* (Public-interest corporations in Japan: An analysis of their present status by means of a national questionnaire survey). Tokyo: Sasakawa Peace Foundation.

Shikata Hiroshi. 1992. *Amerika, firansuropī kikō: Nikkei kigyō no shakai kōken katsudō* (Travels in American philanthropy: The social contribution activities of Japanese companies). Tokyo: TBS-Britannica.

Shimada Haruo, ed. 1993. *Kaika suru firansuropī: Nihon kigyō no shinchi o tou* (Philanthropy blossoms: Asking the true value of Japanese corporations). Tokyo: TBS-Britannica.

Shimokōbe Atsushi, ed. 1996. *Seisaku keisei no sōshutsu: Shimin shakai ni okeru shinku tanku* (The creation of policy-making: Think tanks in civil society). Tokyo: Daiichi Shorin.

Social Policy Bureau, Economic Planning Agency, ed. 1997a. *Shimin katsudō*

no rīdā no tame ni (For leaders of citizens' activities). <http://www.epa.go
.jp/j-j/doc/1997ca2-1-j-j.html> (20 October 1998).

———. 1997b. *Shimin katsudō repōto: Shimin katsudō dantai kihon chōsa hōkokusho* (Citizens' activities report: Basic survey report on citizens' activity
groups). Tokyo: Ministry of Finance Printing Bureau. <http://www.epa
.go.jp/j-j/doc/1997ca1-j-j.html> (20 October 1998).

———. 1998a. *Nihon no NPO keizai kibo: Minkan hieiri katsudō dantai ni
kansuru keizai bunseki chōsa hōkokusho* (The economic scale of Japan's
NPOs: Report of an economic analysis of private-sector nonprofit organizations). Tokyo: Ministry of Finance Printing Bureau. <http://www.epa
.go.jp/98/c/19980610c-minkan.html> (20 October 1998).

———. 1998b. *Open the NPO: Kōkateki na jōhō hasshin no tame ni* (Toward
open NPOs: For the effective transmission of information). Tokyo: Ministry of Finance Printing Bureau.

———. 1998c. *Shimin katsudō dantai ni okeru yūshō jigyō no jittai to kadai ni
tsuite no chōsa* (Study on the status and problems of remunerated projects
by citizens' activity groups). Tokyo: Economic Planning Agency.

———. 1998d. *Shimin no me de mita shimin katsudō* (Citizens' activities seen
through citizens' eyes). Tokyo: Ministry of Finance Printing Bureau.

STB Research Institute, ed. 1994. *Shimin katsudō no hatten wo mezashita josei
no arikata ni kansuru kenkyū: Shimin jigyō ikusei wo tsūjita chiikizukuri ni
kansuru chōsa hōkokusho* (Research on the form of assistance for development of citizens' activities: Survey report on community building through
encouragement of citizens' projects). Tokyo: STB Research Institute.
<http://www.stbri.co.jp/shoroku/93tokyo.html#93025> (20 October 1998).

———. 1996a. *Jūnan na seijuku shakai wo kizuku NPO no tenbō: Shimin katsudō dantai no jittai to NPO suishin hōsaku* (The outlook for NPOs to build
a flexible, mature society: The state of citizens' activity groups and policies
for promoting NPOs). Tokyo: STB Research Institute.

———. 1996b. *Shimin kōeki dantai no jittai haaku chōsa* (Fact-finding survey
of citizens' public-interest groups). Tokyo: STB Research Institute.

Struyk, Raymond J., Makiko Ueno, and Takahiro Suzuki. 1993. *A Japanese Think
Tank: Exploring Alternative Models.* Washington, D.C.: The Urban Institute.

Study Group on Regional Support for Citizens' Activities, ed. 1997. *Shimin
katsudō chiiki shien shisutemu kenkyū pāto 2. Nihon no shimin katsudō to
sapōto sentā* (Study of regional support for citizens' activities, Part 2. Citizens' activities and support centers in Japan). Osaka: Study Group on Regional Support for Citizens' Activities.

———. 1998. *Shimin katsudō chiiki shien shisutemu kenkyū pāto 3. Nihon no
sapōto sekutā: Setsuritsu, katsudō puroguramu, katsudō no jissai* (Study of regional support for citizens' activities, Part 3. The support sector in Japan:
Establishment, activity programs, and activities in actual practice). Osaka:
Study Group on Regional Support for Citizens' Activities.

Tabuchi Setsuya, ed. 1990. *Kōporēto shichizunshippu: 21 seiki no kigyō tetsu-gaku* (Corporate citizenship: Corporate philosophy for the 21st century). Tokyo: Kōdansha.

Takahashi Yōko, ed. 1997. *Firansuropī nyūmon* (Introduction to philanthropy). Osaka: Philanthropic Association of Japan; distributed by Kainan Shobō.

Takenaka Heizō and Ishii Naoko. 1988. *Nichibei keizai ronsō: "Iiwake" no jidai wa owatta* (The Japan-U.S. economic debate: The age of "excuses" is over). Tokyo: TBS-Britannica.

Tanaka Naoki. 1998. *Borantia no jidai: NPO ga shakai wo kaeru* (The age of voluntarism: NPOs will change society). Tokyo: Iwanami Shoten.

Tokyo Volunteer Center, Tokyo Council of Social Welfare, ed. 1997. *Tōkyō ni okeru borantia katsudō suishin no arikata kentō iinkai hōkokusho: Tōkyō Borantia Sentā no arikata wo chūshin ni* (Report of the Committee on the Form of Promotion of Volunteer Activities in Tokyo: With special reference to the form of the Tokyo Volunteer Center). Tokyo: Tokyo Volunteer Center, Tokyo Council of Social Welfare.

———. 1998. *Shimin katsudō shien no arikata kentō iinkai hōkokusho* (Report of the Committee on the Form of Support of Volunteer Activities). Tokyo: Tokyo Volunteer Center, Tokyo Council of Social Welfare.

Tomizawa Kenji and Kawaguchi Kiyoshi, eds. 1997. *Hieiri, kyōdō sekutā no ri-ron to jissen: Sankagata shakai shisutemu wo motomete* (Theory and practice of the nonprofit and cooperative sectors: In search of a participatory social system). Tokyo: Nihon Keizai Hyōronsha.

21st Century Hyogo Project Association, ed. 1995. *Chiiki shakai ni okeru min-kan hieiri soshiki (NPO) no yakuwari to sono kanōsei ni kansuru kenkyū* (Research on the role and potential of private nonprofit organizations [NPOs] in the community). Kobe: 21st Century Hyogo Project Associa-tion. <http://www.pref.hyogo.jp/21C/srvymnu.htm> (20 October 1998).

Wada Jun. 1998. "Applying Track Two to China-Japan-U.S. Relations." In Kokubun Ryōsei, ed. *Challenges for China-Japan-U.S. Cooperation.* Tokyo: Japan Center for International Exchange.

Yamamoto Tadashi. 1995a. "Kokusai kōryū ni okeru minkan no yakuwari" (The role of the private sector in international exchange). *Kokusai Kōryū* 66 (January): 2–13.

———. 1995b. "Minkan no yakuwari ga tsuyomatte iru" (The role of the pri-vate sector is growing). *Gaikō Fōramu* 81 (June): 7–22.

———. 1996. "Taikenteki chiteki kōryū ron: Shimoda Kaigi kara 'Torakku 2' made" (Experience-based theory of intellectual exchange: From the Shi-moda Conference to "Track 2"). *Gaikō Fōramu* 97 (September): 10–20.

———, ed. 1995. *Emerging Civil Society in the Asia Pacific Community.* Tokyo: Japan Center for International Exchange and Institute of Southeast Asian Studies.

————, ed. 1998. *The Nonprofit Sector in Japan.* Manchester, U.K.: Manchester University Press.

Yamaoka Yoshinori, ed. 1997. *NPO kiso kōza: Shimin shakai no sōzō no tame ni* (Basic course on NPOs: To create a civil society). Tokyo: Gyōsei.

Yamauchi Naoto. 1997. *Nonpurofitto ekonomī: NPO to firansuropī no keizai-gaku* (The nonprofit economy: The economics of NPOs and philanthropy). Tokyo: Nihon Hyōronsha.

Zenkoku Yoka Gyōsei Kenkyū Kyōgikai (National Leisure Administration Research Council), ed. 1994. *Shakai sanka katsudō dantai ni kansuru chōsa* (Study of social participation activity groups). Tokyo: Zenkoku Yoka Gyōsei Kenkyū Kyōgikai.

ORGANIZATIONS WITH WEBSITES

Association for Promotion of International Cooperation
    <http://www.apic.or.jp>, <http://www.apic.or.jp/plaza>
Association for Corporate Support of the Arts
    <http://www.mediagalaxy.co.jp/mecenat>
Council of Local Authorities for International Relations (CLAIR)
    <http://www.clair.nippon-net.ne.jp>
C's (Coalition for Legislation to Support Citizens' Organizations)
    <http://www.vcom.or.jp/project/c-s>
JANIC (Japanese NGO Center for International Cooperation)
    <http://www2.coi.te-Tokyo.co.jp/˜janic>
Japan Center for International Exchange
    <http://www.jcie.or.jp>
Japan Environment Association
    <http://www.eic.or.jp/jea>
Japan Environment Corporation
    <http://www.eic.or.jp/jec>
Japan Youth Volunteers Association
    <http://www2.coi.te-Tokyo.co.jp/˜jyva/jyva>
Nara Machizukuri Center, Inc.
    <http://www1.meshnet.or.jp/˜naramati>
National Volunteer Activity Promotion Centre, Japanese Council of Social Welfare
    <http://www.wnn.or.jp/wnn-v/kyougikai/index.html>
NLI Research Institute
    <http://www.nli-research.co.jp>
The Non-Profit Policy Association
    <http://www1.mesh.ne.jp/˜sic/npa>

Osaka Volunteer Association
    <http://www.netv.or.jp/osakavol/index.html>
The Sasakawa Peace Foundation
    <http://www.spf.org>
SCOPE Project
    <http://www.nn.iij4u.or.jp/~scopetr>
Trust Companies Association of Japan
    <http://www.shintaku-kyokai.or.jp>

Index

About the Contributors

YAMAMOTO TADASHI is President of the Japan Center for International Exchange (JCIE), which he founded in 1970. He served as Japanese Executive Director of the Japan-U.S. Economic Relations Group (1979–1981), U.S.-Japan Advisory Commission (1983–1984), and the Korea-Japan 21st Century Committee (1988–1991), and also was a member of the First and Second Prime Minister's Private Council on International Cultural Exchange (1988–1989, 1993–1994). He is currently a member as well as the Japanese Director of the Trilateral Commission, the UK-Japan 2000 Group, the Japanese-German Dialogue Forum, and the Korea-Japan Forum, and a member of the Korea-Japan Joint Committee for Promoting History Studies. He also serves as a member of the board of the Japan NPO Center, which was established in 1996. Mr. Yamamoto studied at Sophia University, continued his education in the United States at St. Norbert College, and received his M.B.A. from Marquette University, Wisconsin. Mr. Yamamoto received the Commander's Cross of the Order of Merit from the German government (1990) and the Honourable Commander of the Most Excellent Order of the British Empire (1998).

IOKIBE MAKOTO is Professor at the Department of Law, Kobe University. He received bachelor's, master's, and doctorate degrees in law from Kyoto University. A specialist in Japanese diplomatic history and U.S.-Japan relations, Professor Iokibe taught at Hiroshima University in 1969–1981, was Visiting Fellow at Harvard University during 1977–1979, became Professor at Kobe University in 1981, and was an academic visitor at the London School of Economics during 1990–1991. He is the author of several books, including *The Policy of the U.S. Occupation of Japan* (Suntory Academic Prize, 1985), *The U.S.–Japan War and the Emergence of Post-War Japan* (Yoshida Shigeru Prize, 1990), *Japan and the Changing World Order* (1991), and *The Occupation Era: The Prime Ministers and Rebuilding of Postwar Japan, 1945–1952* (Yoshino Sakuzō Prize, 1998).

IRIYE AKIRA is Professor of History at Harvard University. He received his B.A. in British history from Haverford College in 1957 and his Ph.D. in American and East Asian history in 1961 from Harvard University. Elected President of the Society for Historians of American Foreign Relations in 1978, Professor Iriye became President of the American Historical Association in 1988 and was Professor of History at the University of Chicago from 1971 to 1989. He has taught at Harvard since 1989, and was made the Charles Warren Professor of American History in 1991. Professor Iriye is the author of many books on East Asian history and Japan-U.S. relations. His most recent publications include *Cultural Internationalization and World Order* (1997) and *Japan and the Wider World* (1997). In 1970 and 1979, he won the Yoshino Sakuzō Prize for the best essay in public affairs and the best book in public affairs.

ŌTA HIROKO is Associate Professor at the National Graduate Institute for Policy Studies. She graduated from Hitotsubashi University in 1976 with a degree in sociology. Professor Ōta took up her current post in 1997, after having worked as a researcher at the Japan Institute of Life Insurance, as Associate Professor of economics at Osaka University, and as Associate Professor of economics at Saitama University. She specializes in economics and economic policy. She has served as a member of the Tax Commission and the Industrial Structure Council. Her publications include *The Economics of Risk* (1995), *A Vision for Economic Reform* (1994), and *The Economics of Safety* (1995).

WADA JUN has been Chief Program Officer and Director for Research Planning at the Japan Center for International Exchange (JCIE) since 1996. He is jointly responsible for the strategic planning and institution building at JCIE, and coordination of policy-related projects. He is also responsible for the feasibility study, commissioned by the Prime Minister's Office, on the establishment of a national archive of historical materials related to modern Asian-Japanese history. Previously, Mr. Wada had been with the Japan Foundation, where he held various posts, including Director, London Office; Director, Center for Global Partnership (CGP) in NewYork; and Director, Japanese Studies Division. Mr.Wada has written and edited numerous books and articles on Korean residents in Japan, philanthropy and intellectual exchange, and Asian arts and culture. His most recent publications include *Locus of and Access to the Historical Materials on Modern Asia-Japan Relations* (1997) and "Applying Track Two to China-Japan-U.S. Relations" (in *Challenges for China-Japan-U.S. Cooperation,* 1998). Mr.Wada received a B.A. in economics and an M.A. in economics and the history of thought from Keio University.

YOSHIDA SHIN'ICHI is Senior Political Correspondent and Columnist at the *Asahi Shimbun.* He joined the *Asahi Shimbun* in 1974, and as a member of the Politics Department has concentrated on Japanese and American politics. As a staff journalist and later a senior reporter, he has reported on the Liberal Democratic Party, with specific attention on the Tanaka faction. During the 1990s, he has served as a Guest Reporter-at-Large for the *Boston Globe,* political correspondent at the *Asahi Shimbun*'s Washington General Bureau (1991–1994), and Chief Correspondent for the Prime Minister's Office. In 1978 and 1995, he received the Japan Newspapers Publishers' and Editors' Association Award (the Japanese equivalent to the Pulitzer Prize) and the Japan Congress of Journalists' Prize. Mr.Yoshida holds a B.A. in law from the University of Tokyo and an M.P.A. from the Kennedy School of Government, Harvard University.

The Japan Center for International Exchange

Founded in 1970, the Japan Center for International Exchange (JCIE) is an independent, nonprofit, and nonpartisan organization dedicated to strengthening Japan's role in international affairs. JCIE believes that Japan faces a major challenge in augmenting its positive contributions to the international community, in keeping with its position as one of the world's largest industrial democracies. Operating in a country where policy making has traditionally been dominated by the government bureaucracy, JCIE has played an important role in broadening debate on Japan's international responsibilities by conducting international and cross-sectional programs of exchange, research, and discussion.

JCIE creates opportunities for informed policy discussions; it does not take policy positions. JCIE programs are carried out with the collaboration and cosponsorship of many organizations. The contacts developed through these working relationships are crucial to JCIE's efforts to increase the number of Japanese from the private sector engaged in meaningful policy research and dialogue with overseas counterparts.

JCIE receives no government subsidies; rather, funding comes from private foundation grants, corporate contributions, and contracts.